D0325685

UNIVERSITY OF DURHAM
PUBLICATIONS

John Henry Newman
and the
Abbé Jager

A CONTROVERSY ON
SCRIPTURE AND TRADITION
(1834–1836)

---

*Edited from the original manuscripts
and the French version*

by

LOUIS ALLEN

LONDON
OXFORD UNIVERSITY PRESS
NEW YORK   TORONTO
1975

Oxford University Press, Ely House, London W. 1

GLASGOW NEW YORK TORONTO MELBOURNE WELLINGTON
CAPE TOWN IBADAN NAIROBI DAR ES SALAAM LUSAKA ADDIS ABABA
DELHI BOMBAY CALCUTTA MADRAS KARACHI LAHORE DACCA
KUALA LUMPUR SINGAPORE HONG KONG TOKYO

ISBN 0 19 713138 7

*Printed in Great Britain
at the University Press, Oxford
by Vivian Ridler
Printer to the University*

IN MEMORIAM
MATRIS FILIAEQUE DILECTISSIMAE

Acknowledgements

LIKE everyone else who has worked on Newman, I owe a great debt to Fr. Stephen Dessain, of the Birmingham Oratory, who has generously given me much relevant information and interpreted difficult manuscript readings. Any errors which remain are, of course, my own. I also thank the Fathers of the Oratory for permission to print the manuscripts of the controversy in their archives.

I take the opportunity to thank the Sir Ernest Cassel Trust and the Research Fund of the Durham Colleges and the University of Durham for assistance given to visit libraries and archives in London, Paris, and Rome.

Contents

x　　　　　　　　　*Contents*

Notation

In the Introduction, the notes run in numerical sequence throughout.

In the body of the work, manuscript variations, or comments on these, are given numerically, numbered from 1 on each page.

Notes from Jager's French edition are given with a symbol (*, †, ‡, etc.)

Editorial notes and references are given alphabetically, numbered from a on each page.

1. Introduction

(i) *The background to the controversy*

THE purpose of this book is to present, for the first time in English, a substantial piece of Newman's controversial writings, which occupies a crucial position in his intellectual history. It is surprising that the work has not been done before. Many of Newman's biographers refer to the polemic with the abbé Jager, in terms which show they have never glanced at it. Others seem to ignore its very existence. In recent years, one or two continental scholars have stressed the importance of the controversy[1] and in 1945 Fr. Henry Tristram, one of the greatest of all Newman scholars, gave a summary account of its origins and themes in his article 'In the lists with the abbé Jager'.[2] This article contains much valuable information which was not readily available elsewhere, but Fr. Tristram treated the controversy as something rather exceptional in the history of the Oxford Movement, as a theological cross-channel excursion all the more surprising because of what he calls 'the astonishing insularity of Tractarian Oxford'. Oxford was not, in the eighteen thirties, as insular as Fr. Tristram thought, and European Catholics, for their part, took a great interest in what was happening there. Several Tractarians, and other Anglicans who were not of the movement but were informed about it, or sympathetic towards it, visited Catholic theologians and writers in the Rhineland, in Louvain, in Rome, Paris, and the French provinces. As far as Rome itself is concerned, the English College in the Via Monserrato was a port of call for visiting Englishmen, Catholic or otherwise. Newman and Froude called there to see its Rector, Nicholas Wiseman, in 1833. Richard Chenevix Trench, later Archbishop of Dublin and author of *On the Study of Words*, was

[1] Cf. G. Biemer, *Überlieferung und Offenbarung. Die Lehre von der Tradition nach John Henry Newman*, Herder, Freiburg, 1961; Jean Stern, *Bible et Tradition chez Newman*, Aubier, Paris, 1967, pp. 111–36; and, more recently, Gary Lease, *Witness to the Faith. Cardinal Newman on the Teaching Authority of the Church*, Shannon, Ireland, Irish University Press, 1971, Chapters 5 and 6.

[2] *John Henry Newman: Centenary Essays*, London, Burns Oates and Washbourne, 1945, pp. 201–22.

there two years later and met not only Wiseman but also his cousin, Charles MacCarthy, that curious friend and disciple of Lamennais, who was later to turn Protestant and end up by becoming Governor of Ceylon. Richard Monckton Milnes, the anonymous author of *One Tract More By a Layman*, spent much time in Italy and France in the circle of Liberal Catholics round Montalembert and Lacordaire. Gladstone was in Italy during 1832 and 1838, and on the latter occasion was much helped by introductions from Montalembert's friend, the art historian Rio.

Through the French Catholic press, an enormous amount of information on the Tractarians was made available not only to French readers but also to Italians, since *L'Univers* and *La Gazette de France*, to mention only two, were regularly read (and occasionally banned) in the Papal States. Between 1830 and 1850, very full articles and reports on developments at Oxford and elsewhere are to be found in *L'Ami de la religion*, *La Gazette de France*, *Les Annales de philosophie chrétienne*, *L'Université catholique*, *Le Correspondant* and *L'Univers*. *L'Univers* was the most regular and most complete source of information, some of it derived from the ecumenically minded Leicestershire squire, Ambrose Lisle Phillipps, some from his friend Jules Gondon, some from French priests living in England, and, on at least one celebrated occasion, from the Tractarians themselves. Gondon, who visited England on a number of occasions to write about Oxford, the English Catholic Revival, and the Irish liberation movement under O'Connell, is, incidentally, the author of what must be the first biography of Newman in any language, the *Notice biographique du R. P. Newman* which appeared in Paris in 1853.

Some of these French periodicals were taken by the Oxford divines. Bloxam, friend of Newman and Phillipps, and host of both Montalembert and Lacordaire at Oxford, was a regular reader of *L'Univers*, and Newman kept copies of it among his papers. It was instrumental in stimulating Dominic Barberi's interest in what was happening at Oxford, and published a letter from John Dobree Dalgairns, proclaiming the passionate adhesion to Rome of the younger Tractarians, to which Barberi replied at great length. Canon Hilaire Lorain, of the seminary at Langres, also came into contact with Dalgairns as a result of reading his letter in *L'Univers*, and Langres later welcomed a number of travellers from Oxford on their way through France. Accounts of life at Langres have been left by Dalgairns and Newman, and of Louvain by Albany Christie.[3] F. W. Faber, T. W. Allies, Tom Mozley, and the Cambridge scholar Christopher Wordsworth (later Bishop of Lincoln) devoted chapters of books or entire volumes to ecclesiastical contacts which they had made during travels on the Continent.

Although the present controversy between Newman and the abbé Jager appeared in print very early in the history of the Oxford Movement, it must therefore clearly be seen as being not only in the mainstream of the perennial debate between Gallicans and Anglicans on the nature of the Church, but also as part of the detailed picture of the Anglican Church which was continuously presented to French Catholic readers between 1830 and 1850. But of course it is much more than that. Although each protagonist dealt with a great many points, each is basically concerned with one issue: the nature of the Church. By being compelled to counter the abbé's arguments, Newman was driven to formulate views which ultimately became the nucleus of a course of sermons delivered in Adam de Brome's chapel in 1836 and then, in 1837, the *Lectures on the Prophetical Office*. In other words, the key text of the Via Media, and the main idea behind the *Essay on Development*, are directly derived from this controversy.

The correspondence arose in the first place as the result of a trip to France made by one of Newman's younger friends, Benjamin Harrison,[4] Student of Christ Church, a brilliant Hebrew scholar, and a contributor to the *Tracts*. He had gone to Paris in the summer of 1834 to study Arabic under the great French orientalist and friend of Pusey, Sylvestre de Sacy. He travelled with William Cureton,[5] later a Syriac scholar of some renown. A few months later, Cureton entertained at Oxford one of de Sacy's friends, Eugène Burnouf, another well-known French orientalist who spent some weeks there early in 1835 as guest of the Professor of Sanskrit, Horace Hayman Wilson. Burnouf's

---

[3] L. Allen, 'Two Letters from the Newman Archives,' *Durham University Journal*, xlvii. 2, March 1955, pp. 57–68.

[4] Benjamin Harrison (1808–87), later Archdeacon of Maidstone (*DNB*, xxv. 31).

[5] William Cureton (1808–64), later chaplain to Queen Victoria and Canon of Westminster.

naïve and chauvinistic letters home during his stay provide some interesting sidelights on the state of learning and religion in Tractarian Oxford.[6]

In the intervals of 'arabicising with de Saci', as Newman put it in a letter to Froude,[7] Cureton and Harrison chanced to meet at dinner the Abbé Jean-Nicolas Jager. Then in his early forties, the abbé had been a schoolmaster and army chaplain, and was well enough equipped with theological and patristic learning to be appointed, a few years later, to the chair of Ecclesiastical History in the Faculty of Theology of the University of Paris. The theological discussion which inevitably arose over dinner was to be continued, they agreed, by correspondence, the letters to be published in the newspaper recently founded by the indefatigable abbé Migne, *L'Univers religieux*. Anonymity seems to have been a minor mania of the Tractarians, and the English correspondents insisted on retaining theirs.

Jager's First Letter appeared on 30 August 1834. Harrison's reply to it was published on 18 September, promptly followed the day after by a Second Letter from Jager. Harrison, who seems to have had from the start the intention of withdrawing from the controversy as soon as possible and persuading Newman to take his place, was forced by Newman's absence from Oxford to compose an answer himself. This appeared on 14 October. Jager's Third Letter to Harrison was of considerable length and appeared in two issues on 23 and 24 October.

Newman agreed to take part but the switchover inevitably delayed the exchange of letters and while awaiting a reply to the charges contained in his Third Letter, the abbé composed and printed a Fourth Letter dealing exclusively with one point Harrison had brought up earlier, the Worship of Images. This topic was not relevant to the main issues of the controversy as they had emerged so far, and which had begun to centre chiefly on the issue of fidelity to the Vincentian canon, as interpreted by Bishop Jebb of Limerick: which, of the Roman Church or the Anglican Church, had observed the more steadfastly the criterion of the rule of faith, given by Vincent of Lérins in his *Commonitorium*, *quod semper*, *quod ubique*, *quod ab omnibus*. Jager's Fourth Letter, does, however, seem to have emphasized the importance

---

6 *Choix de lettres d'Eugène Burnouf*, 1825–1852, ed. L. Burnouf, Paris, 1891.
7 Newman, *Letters & Correspondence*, ed. Mozley. ii. 74, 12 Nov. 1834.

of the Worship of Images issue as far as Newman was concerned and he devoted to it part of his tract *On the Controversy
with the Romanists* (1836).

The *Commonitorium* was hardly new ground for this kind of
controversy but Harrison rather than the abbé seems to have
been responsible for bringing it in. Jager was acquainted with
some of the *Tracts for the Times*, and had read up the classic
statement of the Roman-Anglican controversy from the Roman
side, Milner's *End of Religious Controversy*, Samuel Wix's eireni-
cal *Reflections concerning the Expediency of a Council of the Church
of England and the Church of Rome being holden, with a view
to accommodate Religious Differences* (London, 1818) as well as
Lepappe de Trévern's *Discussion amicale sur l'établissement et la
doctrine de l'Église anglicane et en général sur la Réformation*
(London, 1817). Lepappe de Trévern, Bishop of Vannes and
later of Strasbourg, was one of the hundreds of Catholic clergy
who had found refuge in England during the revolutionary
times, and had repaid the welcome of the Anglican clergy by a
study of their institutions. His book is dedicated to the clergy
of all the Protestant communions and it served as a handbook
of Anglican beliefs for French writers over several decades. Its
purpose had been to open those lines of communication between
the Gallican Church in France and the Church of England which
had remained closed ever since the breakdown of the discussions
between Cardinal de Noailles and William Wake, Archbishop
of Canterbury, early in the eighteenth century. Lepappe de
Trévern quotes a number of Anglican divines, and it is in part
from him, Wix, and Milner, that Jager's reading in Anglican
theology, such as it is, derives. Milner's work had been translated into French[8] and there are times when Jager simply lifts
whole sequences of patristic quotations from Milner's often
approximate renderings, usually though not always without
acknowledgement. But his main source was a little book Harrison let him have to provide points of discussion: the *Pastoral
Instructions* of John Jebb, Bishop of Limerick, which had been
compiled from previous volumes of his sermons and discourses
and was republished in 1831 in a small format volume of nearly

---

[8] *Excellence de la religion catholique, ou Correspondance entre une société de protestans
religieux et un théologien de l'église catholique romaine, ouvrage traduit de l'anglais de
M. Milner*, Paris, A. Le Clère, 1823, 2 vols.

400 pages. The kernel of the book, as far as Jager was concerned, and to which Harrison had no doubt drawn his attention as representing the case for the unique historical and doctrinal situation of the Church of England, was a tract entitled *Peculiar Character of the Church of England; as distinguished, both from other branches of the Reformation, and from the modern Church of Rome*, whose title and theme of 'middle course' anticipated the Via Media by two decades. This tract, of which Jebb's friend, Alexander Knox, has been said to be 'virtually the author',[9] had been reprinted several times as an appendix to reprints of Jebb's *Discourses*; and although Jebb says he found it growing under his hands, its arguments and supporting texts were essentially, in 1831, the same as in 1815, the date of its publication as an appendix to his *Sermons* when he was Rector of Abingdon in the diocese of Cashel. Like Wix, Jebb uses Vincent of Lérins's *Commonitorium* as a touchstone of fidelity to the ideals of the Catholic Church's rule of faith, and this was to be the main area of contention for much of the discussion between Jager and the young divines from Oxford.

Jager's Fourth Letter, as irrelevant to the discussion, was not reprinted when he decided to make a book out of the controversy in 1836, and the numbering of letters in the book, which is retained in the present edition, differs slightly from that used in the *L'Univers*. Part of Newman's first letter (the Third Reply in the present volume) was printed on 25 December 1834, accompanied by Jager's reply. With some justification, Harrison complained to the abbé that this infringed the rules under which they had agreed to proceed: no reply was to be commenced until a letter had appeared in full. In addition Newman's letter was in a type smaller than that used for the abbé's answer. . . . After this complaint, Newman's letter was completed in print without any further intervention by the abbé, on 28 and 29 January 1835.

Immediately, on 30 January, Jager once more took up his reply to Newman and composed in sequence and at great length what now appear in this book as the Fourth, Fifth, and Sixth Letters. The last insertion was on 27 March 1835, after which date the controversy was transferred to the columns of *Le Moniteur religieux*. Jager's reply, apparently, disquieted Newman considerably, and not because of its inordinate length alone. 'I am

9 Overton, *The Anglican Revival*, London, n.d. [1897], p. 18.

at present fidgeted', he wrote to Froude, 'with my answer to the Abbé, who is the most ignorant of men and the most inconsequent of reasoners. It is a great bore, yet with all these sets-off —first it obliges me to get up the controversy; next it shows I am not a Papist.'[10] These were not light 'sets-off' for Newman. A short time later he was to declare that 'The Controversy with the Romanists has overtaken us like a "summer's cloud".' He was in a mood of fair satisfaction with his own talents as a debater in print, and it was a necessity, he felt, to combat the Church of Rome from a position other than that of extreme Protestantism. Pusey wrote to him in 1836: 'As far as I know, most of our old controversy with Rome was carried on upon wrong (Genevan) principles; it would be a good thing to have one on the subject on right principles; it would bring out these principles, people would see that Catholic principles can be maintained against Popish, and would receive them the rather because they are on their own side.'[11] Newman's own draft letter to Jager[12] shows clearly that he thought he could serve a very useful purpose by taking part in such a polemic, anticipating Pusey.

To clarify his own position further, he worked out his views in dialogue form for R. H. Froude's benefit and his own; Froude doing likewise from *his* standpoint. These dialogues, which passed as letters between the two friends, are printed as an appendix to this edition since they contain a distinction, drawn possibly for the first time by Newman and later to play a great part in his work, between the apostolic tradition transmitted by bishops, and prophetical tradition, '. . . the voice of the body of the Church, the received system in the Church, the spirit circulating through it and poured out through the channel of its doctors and writers . . . the system taught, interpretative, supplementary, applicative, of the Scripture doctrine'.

At the end of July 1835 he sent to Harrison, for onward dispatch to the abbé, the first part of his second letter (Fourth Reply, Part One in the present text) which appeared in *Le Moniteur de la religion* in two sections between December 1835 and February 1836. Jager printed his reply to this first part without waiting for the second part to arrive and wrote to Harrison to say he intended to publish the controversy as far

---

[10] Tristram, op. cit., p. 215.   [11] Liddon, *Life of E. B. Pusey*, ii. 4.
[12] Cf. pp. 33–5.

as it had gone, in book form, with his answer to Newman (the Seventh Letter of the present text) as the concluding piece.

At this point the controversy seems simply to have lapsed, as Newman does not appear to have sent off the second part of his second letter. There had been some bitter differences with Harrison over Newman's line of argument in defence of the Anglican position;[13] and the abbé had again defaulted from the strict letter of his promise by splitting Newman's first part into two sections. There seemed little point in continuing to wrangle on procedure. Newman had had enough, and thought the polemic had gone as far as it usefully could. So, in the spring of 1836, after occupying his thoughts on and off for eighteen months at a very important period of his intellectual development, the debate came to an end.

A word about the present text. Newman had prepared a second part of his second letter (Fourth Reply, Part Two), which did not find its way into print either in the French press or in Jager's book and has remained in manuscript ever since, written by an amanuensis whose Latin seems to have been rather shaky. This second part is now published for the first time and gives a more complete voice to Newman than Jager's book did. The book appeared in 1836 with the title *Le Protestantisme aux prises avec la doctrine catholique, ou Controverses avec plusieurs ministres anglicans, membres de l'Université d'Oxford* (Tome premier, Paris, Debécourt, 1836) and was never reprinted. Stern notes (op. cit., p. 112) an edition published by de Lossy dated Paris, 1835, with the same pagination, and assumes that date refers to a fascicule only. The de Lossy edition omits the aggressive first phrase of Jager's title, and calls itself merely *Controverse religieuse avec plusieurs ministres anglicans, membres de l'Université d'Oxford soutenue par M. l'abbé Jager*. Nor did any second volume appear. Even a dozen years after its first appearance it was already out of print, and Christopher Wordsworth, then headmaster of Harrow, recalls visiting the abbé Jager in the late summer of 1844 and being told the book was no longer available.[14]

Newman's sisters seem to have undertaken the task of translating his drafts for *L'Univers*, which printed them with reasonable fidelity. In order that the present edition should not be

---

[13] Cf. Appendix II.   [14] C. Wordsworth, *Diary in France*, 1845, p. 114.

merely a rendering back into modern English of Newman's French text, I have used in full the original manuscript drafts of his Third Reply, and Fourth Reply, Part Two. Where no draft exists, as in the case of the Fourth Reply, Part One, I have used the earliest printed version of the *Lectures on the Prophetical Office of the Church*[15] wherever the text is manifestly a reproduction of some form of the text of the Jager controversy. The text of Newman as here printed is therefore not a retranslation from the French but, almost *in toto*, his own English text.

Its importance will, I think, be immediately evident to anyone versed in the history of the Oxford Movement and in the development of Newman's Anglican theology. It would not have been enough, though, merely to have reprinted Newman's text, even if readers are likely to be chiefly interested in what he has to say, and not in the abbé Jager or Benjamin Harrison. Many of Newman's points were raised in the first instance by the abbé, or to combat him. In particular the amplification of the very notion of prophetical office is given in the dialogue Newman wrote to develop his ideas for Froude, and this idea of prophetical office is clearly most relevant to the growth of the idea of doctrinal development. No doubt it was this the abbé had in mind when he wrote to Newman after hearing of his conversion in 1845—it was reported almost at once in the columns of *L'Univers*—to inquire if their polemic had played any part in that event. 'I was obliged to answer, No,' he recollected in 1868, but the letter he sent to Jager, early in 1846, is by no means so direct: 'I thank you very much for your kind letter,' Newman wrote, 'which circumstances hindered me from answering at the time I received it. Since it was written, you will see I have published a work, giving some of my reasons for my change of opinion. I have no wish at all that it should be kept secret that I was your opponent 11 or 12 years ago in the correspondence you inserted in the *Univers* newspaper, and afterwards published separately; Many thanks, indeed, for your kind wish to know me, if I went to Paris. I should rejoice in such an opportunity.'[16] Newman's negative, however polite, is one which might be questioned. He seems ready to acknowledge general formative influences, particularly on his early life, but he is averse to

---

[15] London, Rivington; Parker, Oxford, 1836, xi+422.
[16] *Letters & Diaries*, ed. C. S. Dessain, xxiv, 37 and xii, 81.

recognizing the effect upon his decisions of arguments put forward by his contemporaries—if we exclude the celebrated *Securus judicat.* Wilfrid Ward comments that his memory seems to have been selective about this kind of thing and in the case of the revision of the *Essay on Development* I think it can be shown he reacted to Christopher Wordsworth's criticisms, though he claimed in a letter to Bloxam never to have read Wordsworth's attack on the Essay.[17] Looking back on this period of his life, he wrote to Henry Wilberforce (27 January 1846):

> Now in the year 1834 or 35 my belief even in this theory [the Via Media] was so strong, that I recollect feeling an anxiety about the Abbé Jager, with whom I was controverting, lest my arguments were unsettling him and making him miserable. Those arguments were not mine, but the evolution of Laud's theory, Stillingfleet's, etc which seemed to me clear, complete, and unanswerable. I do not think I had that unhesitating belief in it in 1836–7 when I published my *Prophetical Office*, or rather I should say that *zeal* for it—for I believed it fully or at least was not conscious I did not. It is difficult to say whether or not a flagging zeal involves an incipient doubt. The feelings under which I wrote the volume will be seen in the commencement of the last Lecture. I thought the theory true, but that all theories were doubtful and difficult and all reasoning a weariness to the flesh.[18]

Whatever the value of his recollection may be, ten years after the event, the reader of the controversy might prefer to judge for himself the effect of the abbé Jager's attacks on Newman's Anglican theology, the arguments found by Newman to parry them, and, in so doing, to develop his theory of the rule of faith. The abbé is prolix, but to be fair to him his arguments have been summarized in the present edition and inserted in the same place they occupy in his own publication of the controversy in book form, to preserve the connection between Newman and his opponent.

(ii) *The influence of the controversy on Newman*

The controversy occurred at an interesting moment in Newman's life. He had been a fellow of Oriel for more than a decade,

---

[17] Cf. my article 'Newman and Christopher Wordsworth', *Essays presented to C. M. Girdlestone*, Newcastle-upon-Tyne, 1960, pp. 13–26, and W. Ward, *Life of Cardinal Newman*, i. 58: 'Some writers have, I observe, quoted Newman's letter in old age stating that he "never read a line of Coleridge". It is not the only instance in which his memory was in later years seriously at fault.'

[18] *Letters and Diaries*, ed. Dessain, xi. 100.

and Vicar of St. Mary's, the University church, since 1828. His first book, *The Arians of the Fourth Century*, was finished in July 1832 and published the following summer. On 9 July 1833 he returned from Sicily, convinced that God had preserved him for some great work. Three months later, on 9 September 1833, the first of the *Tracts for the Times* was issued, anonymously. It was Newman's work, and made a strong appeal to the clergy of the Church of England to stand by their bishops, as the successors of the Apostles, and the guardians of the Church's heritage. He returned to the theme in Tract No. 15, *On the Apostolical Succession in the English Church*, in which he makes the same point which he uses against Jager, that the Church of England had undoubtedly received its orders from the Church of Rome which he now considered to be heretical; but that Church was not heretical in primitive times and had kept the Rule of Faith 'until that rule was changed and altered by the Council of Trent' (p. 10, note).

What he was later to call, in the *Apologia*, 'the intolerable offence of having added to the Faith' (*Apologia pro vita sua*, Longmans, 1882, p. 107) was the chief head of accusation against Rome by the Anglican Newman in the controversy between Antiquity (or Apostolicity) and Catholicity. The Jager polemic is the principal episode in this controversy.

From 23 April 1834 he began a series of sermons in Adam de Brome's Chapel in St. Mary's, which developed the theme of the Church of England as the representative of the Via Media— Bishop Jebb's 'middle way'—between the exaggerations of popular Protestantism on the one hand and the corruptions of the Church of Rome on the other. These sermons and the letters to Jager became the *Lectures on the Prophetical Office of the Church, viewed relatively to Romanism and Popular Protestantism* (London, Rivington; Parker, Oxford, 1837). Thirty years later, when he reviewed his religious development from 1839 to 1841 in the third chapter of the *Apologia*, he sketched the elements of the controversy between Rome and the Church of England again, and pointed out that he was not fundamentally concerned with the issue of the Pope's position as the centre of unity or the source of jurisdiction, but rather with the more general question of the relation between the Faith and the Church. 'This was my issue of the controversy from the beginning to the end', he wrote 'There was a contrariety of claims between the Roman and Anglican religions, and the history of my conversion is simply the process of working it out to a solution' (*Apologia*, London, Longmans, 1882, p. 112).

In the same chapter he reports the controversy as he had out-lined it in *Home Thoughts Abroad* (1836) in terms of two friendly antagonists, one putting the Roman view, the other the view based on the Via Media. Jager is nowhere specifically mentioned; but some of the points made are Jager's, and some of those made against the Roman case are similar to those Newman used to defend himself against Jager (*Apologia*, 1882, pp. 110–12).

If we view Newman's movement towards the conversion of 1845 as paralleled by a growth in the idea of development, it is not difficult to see why Jager thought his polemic had had some effect in changing Newman's opinions.

Clearly, the idea of development does not occur for the first time in the *Essay on the Development of Christian Doctrine* (London, Toovey, 1845) nor in the sermon on 'The Theory of Developments in Religious Doctrine' (*Fifteen Sermons preached before the University of Oxford*, 1843) which dealt, as he wrote to Manning later, with 'a subject intended for years'.[19] But where it is referred to in Newman's early work it is usually an attribute of 'Romanism', in other words it is a case *against* which he argues.

While proclaiming the stability of Anglican doctrine and at the same time being aware of change, Newman brings forward at various times interpretations of change which gradually expand and are clarified under his hostile gaze until at last he finds that this elaboration of arguments to render change and development explicit is beginning to act as a justification of it. The Newman who wrote *Arians* used the argument of the 'economy' of hidden truths. For reasons connected with venera-tion of Christ's teaching, the Church had allowed revelation to be shown piecemeal, as occasion required and as the recipients were fitting. Not everything was appropriate for every genera-tion. As Walgrave indicates, the nature of the process of making explicit was a transposition into abstract language of a vision supported by the concrete language of the Scriptures: a transla-

[19] Letter dated Oct. 25, 1843, in *Correspondence of John Henry Newman with John Keble and others*, ed. F. Bacchus, London, Longmans, 1917, p. 277.

tion of what was essentially a sort of intuition into systematic concepts and discursive reflexions.[20]

In the second chapter of *Arians*, he had given an account of the principle of formation of creeds.

As the mind is cultivated and expanded, [he wrote] it cannot refrain from the attempt to analyse the vision which influences the heart, and the Object in which that vision centres; nor does it stop till it has, in some sort, succeeded in expressing in words, what has all along been a principle both of its affections and of its obedience. But here the parallel ceases; the Object of religious veneration being unseen, and dissimilar from all that is seen, reason can but represent it in the medium of those ideas which the experience of life affords . . . and unless these ideas, however inadequate, be correctly applied to it, they re-act upon the affections, and deprave the religious principle. This is exemplified in the case of the heathen, who, trying to make their instinctive notion of the Deity an object of reflection, pictured to their minds false images, which eventually gave them a pattern and a sanction for sinning. Thus the systematic doctrine of the Trinity may be considered as the shadow, projected for the contemplation of the intellect, of the Object of scripturally-informed piety: a representation, economical; necessarily imperfect, as being exhibited in a foreign medium, and therefore involving apparent inconsistencies or mysteries; given to the Church by tradition contemporaneously with those apostolic writings, which are addressed more directly to the heart; kept in the background in the infancy of Christianity, when faith and obedience were vigorous, and brought forward at a time when, reason being disproportionately developed, and aiming at sovereignty in the province of religion, its presence became necessary to expel a usurping idol from the house of God.[21]

At the stage of *Arians*, Newman's attention was not focused on the increase of doctrine. He merely saw another way of expressing the object of faith. That object itself remained identical and invariable. Far from approving this need to find other ways of expressing the object of faith, he seems to regard the translation of it as inadequate and dangerous. It is nothing more than a necessary evil. His idea of the faith is therefore, at this time, a static one.

When he came to publish *Lectures on the Prophetical Office*

(1837), not only was his attachment to the Via Media cooler, he had also begun to consider the role of ecclesiastical tradition as the agency interpretative of Scripture. As he recalled it in 1846, in his letter to Henry Wilberforce, his belief in the Via Media was so strong in 1834 and 1835 that he recollected feeling an anxiety lest his arguments were unsettling the abbé Jager and making him miserable.[22] The arguments were not his own, they were derived from Laud and Stillingfleet, but his evolution of them seemed to him 'clear, complete, and unanswerable'.[23] He did not have that unhesitating belief in 1836–7 when he published the *Prophetical Office*. Or rather, he adds, he did not have the former unflagging zeal for it, and although he believed it fully he wondered later whether flagging zeal involved an incipient doubt. He concluded by affirming that he thought the theory true, but that all theories were doubtful and difficult, and all reasoning a weariness to the flesh.[24]

Between the beginning of the Jager controversy, then, and its termination in book form in the *Lectures on the Prophetical Office*, Newman had sensed a weakening in his adhesion to the middle way of Anglicanism. *Pari passu*, he had begun to elaborate the notion of a prophetical office in which lay the seeds of the idea of development. This notion was worked out in a letter to Hurrell Froude, since printed in part of Froude's *Remains*, and given in full in Appendix III to the present edition. There are two kinds of tradition, one official and precise, transmitted from one definite person to another throughout the history of the Church. This is episcopal tradition, ultimately derived from the Apostles. The second is less precise, and he defines it as

the voice of the body of the Church, the received system in the Church, the spirit circulating through it and poured out through the channel of its doctors and writers . . . which I may call *prophetical Tradition* [Newman's italics], or the system taught, interpretative, supplementary, illustrative, applicative of the Scripture doctrine. Now I maintain that Tradition in this sense, and this is the sense in which I contrasted it to Scripture, does not carry with it any witness of its reception being necessary for Church Communion. Its reception is the privilege of the Christian when admitted, not a condition of his admission.[25]

This qualification makes prophetical tradition less authoritative than episcopal tradition which, Newman is prepared to concede, 'carries the sanction with it as fully as Scripture does'. But that he was unsure of the precise relationship of the two kinds of tradition to his notion of fundamental doctrines is shown by his penultimate paragraph, in which he asks Froude to keep the letter so that he might think over it, and to help him out of a puzzle he might have got into. He emphasized, writing to Froude on 9 August 1835, that he thought the abbé would be obliged to grant that prophetical tradition had no innate self-sanction. The more he studied the question, the more convinced he was that the Fathers insisted on Scripture as the Rule of Faith. Scripture came with a claim, and Tradition did not. For Vincent of Lérins, for instance, tradition was only interpretative.

When he amplified this theory in his lectures on the prophetical office, he was less intent on diminishing the authority of prophetical tradition. Having defined episcopal tradition as the Creed, a collection of definite articles committed and received from bishop to bishop and forced upon the attention of each individual Christian, he defines prophetical tradition as exposition, in contrast to the ruling and preaching function of the Apostles:

Prophets or Doctors are the interpreters of the revelation; they unfold and define its mysteries, they illuminate its documents, they harmonize its contents, they apply its promises. Their teaching is a vast system, not to be comprised in a few sentences, not to be embodied in one code or treatise, but consisting of a certain body of Truth, permeating the Church like an atmosphere, irregular in its shape from its very profusion and exuberance; at times separable only in idea from Episcopal Tradition, yet at times melting away into legend and fable; partly written, partly unwritten, partly the interpretation, partly the supplement of Scripture, partly preserved in intellectual expressions, partly latent in the spirit and temper of Christians; poured to and fro in closets and upon the housetops, in liturgies, in controversial works, in obscure fragments, in sermons. This I call Prophetical Tradition, existing primarily in the bosom of the Church itself, and recorded in such measure as Providence has determined in the writings of eminent men. This is obviously of a very different kind from the Episcopal Tradition, yet in its origin it is equally Apostolical, and equally claims our zealous maintenance. . . . This is that body of teaching which is offered to all Christians even at the present day, though in various forms and measures of truth, in different parts of Christendom, partly being a comment, partly an addition upon the articles of the Creed.[26]

The truths revealed by this means may not have the same compelling force or sanction as those defined by the episcopal tradition. 'These developed and fixed truths', he writes later, 'are entitled to very different degrees of credit, though always to attention.'[27] Some councils spoke more authoritatively than others, though all which appealed to Tradition might be presumed to have an element of truth in them. And this is the view Newman then took of the Council of Trent. Its decrees claimed to be Apostolic, but in his view they were 'the ruins and perversions of Primitive Tradition'.[28]

The notion of a developing agency is obviously contained in this idea of a prophetical tradition. That there were dangers in it had already been pointed out by Jager in his Fourth Letter. Newman had agreed, he says, that the task of seeking out the Faith in Scripture and the Fathers was not incumbent upon every individual, but was the task of the Church, 'who is the guardian and judge of Catholic doctrine, and who has the right to expound it, to proclaim it, to resolve its difficulties and to exclude rebellious innovators from her midst. You even confess that she is infallible, at least in the chief points. You go further, and grant to the Church more than we desire, and more than we can accept, the right to make articles of faith *according to time and circumstances*, a right we are far from recognising, and which the Roman Church has never attributed to herself.'[29]

Newman rejects this. 'My words were', he replied to Jager, '*The power to develop its fundamental Creed* [Newman's italics] into Articles of *religion* [Newman's italics], according to times and circumstances; to develop is not to create. Articles of religion are not essentially fundamental articles as articles of faith are.'[30]

In his Seventh Letter, Jager returns to this point.

'To develop is not to create' you say. That is true. But show me, then, first of all, that your Thirty-nine Articles are the development

---

[26] *Lectures on the Prophetical Office of the Church*, London, Rivington; Parker, Oxford, 1836, pp. 298–9; 3rd ed., 1891, pp. 250–1.

[27] Op. cit., p. 300; 3rd ed., p. 252.   [28] Op. cit., p. 301; 3rd ed., p. 252.

[29] Jager, *Le Protestantisme aux prises avec la doctrine catholique*, p. 129. Henceforth referred to as 'Jager'.

[30] pp. 96–7.

of the Creed. To develop a principle is to show the consequences which flow from it. So one develops Protestantism when one shows that it leads directly to the destruction of all truth. *You* claim to develop the Creed when you say that Scripture contains all things necessary to salvation; that we are justified by faith alone; that there are only two sacraments; that the Roman Church has erred in matters of faith and discipline; that she worships and adores images; that the Pope has no jurisdiction over the Catholic Church; that Queen Elizabeth has the chief power in all kinds of causes, whether ecclesiastical or civil, and so on. Now what connection is there between these curious propositions and the articles of the Creed? When you recite this creed, you make a profession of believing in one *Church, Holy and Catholic,* which will remain so until the end of time. And then you declare before the whole world that she can become corrupt and lost, and fall into error and idolatry! Is this a development of the Creed?[31]

But there is more than polemical abuse to what Jager affirms. Earlier in the same letter he had taken up Newman's point about the prophetical tradition.

No doubt, there is a difference [he wrote] between apostolic tradition and prophetic exposition. The prophets or the doctors of the Church are obliged to define, to comment, to develop the mysteries of religion, and to put them within the people's reach. But as Vincent says, they must do it 'while preserving the same doctrine, the same sense, the same judgement'. When you develop a truth, you do not change it, on the contrary, you give it more force, more lustre, greater scope. That is what the Fathers and the Doctors of the Church did. The Church took care to warn those who had the misfortune to stray from the apostolic doctrine in their explanations, she pointed out their errors, and condemned them when necessary. And so apostolic tradition has remained pure and intact until our own day, and will remain so until the end of time.[32]

It was Vincent whom Newman quoted when he came to make the same point as Jager in Chapter I of the *Essay on Development.* Defining the first note of a genuine development as 'preservation of type', he points out that healthy development is distinguished from the corruption of an idea if it retains 'one and the same type, the same principles, the same organization'.[33] A test is suggested by the analogy of physical growth, in which the

[31] Jager, op. cit., pp. 425–6.   [32] Ibid., p. 424.
[33] *An Essay on the Development of Christian Doctrine,* 1845 edn., Chap. I, sec. iii; new ed. 1878, Chap. V, sec. i.

parts and proportions of the adult correspond to the rudimentary forms at birth.

The adult animal has the same make, as it had on its birth; young birds do not grow into fishes, nor does the child degenerate into the brute, wild or domestic, of which he is by inheritance lord. Vincentius of Lérins adopts this illustration in distinct reference to Christian doctrine. 'Let the soul's religion,' he says, 'imitate the law of the body, which, as years go on, develops indeed and opens out its due proportions, and yet remains identically what it was. Small are a baby's limbs, a youth's are larger, yet they are the same.'

Little wonder that Jager thought he had had some effect on Newman's idea of development. Another point arises, which may seem trivial, but which Newman himself elevated to a position of some importance. In the *Dublin Review* (7, 1839, pp. 139–80), Nicholas Wiseman had published an article entitled 'The Anglican Claim of Apostolic Succession' in which he compared the Anglicans to the Donatists. Newman was, of course, familiar with the Donatist controversy. In his view the cases were not parallel and as a result he 'did not see much'[34] in Wiseman's article when he first read it. He was then pressed by a friend to notice St. Augustine's words in an extract quoted by Wiseman: *Securus judicat orbis terrarum.*

They gave a cogency to the Article [he later wrote], which had escaped me at first. They decided ecclesiastical questions on a simpler rule than that of Antiquity . . . the deliberate judgment, in which the whole Church at length rests and acquiesces, is an infallible prescription and a final sentence against such portions of it as protest and secede. . . . For a mere sentence, the words of St. Augustine, struck me with a power I never had felt from any words before. To take a familiar instance, they were like the 'Turn again Whittington' of the chime; or, to take a more serious one, they were like the 'Tolle, lege', of the child, which converted St. Augustine himself. 'Securus judicat orbis terrarum!' By those great words of the ancient Father, interpreting and summing up the long and varied course of ecclesiastical history, the theory of the *Via Media* was absolutely pulverized.'[35]

A glance at the Fourth Reply, Part One, of the present text, will show not merely that Newman was familiar with the Donatist controversy years before the impression made by Wiseman's article but that, in spite of his assertion that the

34 *Apologia*, p. 116.   35 Ibid., p. 117.

parallel with Anglicanism was not a true one, he had in fact himself drawn a parallel between the Donatists and the Church of England. 'You hurl at me darts which you think are lethal,' he says to Jager, 'namely, that the Donatists were considered by the Church as excluded from salvation, although their error was against Scripture. I answer, almost in your own words, that to maintain an opinion against the voice of the whole Church stubbornly and publicly is of itself without any doubt a mortal sin, and that such was the flagrant sin of the Donatists, as St. Augustine tells us . . .' A little further on, Newman points out that Jager had argued that if St. Cyprian, in acting against the tradition (of validity of heretical baptism), appeared excusable to St. Augustine, it was because in his day the question had not been sufficiently clarified; it was because Cyprian could still doubt the universality of the ecclesiastical teaching, since many shared his views. 'My dear Sir,' counters Newman, 'that is precisely the situation in which we find ourselves in England. We believe that your particular points of doctrine are not yet sufficiently clarified. We are, like St. Cyprian, in that stage of doubt on the *universality of the teaching*, and *many bishops* share our views' [Newman's italics].[36] And, of course, in his Sixth Letter (Fifth in the present numbering), Jager himself had made the parallel towards the end, in attacking Newman's notion of fundamental doctrines.

So reason, Scripture and the Fathers unite to demonstrate to you the infallibility of the Church. What answer will you make to proofs which are so numerous and so striking? That the Church is infallible in fundamental points? That, in effect, is what you say in your letter. But what an odd infallibility! She is infallible in fundamental points, and can err in the discernment of them, and offer us for fundamental that which is not so! Moreover, when you make this distinction, you must begin by agreeing among yourselves. You proclaim the Church to be infallible on the chief points, and yet you accuse the Roman Church of having erred on dogma and morals, of having fallen into idolatry and superstition, of having added to the religion of Christ *strange* and *monstrous* dogmas, opposed to the word of God. One thing or the other: either those errors are fundamental, or they are not. If they are fundamental, your opinion is false; if they are not, you are schismatics, condemned by St. Vincent as the Donatists were, since, like them, you separated yourselves from the Church for articles which

[36] Fourth Reply, Part One, para. 60.

were not fundamental. Again, what is more fundamental in religion than the dogma of infallibility, since upon this dogma depends the certainty or uncertainty of our faith. So if the Church cannot err on fundamental points, she could not have erred when she believed herself to be infallible. The dogma of infallibility is therefore supported by your own assertion.[37]

Indirectly, then, the conjunction which so startled him in 1839, of Donatists, Anglicans, and St. Augustine, had been present to his mind in 1835; without producing the dramatic effect it had later. In this point too, though, Jager might well make a claim that his arguments had, however circuitously, produced their effect.

(iii) *The course of the controversy*

    (a) Jager's First Letter
    (b) Harrison's First Reply
    (c) Jager's Second Letter
    (d) Harrison's Second Reply
    (e) Jager's Third Letter
    (f) Newman decides to intervene

(a) *Jager's First Letter*

Jager's first letter appeared in the columns of *L'Univers* on 30 August 1834. After the customary initial protestations about the calm frame of mind in which the controversy was to be conducted on both sides, Jager described what he had learned about the present state of Anglicanism from conversations with Harrison and Cureton. They did not share what he termed the indifference of Protestantism. Oxford attached great importance to the preservation of what had been revealed. Hence nowhere in the books Harrison had lent him had he found that distinction between fundamental and non-fundamental doctrines which had been the cause of so much dispute between Catholics and Protestants. Anglicans admitted a visible Church, One, Catholic and Apostolic, and also that the Roman Church was a part of it. They rejected as dangerous the private interpretation of Scripture, believing with St. Vincent of Lérins 'what has been believed everywhere, at all times, and by all the faithful'. This theme had been developed by Bishop Jebb of Limerick in his *The peculiar character of the Church of England*. As he saw it, Pro-

---

[37] Jager, pp. 268–9.

testants had destroyed all authority and the Anglican Church
had avoided this extreme. Jebb developed the failures of private
interpretation: it placed an intolerable burden on the individual
seeker for truth, in terms of what he had to know of what went
before him; Scripture was not clear, and if we clung only to what
was clear, we should end up with nothing more than natural
religion. Where, then, was Jebb's rule? He found it in the fifth
century in the works of Vincent of Lérins, who defined it as
Scripture plus the line of prophetic and apostolic interpretation.
Vincent's criterion was 'the *universality, antiquity*, and *consent*
of the Catholic and Apostolic Church' (Jebb, op. cit., p. 282),
the decrees of General Councils or, failing them, the concurrent
sentiments of the greatest doctors. Jager praised the Anglican
Church for its rejection of private interpretation, and asked
where its tradition ended, in the fifth century, as Jebb saw it,
or in the sixth, in Hall's view. He finally proposed that they
should take the first six centuries of the Church as the basis of
their discussion.

(b) *Harrison's First Reply*

Where Jager had stressed grounds of agreement, Harrison
in his reply indicated difference. His letter was published in
L'Univers on 18 September 1834, and in it he stressed that the
principles of Anglicanism as explained by Jebb had been ob-
scured during the eighteenth century. He hoped the controversy
would show them forth, though the teaching duties of the
Oxford participants might delay their replies. He also hoped
that an Oxford periodical would publish the controversy. None
was named, but it seems likely the *British Magazine* was meant,
though nothing seems to have come of this.

Then he moved to the attack, basing his points on the *Churchman's Manual* (Oxford, 1833) which he had left with Jager. The
Church of Rome had imposed doctrines for which no warrant
could be found in Scripture or antiquity:

(1) the adoration of images
(2) the invocation of the Virgin Mary and the other saints
(3) the doctrine of Transubstantiation
(4) communion under one kind
(5) celibacy of the clergy
(6) the doctrine of purgatory

(7) the authority of Rome over all other churches
(8) obedience due to the Pope
(9) the seven sacraments

He did not dispute that Rome had the character of a true church, but he affirmed that Jager could not deny that title to the Church of England, possessing as it did an uninterrupted apostolic succession; and he claimed the title 'Catholic' for it. As far as Jebb was concerned, the issue was which of the two churches, Rome or Anglican, had been the more faithful to Vincent's maxim, since both appealed to it. The Anglican Church had observed it, the Roman Church had not.

(c) Jager's Second Letter

Jager's reply appeared the following day in *L'Univers*. He would, he said, willingly concede the title of Catholic to the Anglican Church. The public, however, would not. He proposed they should not leave a subject once begun, and found an ideal way of observing this rule by dealing with Harrison's claim, derived from Jebb, that the Roman Church had violated Vincent's rule.

Jager then examined Jebb's three proofs of his assertion. First, the Church of Rome maintained that there were two rules of belief, an unwritten as well as a written word of God, the former's authority being as definitive as the latter's; whereas for Vincent there is but one authority, the divine canon of the sacred scriptures. He admits the tradition of the Catholic Church, but not as a rival to the sacred word.

Now, says Jager, if we examine St. Paul and the Fathers, we find that they admit an unwritten word, and declare explicitly that *not* all things are to be found in the scriptures. Vincent himself says we should hold as true the doctrine the Church professes, and as certain what doctors have constantly taught. There is only one authority, the word of God, transmitted through scripture and tradition. Even Jebb seems to say as much when, in his *Pastoral Instructions* (p. 317), he declares 'Where the Scripture clearly and freely speaks, she receives its dictates as the voice of God. When Scripture is either not clear, or explicit; or when it may demand expansion and illustration, she refers her sons to an authoritative standard of interpretation *(tradition)*. . . . Thus, her appeal is made to past ages, against every possible error of the present.'

Jebb's second objection is this. Vincent proposes to assist, not supersede, the faculty of private judgement. The Church of Rome merely imposes her own summary decision, to which her children must submit. This is a direct violation of Vincent's rule, for he says,

> *Sive* EGO, *sive* ALIUS; whether, I MYSELF, *or* ANY OTHER PERSON, *wish to detect the frauds, and shun the snares of rising heretics, he must, through Divine assistance, fortify his faith in a twofold manner: by authority of the Divine law, and by the tradition of the church.*

This means that each individual member of the Church is to look to his own faith, says Jebb, something which the Roman Church allows to none.

Can Dr. Jebb seriously maintain, asks Jager, that each individual is compelled to study the collections of the Fathers to discover sacred truth? Of course not, even to state it shows how absurd it is. And Vincent exhorts us to adhere to the decision of the Church, either in terms of a general council or in terms of the sentiments of the fathers (*Commonitorium*, XXIX). Vincent knew the Church had exercised the right of decision in religious matters, every time a new heresy had arisen. The Church of England reserves this right to itself as well (Article 20). So Jebb, in declaring the Church's decision to be at variance with Vincent's rule, is himself opposed to Vincent and to his own Church's doctrine. What does the *sive ego, sive alius* text, adduced by Jebb, mean? Vincent is speaking of *new* heresies (*exsurgentium, Commonit.* II) and he means that if a heresy already condemned should rise up, hold to the Church's past decision. If there is a new one, hold to the faith of the majority of Christians. If the majority is infected, then have recourse to the ancient faith.

Jebb's third instance of dissonance between Vincent and Rome lies in the appeal to antiquity against innovation. Vincent urges this as a duty; the Church of Rome represses it. . . . Unconditional submission is required from those who from time to time occupy the seats of power in the Church, *which they constitute*. There is then no room for the appeal Vincent recommends.

Not so, says Jager. The church's pastors ascertain the true and ancient faith, and proclaim it by a short and precise decision —this protects the flock of Christ from an intolerable burden: 'What should become of us in the immense labyrinth of human aberrations, if we had neither a guide to lead us nor a torch to light our way?' This does not mean her choice is arbitrary: she is incapable of deciding anything new. In the words of Tertullian, 'we have for our authority the Apostles of the Lord, who did not even themselves choose to bring in anything of their own will, but faithfully delivered over to the nations the Religion which they had received from Christ' (*de Praescriptione*, VI).

(d) Harrison's Second Reply

Harrison had hoped Newman would be able to step into the breach at this point, and was chagrined to learn, as he wrote to Jager in his Second Reply (*Univers*, 14 October 1834) that Newman, referred to not by name but as the *ami d'Oxford*, was visiting friends and did not intend to return to Oxford before the end of the Long Vacation. Harrison's reply is disappointing. He reaffirms that, for Anglicans, Scripture contains all things necessary to salvation, and that what is not in Scripture cannot be imposed as an article of faith. This is consonant with Vincent's phrase in the *Commonitorium* (II), he declares, in which Vincent says 'Not that the Scripture *is not sufficient for all* . . .' It is all-sufficing, but must be interpreted with the tradition of the Church. Jager had not understood Article 20, in which it is clear that the Church has the right to add rites and ceremonies but not to command anything as necessary to salvation which is not in Scripture. Vincent likewise declares his rule is only to be observed 'in those questions upon which the foundations of the whole Catholic doctrine do depend' (*Commonit.* XXIX).

Jager had affirmed that when a nascent heresy arose, not yet condemned by the Church, recourse should be had to the majority view, and then, failing this, to the ancient faith. This is no easy task, replied Harrison. The majority must be ascertained, and how can the individual do this? In any case, is this what Vincent recommends? No, he says quite clearly that if a new infection of heresy seems to corrupt the whole church, the seeker for truth must consult the ancient councils. If there is no decision there, then he must consult the ancient writers. Jebb is right, then, it is the duty of every individual to 'hold to the faith of the fathers' (*Commonit.* XXXIII). Vincent would not have imposed the duty of search had he been aware, as Jager claimed he was, that the Church reserved to herself the right of decision in every case. When nearly all the Latin bishops were infected with heresy, in the days of Arianism, those who preferred ancient faith to new error were, says Vincent, untouched with the spot of infection (*Commonit.* IV). After discussing other examples, such as Nestorius and Photinus, Vincent concludes 'that all true Catholics may know that with the Church they ought to receive doctors, and not with doctors to forsake the faith of the Church' (*Commonit.* XVII). There was the true and sincere Catholic.

Jager had touched very lightly on the third discrepancy he alleged between Vincent and Rome. Vincent recommends the Christian not to acquiesce in error even when it is maintained by existing authorities. But the Church of Rome demands unconditional submission. Now Vincent is writing, says Harrison, in a time of general corruption and of a dominant heresy in which the voice of the true Church is stifled or silent. No matter what the eminence of the doctors concerned, Vincent affirms, it was never lawful, is nowhere lawful, nor ever shall be lawful 'to preach unto Catholic Christian men beside that which they have received' (*Commonit.* IX). Hence the point of Article 20, that it is not lawful for the Church to ordain anything contrary to God's witness or expound one place of scripture so that it shall be repugnant to another.

Finally, Jager had said that Harrison accused Rome of errors and corruption; and he, Jager, accused the Church of England of schism. But, concludes Harrison, we accuse you of that too. We appeal to antiquity. We accuse your church of new inventions and additions to the word of God.

(e) *Jager's Third Letter*

In his third letter, published in two parts in consecutive issues of *L'Univers* (23 and 24 October 1834), Jager remained unimpressed by Harrison's arguments. Although he recognized their zeal and learning, he saw them to be without any solid foundations. It was more important now, he declared, to discover whether, as Harrison claimed, the Roman Church had violated Vincent's rule than to continue to debate as to which church adhered more closely to that rule.

He begins his defence by pointing out that during the three centuries of controversy with the Protestants, the Roman Church has openly and unwaveringly affirmed that Scripture alone is not sufficient to reveal the whole of the religion of Jesus Christ and, to know its real meaning, we must turn to the authority of the Church which preserved the antiquity, uniformity, and universality of its teaching against the arbitrary and multiple interpretations of private judgement. Although this, in itself, confutes Harrison's entire argument, he decides to comment in detail on Harrison's observations.

He acknowledges that part of the essential faith of the Roman Church consists of certain things unwritten and yet regarded as divine; in fact, Christianity, if it is not to be an empty word, must recognize the divine sources of the interpretative tradition and that it is the necessary base of a general and universal belief. If, on the grounds that Vincent never speaks of them, Jebb condemns the Roman Church for regarding certain unwritten things as divine, so must the Anglican Church also stand condemned for accepting as divine things unwritten, such as its rites and ceremonies. Jebb *should* have attempted to prove that the Roman Church had rejected the interpretations of the fathers recommended by Vincent—but that would have been an impossible task, for the Roman Church reveres them as she does Scripture, because they derive from the Apostles and Jesus Christ himself.

He studies in more detail Vincent's statement that Scripture is self-sufficient and the question arising from it: why is the interpretation of the Fathers necessary? It *is* self-explanatory and needs no interpreters, Jager agrees, but Vincent nowhere says that Scripture contains everything necessary for salvation. On the contrary, he makes constant reference to the early decisions and ordinances of the Fathers. He acknowledges the unwritten word when, in exposing the errors of Nestorius, Apollinaris, and Photinus, he sets against them the belief of the Catholic Church that the Trinity is but one Divinity. Although the Anglican bishop, Beveridge, cannot find this belief in full in the Scriptures, he regards it as a divine truth because it has been deduced from them by the universal consent of Christians. In fact, Jager continues, Vincent explicitly upholds the unwritten word when he says, at the beginning of his treatise, that we must believe in the decrees of a general council, which confirm to posterity in writing what the Church had formerly received by tradition alone. If this unwritten word is called *interpretation*, then their dispute is merely verbal.

Jager says he cannot understand how the Anglican Church can admit—according to *Tracts for the Times*, No. 34—rites and ceremonies derived from tradition and yet feel justified in rejecting dogmatic truths from the same source.

Anglicans agree with the Roman Church that Christ descended into Hell, that the Mother of God remained a Virgin, that the Lord's Day, not the Sabbath, must be kept holy and that baptism may be administered by anyone, is not renewable, and may be conferred on infants. These are new unwritten articles and yet they form part of Anglican teaching. Some of them must surely be regarded as necessary to salvation.

Jager examines the Thirty-Nine Articles and finds proof of acceptance of more unwritten articles than Catholics admit. They are entitled Articles of Faith, so must be considered necessary to salvation. But there is no trace of them in Scripture. They must, therefore, be founded on tradition. The Roman Church does not admit so many unwritten articles. It is the Church of England, concludes Jager triumphantly, which has violated Vincent's rule by acknowledging unwritten laws.

In his second accusation, Jebb accused the Roman Church of making its people slaves to her summary decisions, thereby violating the rule of Vincent which says the church must assist its members' private judgement, not supersede it. The point of Vincent's rule, says Jager, is to emphasize the unchangeable nature of Christian doctrine. This is precisely what the Roman Church does, innovating nothing, rewriting nothing, merely transmitting what she has received. As Vincent affirms, 'what hath she else at any time endeavoured by the decrees of councils, but that what before was simply credited, the same afterward should be more diligently believed; . . . that what before was more securely reverenced, the same afterward should more carefully be cherished?' (*Commonit*. XXIII). This seems to Jager an adequate answer to Jebb's second charge.

To answer the accusation completely, Jager sets out his argument in more detail.

The Church cannot stay silent in the face of error and novelty. Vincent confirms that the Church's duty is to speak out in time of heresy and he quotes Paul's severe words to heretics: 'But although we or an angel from heaven evangelize unto you beside that which we have evangelized, be he anathema' (Gal. 1: 8). Vincent points out that the Catholic Church inherits the Apostles' right to condemn heresy. 'It is truly proper to all Catholics', he says, 'to keep those things which the Holy Fathers have left, and committed to their charge, *to condemn profane novelties . . .*' (*Commonit.* XXIV). If the Anglican Church has given up that responsibility, it has lost the title of Catholic.

He next examines Jebb's assertion that Vincent recommends each individual, in time of heresy, to seek his own faith in antiquity. This is an impossible task. Lack of learning, intellect, resources, and time make the task of perusing all ancient theological documents completely impracticable for the majority of Christians. Were such a task possible, its only results must be to reduce the authority of the Church to ceaseless and insoluble wrangling. Instead of allowing free rein to all private interpretations, Vincent himself acknowledges the necessity for courts of final appeal within the Church and insists that the true Christian has a corresponding duty to obey their decrees. Whoever despises the divinely inspired courts, says Vincent, 'doth not condemn man but God' (*Commonit.* XXVIII).

To answer Harrison's points on nascent heresy, Jager repeats the procedure, set out in his second letter, for a Christian to follow in the face of a new heresy.

1. If the nascent heresy is condemned by a council, its decision must be upheld.

2. If no pronouncement has yet been made by the Church, the faith of the majority must be followed. Vincent's rule affirms that we must 'prefer the health of the whole body, before the pestiferous and corrupt member' (*Commonit.* III). Contrary to Harrison's opinion it is not difficult to ascertain the majority, for a heresy, by its very nature, always begins with a small number. It is easy for the Christian to hold to the generally accepted belief—certainly much easier than delving through antiquity.

3. Supposing the heresy to infect almost the whole body of

the Church as in the period of Arianism, Vincent says the Christian *'by preferring ancient faith before new error*, was untouched with any spot of that infection' (*Commonit.* IV). This advice is completely in accord with the practice of the Roman Church.

4. Vincent goes further and supposes a very rare case where antiquity itself might be divided and there is uncertainty about the ancient faith. Then the Catholic must himself labour to establish true faith by consulting and comparing the opinions of those ancient fathers who were 'approved masters' (*Commonit.* III). . . . But Harrison cannot regard this as a victory for he can nowhere find that the Roman Church has *forbidden* this sort of research as Jebb suggests. Rather, she does not make it a duty.

Far from denying the guidance of the Church, Vincent recommends it. To prelates, priests, and teachers he says 'That which before men believed obscurely, let them by thy exposition understand more clearly' (*Commonit.* XXII). In fact, he believes the guidance of the bishops, who constitute the Church, to be infallible. 'We inveighed also against the wicked presumption of Nestorius, who maintained that the whole Church both doth now err, and always had erred' (*Commonit.* XXI).

5. Jager deals briefly with Jebb's third accusation that, although Vincent says the Christian must not acquiesce in error however generally maintained by existing authorities, the Roman Church always demands complete submission to its teachings. We must, agrees Jager, anathematize *anyone* who falls into error, but this does not exclude the necessity of submitting to universal Church authority, which maintains the ancient faith and rejects novelties, a view of Vincent's already established. Besides, Vincent was referring to a special case: that period between the rise of heresy and a decision by the Church. The Roman Catholic still has recourse to antiquity and Scripture because they are the Church's guide.

Hence the doctrine of the Roman Church is in complete harmony with Vincent's treatise.

(f) Newman decides to intervene

At this point, the controversy took an odd turn. Jager believed that the elucidation of Vincent's rule would occupy them no

further, and passed on to discuss some of the items in Harrison's
first reply. This became a fourth letter, devoted to the Cult of
Images, and appeared in *L'Univers* in two parts on 7 and 8 November 1834. When Jager reprinted the controversy in book
form, this letter was omitted, because Newman, when he entered
the controversy, turned the debate back to Jebb's interpretation
of Vincent's *Commonitorium* and ignored the images discussion
completely. What is called the Fourth Letter in Jager's book,
and consequently in the present work, is strictly speaking the
fifth in his original sequence, the other letters being renumbered
to conform with this.

Whatever Jager's merits as a controversialist, he seems to
have proved too much for Harrison. After the publication of
Jager's Third Letter, Harrison pressed Newman to take over.
'I have got into controversy', Newman wrote to Hurrell Froude
(12 November 1834, quoted in Tristram, *John Henry Newman:
Centenary Essays*, p. 211), 'with a Parisian Abbé. . . . The war
is to be on the whole Romish question, and I have been reading
Laud, Stillingfleet, etc.'

Where Jager was only too impatient to fill the columns of
L'Univers with his arguments, Newman spent the entire first
term of the academic year 1834–5 in composing his first letter—
here called, in proper sequence, the Third Reply. It is quite clear
that Newman relished the prospect of engaging in controversy,
and felt it served his purpose very well, as a draft of a letter to
Jager shows. Newman finally refrained from sending this draft;
but it is an interesting reflection on his motives for entering into
debate at this juncture:

Before availing myself of the honour you have offered me [he writes],
of submitting to you my thoughts upon certain tenets of the English
Church, you must allow me to state the position I consider myself to
occupy towards you. My opponent is, as all know, a learned man. His
name is known as such; whereas I am a nameless individual, who have
been occupied ever since I went into orders (tho' I trust not unpro-
fitably) in humble parochial duties and the classical education of youth,
and am no theologian. You will naturally ask, why then have you
undertaken to write to me; it is a reasonable question; at first sight
there is a great presumption in my doing so. But in your late message
to Mr. H[arrison] you so earnestly requested in the most kind and
polite manner to be suffered to contend with some of us at Oxford,
you were so sollicitous [*sic*] to find an adversary; and when our mutual

friend applied to me on the subject there were several reasons which induced me to be venturesome.

First because I felt it likely that if I did not engage with you, no one else would; so that it seemed a duty for some one, if possible, to attend to your wish. Yet who was to be found disengaged among us for such a service? Indeed we are too busy here in our various ways to take up matters which are not immediately *practical*; and such at present are the differences between your and our theology [that it] is not a practical question in the eyes of English divines. And it must be confessed in proportion to our long security in that matter such I frankly own is the ignorance of the English clergy as to these differences and of the controversy arising out of them. Almost all of us, excepting our Theological Professors and other high organs of our religious opinions have laid aside their arms; which were formerly wielded by an Andrews, a Laud and a Barrow. So that little as I have studied the subject I dare say I know as much as most of them. I considered with myself that I probably had thought as much on the subject as most of us tho' I had never practised myself in polemical exercise that if the controversy between the Churches was to be renewed there must be a beginning; and that on our side that beginning must be attended with some mistakes in detail in the mode of conducting the argument;—that the Romans once had as model for a ship of war but a chance vessel of the enemy's flung upon the beach, yet at last they became lords of sea as well as land; and that the challenge had come directly to me not to another. For these reasons I considered I ought not to decline the challenge, believing as I do that truth is on my side. And this is a second reason why I should not shrink from a challenge which has come fairly before me.

But my chief reason is a profound persuasion that the truth is mainly on the side which I should have to advocate; so that even an unskilful person, such as myself, though destitute of the advantage of years, experience and learning would be unlucky if he did not make his leaders think better of his cause than they did before.

As to converting any Romanists, that is not my aim, much as I should rejoice to convince them of the superior purity of my own Church knowing as I do that religious principles depend for the most part not on reasoning but on habit and association. Well were it for both the Gallican and the Anglican Churches, if they would be content to be silent on their respective differences, except as they saw a probability of removing them and would unite together in a mutual communion, as formerly in disputes about Easter and the baptism of heretics.

All I can hope to do then, all I propose to myself, is to contribute towards lessening the jealousies with which the French Catholics and yourself perhaps in particular regard us of the Anglican Church. Why should they not look forward to a time when, without any of those untrue conciliations which are [a] portion of the liberalistic spirit which is fashionable in the comprehensions of the day, the two Churches should enjoy that mutual peace and love which some of its [*sic*] eminent men on both sides have before now desired to bring about?

It remains only that I should state distinctly, what I have above implied, that I have no authority, office or station in the University which might give weight to my words. I am but an individual member of one of the Colleges; and have no claim to represent any one besides myself.

Newman's first contribution to the controversy, and appearing in it as the Third Reply, was printed in part in *L'Univers* on 25 December 1834. This partial printing contravened the rules of debate which Harrison and Jager had agreed at the start. Each protagonist's letter was to be printed in full before the other's reply began; whereas *L'Univers*, after printing less than a column of Newman, offered nearly six times that amount of space to Jager, and in far larger type, in the same issue. Harrison reacted at once to this, and wrote to Jager protesting at this infringement of the rules. He reported what he had done to Newman on 3 January 1835:

Here is the Abbé again at his former tricks. I have written to him at once telling him that it would never do to take your letter piecemeal; and begging him to insert your letters as a whole, in numbers as closely consecutive as possible, and then give us his reply as a whole. I have argued fairly out with him the endless confusion into which the controversy will be brought, if we are to have half a dozen answers awaiting a reply, while there is one long letter lying by him which is to be taken bit by bit, to the utter ruin of its meaning as a complete argument. I hope this may produce some effect; if not, I shall be sorry for my friend and ashamed of the 'Univers's' tactics. (*Letters and Correspondence of John Henry Newman*, ed. Anne Mozley, ii. 81–2.)

Perhaps as a result of this intervention, Jager saw to it that Newman's letter was completed in *L'Univers* on 28 and 29 January. Fr. Tristram describes it as 'a clear and incisive piece of work, not unworthy of the hand responsible for the early *Tracts for the Times . . .*' (Tristram, op. cit., p. 212). The full text of this letter now follows.

2. Newman's First Letter[a]

SIR,

In taking up this argument, hitherto sustained by Mr. H . . .
I beg to thank you for the kind and amiable way in which you
have begun[1] the controversy. You have adopted the style of
those, who wish,[2] according to the Apostle's words, to 'hold
the truth in love' (*Eph.* iv, 15) and I can desire nothing better
than to be able to follow your example in this respect in maintaining my own views of Gospel doctrine. Allow me to premise
one or two remarks, on the introduction[3] of your last letter, and
then I will proceed to make my reply to you under Bishop Jebb's
three heads, as by you made the basis of discussion.[4]

First I do not wish[5] to be supposed[6] to grant you six centuries
as the range of Apostolic[7] purity in the Church. Bishop Hall[b]
indeed has taken[8] it; so, as it would seem, has Jewell.[c] The more
usual period however for our divines to take[9] is about the period
of the first four Councils, i.e. down to the middle of the fifth
century.[10] I will say no more on the subject here, than make this
memorandum.

Next suffer me to dissent from your representation that Mr.
H. and I have[11] been acting on the offensive against[12] Romanism.
Not so. Mr. H. puts[13] a number of English publications into your
hands[14] in order that you may gather from them our sentiments

[1] conducted	[2] would	[3] after the example
[4] commented on		[5] not
[6] committed		[7] Church
[8] sa[id]	[9] Laud takes between four and five, Stillingfleet four	
[10] A.D. 451	[11] both	[12] attacking
[13] Jebb's book		[14] among others

[a] The Third Reply in the original sequence of the controversy. Unless otherwise
indicated, numbered footnotes in this Letter give words or phrases deleted by
Newman from his MS. A later note adds at this point: Beginning of the controversy
with the Abbé Jager, vid. Advertisement to 'Prophetical Office'.

[b] Joseph Hall (1574–1656), Bishop of Exeter and Norwich. Hall was one of
a number of Anglican divines who treated the question of Fundamentals. Cf. *The
Peace-Maker*, Ch. 1, Sect. 3, 'Of the Fundamental Points of Religion', in *Works*,
vol. vii, Oxford, 1837.

[c] John Jewel (1522–71), Bishop of Salisbury, author of *Apologia pro Ecclesia
Anglicana* (1562).

of the[1] English Church. You single out Bishop Jebb; and because he, in showing our peculiar position, indirectly assails Romanism, but not Romanism alone, Puritanism also, therefore you begin, which you had a full right to do, to attack Jebb. You call upon us to meet[2] you and defend[3] him. We are willing to do so; but do not say we have volunteered an attack on you, rather than made a defence of ourselves. We are very happy to be allowed to attack you, but you have begged us to do so.

Lastly you observe that Bishop Jebb[4] accused the Latin Church of innovating[5] with a very bad grace, seeing she[6] has ever professed[7] to abominate innovation; whereas our Church's hatred of it, if she[8] has it, has slept in libraries, and has been unknown of late even to her own members.[a] To this I reply that we are engaged in a mere historical question: *why* did our Church reform herself in the 16th century, on *what principles?* a question to be determined by our acts[9] and formularies ascertained in the history of that period,[10] and by our great divines. Doubtless, with a few great exceptions such as Bishops Butler,[b] Wilson[c] and the like, the last century was the age of little men; i.e. little men[11] were in chief repute and honor in the Church. Such is the force of political influence. Yet the true succession of the school of Ridley,[d] Laud,[e] and Kenn[f] [*sic*] was continued

[1] our	[2] follow	[3] in [defend]ing	[4] Mr. H
[5] [innovat]ion	[6] it	[7] proclaim	[8] it
[9] deeds *added above the line*		[10] then executed	[11] they

[a] The French of this reads as follows: 'Enfin vous observez que l'évêque Jebb a mauvaise grâce d'accuser l'Eglise latine d'innover, puisqu'elle a toujours professé de l'horreur pour toute innovation, tandis que la haine que notre église y porte, si toutefois elle en est imbue, a dormi dans nos cartons restant inconnue pendant long-temps à ses propres membres.' Jager adds the following note: 'Nous n'avons pu comprendre le sens, ni le but de cette observation. Si elle est importante nos adversaires sauront la reproduire.' Jager, p. 93.

[b] Joseph Butler (1692–1752), Bishop of Durham, author of the *Analogy of Religion* (1736).

[c] Thomas Wilson (1663–1755), Bishop of Sodor and Man. He was a friend of the abbé Claude Fleury, author of *Histoire ecclésiastique*. Keble edited his works in the 'Library of Anglo-Catholic Theology' (Oxford, 7 vols., 1847–63).

[d] Nicholas Ridley (? 1500–55), Bishop of Rochester, then of London, burned for heresy under Queen Mary.

[e] William Laud, Archbishop of Canterbury (1573–1645). The account of his controversy with the Jesuit, Fisher (*A Relation of the Conference*, etc.), and Stillingfleet's defence of it, were among Newman's sources for his discussion of fundamentals.

[f] Thomas Ken [or Kenn] (1637–1711), nonjuror, Bishop of Bath and Wells.

in our cloisters[1] and our retired[2] parsonages, to come to light again in due time. No one knows so well as the Church of Rome,[3] that to suspend the enforcement of a claim, is not to relinquish it.

Bishop Jebb's first remark upon Vincentius is this, that he agrees with the Church of England, not with the Church of Rome in his judgment concerning the Rule of Faith. 'The Church of Rome' says the Bishop, 'maintains, not only that there are two rules of belief, but that these two rules are co-ordinate; that there is an unwritten, no less than a written word of God, and that the authority of the former is alike definitive with the authority of the latter' (p. 283).[a] The Church of England on the other hand receives Tradition as well as Scripture as a rule, i.e. a guide in faith and conduct, in various ways, but in all ways as altogether subordinate and subsidiary, as shall directly[4] be explained.[5]

[6]Now I shall first attempt clearly to state, in detail, what is your[7] doctrine and what our doctrine is in this matter; and then will apply my statement to the elucidation of the points contained in your last letter.

[8]The main principle which we of the Anglican Church maintain, is this: that Scripture is the ultimate basis of proof,[9] the place of final appeal, in respect to all fundamental doctrine. Let

[1] colleges   [2] priv[ate]   [3] itself knows well   [4] by and bye

[5] Further, the words of Vincentius quoted by Jebb are these: 'duplici modo munire fidem suam, Domino adjuvante, deberet; primo scilicet, divinae legis auctoritate, tum deinde, Ecclesiae Catholicae Traditione' ['. . . he ought two manner of ways by God's assistance to defend and preserve his faith; that is, first, by the authority of the law of God; secondly, by the tradition of the Catholic Church'] [*Commonit. II*]

[6] *At this point some suggestions for translation have been pencilled on the draft*: ultimate appeal—dernier ressort

                        doctrine—doctrine

                        fundamentals—doctrines fondamentales [vérités]

immediately   —directement

ultimately   —à la longue

canon of Sc.   —le canon de l'écriture

                        la doctrine de Transubn

                        la communion sous une seule espèce.

[7] the   [8] your Church considers

[9] *marginal reference* Marsh p. 28 [i.e. Herbert Marsh, 1757–1839, *A Comparative View of the Churches of England and Rome*, Cambridge, 1814].

[a] John [Jebb], Bishop of Limerick . . . *Pastoral Instructions on the Character and Principles of the Church of England, selected from his former publications* . . . London, Duncan Cochran & Key, 1831, p. 283.

these words be well weighed. We do not deny that ceremonies and practices may lawfully be made to rest upon tradition, but that doctrines may so rest; nay not simply all doctrines, but fundamental doctrines. Nor do we say that the proof of even fundamental doctrines must rest immediately on Scripture, but ultimately. These three words, *ultimate appeal, doctrines,* and *fundamentals* must be clearly understood. E.g. we should be[1] ready to receive the three orders of the Ministry even on[2] *tradition,* as being a point of *discipline*; we receive the validity of heretical baptism on *tradition,* as being a *doctrine not fundamental*; we receive the doctrine of the Trinity, *a fundamental, immediately* from tradition, *ultimately from Scripture.* If we are asked what we mean by fundamentals,[3] we answer that we mean such doctrines as are necessary for Church Communion; if we are asked which these are, we answer briefly the articles of the Creed. Further, if we are asked what we consider to be the obligation of receiving doctrines *not* fundamental, or of matters of discipline, (such as[4] come to us on the voucher of tradition), we answer we consider it *pious* to receive them, but not *necessary*[5] for Church communion. Thus we make a[6] distinction between the authority of pure tradition and[7] the[8] authority of tradition based on Scripture in fundamental points, somewhat answering to your distinction between a praeceptum and a consilium of the Church. The reception of [9]pure tradition is pious, of [10] doctrines conveyed to us by Tradition but proved by Scripture is imperative.[11]

This statement gives great and extensive influence[12] to tradition. Doubtless, we consider that it tells us all that Scripture tells and much besides.[13] It is evident, from what has been said, we make 1. a tradition interpretative of Scripture.[14] 2. a tradition of doctrine not in Scripture. 3. a tradition of discipline, ceremonies,[15] historical facts, &c. &c. extending to a variety of

---

[1] even   [2] more   [3] are fundamentals   [4] which
[5] (as is the reception of fundamentals   [6] this
[7] in matters of doctrine not fundamental and of discipline   [8] of
[9] the former
[10] the latter. *Newman has substituted for this phrase and then in turn deleted* tradition based on Scripture is imperative.
[11] *Newman adds a later note in the MS.:* (somewhat loosely said) July 26-35 imperative for salvation, but (it being a secret how far such unbelief is sinful) not necessary for Church communion.   [12] and extent   [13] more too
[14] or corpus hermeneuticum   [15] in ceremony

matters. But in every way of regarding it, you will see we consider tradition subordinate, not coordinate to Scripture, which is all along the one basis of the Rule of Faith, containing expressly or implicitly the fundamental doctrines.

You on the other hand, allowing our three uses of Tradition, add a fourth,[1] which we deny. You consider[2] Tradition per se the sufficient authority for the Church's considering a doctrine fundamental. 'Quia . . . [Scriptura] non est regula totalis, says Bellarmine, sed partialis, inde illi accidit, ut non omnia mensuret, et propterea aliquid sit de fide, quod in ipsa non continetur' (Bellarm. *de Verb. Dei* iv, 12 §).[a] This point will be best illustrated by taking some specimens from the decrees of the Council of Trent, which with you are fundamental, and which specify the ultimate authority on which they are made.

You know we do not receive your doctrine of Transubstantiation and the Adoration of the Host, on the ground that they are[3] unscriptural.[4] Now the Council of Trent promulgates them; but on what authority? Take the words with which the decretum de Sanctissimo Eucharistiae sacramento is prefaced; the Church of Rome decrees it 'doctrinam tradens, quam *semper* Catholica Ecclesia, ab ipso Jesu Christo Domino nostro et ejus Apostolis erudita,[5] atque a Spiritu sancto, illi omnem veritatem indies suggerente, edocta, *retinuit*, et ad finem usque saeculi *conservabit*.'[b] Here there is no appeal to the written word.

Again, take the beginning[6] of the decree concerning[7] the Sacrifice of the Mass. 'Quare non solum pro fidelium vivorum peccatis, poenis, satisfactionibus, et aliis necessitatibus, sed et pro *defunctis* in Christo, nondum ad plenum purgatis, rite juxta Apostolorum *traditionem*, offertur.'[c]

Again the decree concerning[7] Indulgences is made to rest[8] solely on the power of the Church, 'divinitus sibi *tradita*'.[d]

[1] further   [2] pure   [3] contrary   [4] *Marginal reference* Marsh, p. 28.
[5] *This word is first underlined, then the underlining is deleted*   [6] part
[7] Purgatory 'Cum Catholica Ecclesia, Spiritu Sancto edocta ex   [8] solely

[a] *This reference is omitted from the French text. Cf. p. 38, n. 5.*

[b] 'delivering the doctrine which the Catholic Church, instructed by our Lord Jesus Christ himself and by His Apostles, has always preserved, and will preserve until the end of the world.' Labb. t. xiv, p. 804.

[c] 'wherefore it is offered not only for the sins, punishments, satisfactions, and other necessities of the living, but also for those who are deceased in Christ, and are not yet fully purged of their sins', ibid., p. 853. [*Quoted in Marsh, op. cit., p. 33.*]   [d] 'divinely handed down to it,

These instances are given, not by way of ascertaining[1] your view,[2] that we may clearly have before us the points on which we are at issue[3]; viz. Whether or not Tradition per se is a sufficient authority for the Church to go by in settling *fundamentals*.[4] You answer in the affirmative;[5] we in the negative.

Now let us go on to another part of the subject, viz. the relation of the Church towards these two sources of Truth. We[6] say the Church first is *keeper* of Christian doctrine,[7] next *declares* it,[8] thirdly has authority[9] in regard to it, i.e. speaks[10] definitively about it. You argue as to the two first, and differ as to the last; so let me explain myself.

We consider the Gospel Faith to be the foundation on which the Church is built; prior to it, the essential[11] deposit committed to it,[12] the main object[13] proposed thro' it to mankind,[14] the ground[15] of communion, ever one and the same,[16] admitting of no[17] addition,[18] and imperishable.[19] It is the foundation according to the words: 'on this Rock, (i.e. St. Peter's confession) will I build My Church'.[20] It is prior to it, *because* it is its foundation, just as revelation itself[21] is prior in turn to the Gospel Faith.[22] It is the deposit committed to the Church, which in Scripture is expressly called the pillar and seat of the Truth, and is exhorted

---

[1] proving what I suppose you will grant   [2] which I fear is too

[3] in question   [4] in fundamental matters, i.e. points of faith

[5] *A note is inserted at this point, then deleted*: 'Quia non est [Scriptura] regula totalis, sed partialis, inde illi accidit, quod *non omnia* mensuret, et propterea aliquid sit de Fide quod in ipsa non continetur', Bellarmine, De Verbo Dei. iv. 12. ['Because Scripture is not a complete rule, but a partial one, hence it happens that it does not comprise all things, and as a result something may be of faith, which is not contained in it.' *This reference is quoted by Marsh, op. cit., p. 47.*]

[6] You   [7] is a witness and keeper of the divine oracles

[8] and has them   [9] *This word is underlined, then the underlining is deleted*

[10] proclaims   [11] sole

[12] the Church's case   [13] sole condition of faith

[14] to be received in order to / as the means of / salvation and as

[15] condition   [16] each unalterable / and the

[17] neither increase   [18] novelty or

[19] immortal

has no authority

[20] we consider the Church cannot add to it

it to be contained in the Apostles' Creed, or

rather to paraphrase in those Articles of the early Creed

which are found the same in all the

early Creeds, of which our particular

Creed is one form.

[21] the Verbum Dei i.e. Scripture   [22] doctrines

in the person of Timothy to hold fast the deposit. It is the main object proposed for Church communion,[1] for it is said 'he who believeth[2] and is *baptized* shall be saved.'[a] It is ever one and the same, by which I mean that what St. Paul committed to Timothy is to be handed on 'by faithful men' for ever. It admits of no increase, i.e. no more[3] than the foundation of an house; the Church having no power over that on which it stands. It is imperishable;[4] by which I mean that the time[5] will never come for[6] it to sink into oblivion like Greek and Roman polytheism. The only question you have to ask me is, in what doctrines this foundation[7] consists. [8]We consider that in the first instance the doctrine of Christ is the foundation, according to the Apostle's words 'Other foundation can no man lay than that is laid, which is Jesus Christ;' or again the doctrine of the Trinity, as confessed in the baptismal form. These are certainly fundamentals,[9] [10]and the fountain heads of all doctrines; but they are not all the fundamentals,[11] for we are accustomed by the guidance of Scripture to add to them, or rather to develop them into, the Articles of the primitive Antenicene Creed. Such then are the doctrines which we consider to have been revealed[12] as the basis of the Church, the condition of baptism, the profession of Churchmen.

Further, as we consider (according to the above statement) that the Church Catholic will never lose the deposit committed to her, (as it is said, The gates of hell shall not prevail against it), we believe her so far to be infallible, infallible in fundamentals.[13]

[1] belief unto salvation   [2] *This word is underlined, then the underlining is deleted*
[3] that   [4] never ending indestructible
[5] matters   [6] when   [7] it
[8] a question which the Church of England is not very careful to answer accurately
[9] but   [10] Church Communion i.e. the conditions of baptism
[11] laid down in Scr   [12] by means of/through the Word of God in order to be
[13] *Newman later notes:* (awkward expression) July 26/35 yet Stillingfleet seems to use it. [*Newman refers to the following passage:* 'But yet further, I add, that taking *Fundamentals* in your sense, you prove not the thing you intended, but only to such as do acknowledge, and as far as they do acknowledge, that *General Councils cannot err.* For, they who acknowledge them infallible only in *Fundamentals*, do not judge anything *Fundamental* by their *Decision*, but judge their *Decisions infallible*, so long as they hold to *Fundamentals*; and so (for all that I can see) leave themselves *Judges, when General Councils are infallible* and *when not*: And therefore if they go about to testifie any thing as revealed from God, which is not Fundamental, they do not believe that their Testimony cannot err, and so are not bound to believe that it is from God.' Stillingfleet, *A Rational Account of the Grounds of Protestant Religion, Works,* London, 1710, vol. iv, p. 65.]

[a] Mk. 16:16

Further still, we allow to the Church, nay to separate branches of it, a power to develop[1] its fundamental Creed into Articles of religion,[2] according to times and circumstances,[3] not however as necessary to be believed for communion,[4] but useful for all her[5] people as necessary for holding rule or influence.[6] These will be either doctrines and[7] points of discipline handed down by tradition, as the baptism of infants, or doctrines or propositions deduced from Scripture, as the procession[8] of the Holy Spirit from the Son. The object of these additions is either to secure the fundamentals, as was[9] effected at Nicaea by the Homoousion, or to fortify the Church itself, as our article denying the jurisdiction of the Roman See in England. And in this respect it is that the Church has 'authority in controversies of faith'; viz. first to oblige her Ministers to take her view and[10] exposition of the fundamentals, next to hinder individuals from openly professing or teaching any other exposition. For a while the whole Church agreed together in these voluntary developments; but, at length, separate[11] branches spoke for themselves according to circumstances. It is evident that the authority of these authoritative declarations will vary with the circumstances under which they are made. If made by the whole Church in early times, and professing to come from Apostolic tradition,[12] they will come[13] with great weight to all Christians in every age. Thus our Church professes to hold the decrees of the four first General Councils as the rule of orthodoxy against heresy. But according as the distance from the Apostles is[14] greater, the portion[15] of Christendom represented smaller, external influences,[16] political and other, more apparent, or the subjects debated of a less fundamental character, we make the less account of them. In no case however do we impose any of them as terms of communion.

Lastly, as[17] we do not consider the Church[18] infallible so far forth as she thus exercises her own judgment, (i.e. in explaining,

---

[1] add to   [2] doctrine
[3] but   [4] or salvation
[5] its   [6] in the Church
[7] or   [8] Hypostasis
[9] or to   [10] of   [11] each
[12] traditions *then the* s *has been deleted*   [13] be
[14] becomes *superscribed*   [15] branches of
[16] causes   [17] seeing   [18] Her

commenting on, guarding her deposit,) we are not unwilling to allow that at various times various errors have incrusted the faith of the Gospel. Such indeed is the view which we actually take of the Churches of the Roman communion; accounting them true Churches, Churches holding the fundamentals but overlaid with corruptions.

On the other hand you Romanists believe the Church Catholic[1] to have the power of adding to the fundamentals of faith, as was done[2] abundantly at Trent; and in order to this, you[3] draw[4] the line of infallibility much higher than we do, not including indeed within it decisions respecting discipline or matter of fact or civil policy, but maintaining that absolutely no doctrine small or great, propounded by the Church can be other than true, and entitled to our cordial and unhesitating acceptance. But with this part of the subject we are not yet concerned.

Summing up then all that has been said, it appears we acknowledge[5] 1. Scripture as[6] the repository[7] of the fundamentals 2. [8]a corpus of traditions professedly apostolical, partly interpretative of Scripture, partly independent of it though agreeable to it. 3. the Church's teaching as based on the fundamentals,[9] authoritative, of an argumentative[10] and systemizing character[11]; whereas you [12]rest the fundamentals on Infallible Definitions of the existing Church, [13]availing itself of the materials contained in Scripture and Tradition.

Now to recur to Vincentius, about whose doctrine is our dispute. His work contains[14] the following positions agreeable to the Anglican[15] view.

1. that tradition is secondary to Scripture. 'Quod sive ego sive quis alius vellet exurgentium haereticorum fraudes &c., duplici modo muniri fidem suam, Domino adjuvante, deberet; primo scilicet divinae legis auctoritate, tum deinde Ecclesiae Catholicae

---

[1] the Church of Rome believes herself   [2] she did   [3] they/she
[4] draws *then* s *deleted*   [5] consider
[6] containing   [7] storehouse   [8] we acknowledge
[9] a power in the Church to impose   [10] authoritative
[11] argumentative given to system and arrangement
[12] supersede Scripture and Tradition by the believe but simply on Tradition by the
[13] not as   [14] tells us   [15] English

traditione.'[a1] Here I make this remark. Tradition is prior[2] to Scripture in *order of time*, both historically,[3] and in its use as respects individual Christians. As such your[4] writers insist on its claims to deference. 'Jesus Christ' says Bossuet, (*Expos.* ch. xvii)[b] 'having laid the foundation of His Church by preaching, the unwritten word was consequently the first rule of Christianity; and, when the writings of the New Testament were added to it, its authority was not forfeited on that account'. There is great force then in Vincentius's putting the written word first; it was natural to have put Tradition first, had not Scripture been in his opinion first in dignity and consideration.

2. that it is interpretative of Scripture. 'Cum sit perfectus scripturarum Canon, sibique ad omnia satis superque sufficiat, quid opus est, ut ei Ecclesiasticae *intelligentiae* jungatur authoritas?'[c] He answers, that, because there are different interpretations, therefore it is necessary that the true *interpretation* 'secundum Ecclesiastici et Catholici *sensus* normam dirigatur.'[d]

3. [5]the fundamentals of faith are ever one and the same.[6] 'Depositum', inquit, 'custodi.' Quid est depositum? id est quod

inform

1 This passage is not explicit enough to say to us what he considered the province of the Church, (n)or the specific uses of Tradition. As far as it goes however it agrees with the Anglican view as above stated; viz. that Tradition is subordinate to scripture.

2. that it is interpretative of Scripture 'Cum sit perfectus scripturarum Canon, sibique ad omnia satis superque sufficiat, quid opus est, ut ei Ecclesiasticae intelligentiae jungatur authoritas?' ['Seeing the Canon of the Scripture is perfect, and most abundantly of itself sufficient for all things, what need we join unto it the authority of the Church's understanding and interpretation?' *Commonit.* II] Here, we maintain, is declared the

2 *Superscribed* Laud P. 101   3 as regards   4 These
5 that the Church makes use of this interpretative tradition
6 admit of written addition
do not admit of

a '... whether I or any other desired to find out the fraud of heretics. . . . that he ought two manner of ways by God's assistance to defend and preserve his faith; that is, first, by the authority of the law of God; secondly, by the tradition of the Catholic Church.' [*Commonit.* II]

b i.e. *Exposition de la doctrine de l'Eglise catholique*, chap. 17 [quoted in *Proph. Office*, 3rd ed., p. 233].

c 'Seeing the Canon of Scripture is perfect, and most abundantly of itself sufficient for all things, what need we join unto it the authority of the Church's understanding and interpretation?' [*Commonit.* II]

d '... be directed according to the rule of the Ecclesiastical and Catholic sense.' [*Commonit.* II]

tibi creditum est, non quod a te inventum; quod accepisti non
quod excogitasti; rem non ingenii, sed doctrinae, non usurpa-
tionis privatae, sed publicae traditionis,[1] rem ad te perductam,
non à te prolatam, in qua non auctor debes esse, sed custos; non
institutor, sed sectator, non ducens sed sequens.'[a] Now if we
ask who the person addressed is, the answer is ready; it is (in
the person of Timothy,) the Church and[2] its Rulers. 'Quis est
hodie Timotheus? nisi vel generaliter universa Ecclesia, vel
specialiter totum corpus Praepositorum?'.[b] These fundamentals[3]
may not be added to by the Church nor may they be curtailed.
'Abdicatâ etenim qualibet parte Catholici dogmatis, alia quoque
atque item alia, ac deinde[c] alia et alia jam quasi ex more et licito
abdicabuntur.'[d] c. 31 Thus the Church has no power [4]over the
fundamentals one way or the other.

4. the Church may explain, and develop the fundamentals,
though it cannot make new ones.[5] 'Crescat igitur oportet, et multum vehementerque proficiat, tam singulorum quam omnium,
tam unius hominis quam totius Ecclesiae aetatum ac saeculo-
rum gradibus intelligentia, scientia, sapientia; sed in suo duntaxat genere, in eodem scilicet dogmate, eodem sensu, eademque
sententiâ.'[e] c. 23. vid also[6] c. 32.

---

[1] *underlined then underlining deleted*   [2] or
[3] Nor may fundamentals   [4] of any kind
[5] Fideliter coapta, adorna sapienter, adjice splendorem, gratiam, venustatem.
Intelligatur te exponente illustrius quod antea obscurius credebatur. ['. . . faithfully set them, wisely adorn them, give them brightness, give them grace, give
them beauty. That which men before believed obscurely, let them by thy exposition understand more clearly.' Vincent, *Commonit.* XXII]   [6] again

[a] ' "Keep (quoth he) the *depositum*." What is meant by this *depositum*? that is,
that which is committed to thee, not that which is invented of thee; that which thou
hast received, not that which thou hast devised; a thing not of wit, but of learning;
not of private assumption, but of public tradition; a thing brought to thee, not
brought forth of thee; wherein thou must not be an author, but a keeper; not a
founder, but an observer; not a leader, but a follower.' [*Commonit.* XXII]

[b] 'Who at this day is Timothy? but either generally the whole Church, or
especially the whole body of Prelates . . .' [*Commonit.* XXII]

[c] *deinceps* in printed note of the Latin text, Jager, p. 466.

[d] 'For if we give up any part of the Catholic Faith, straightway other parts, and
after that other, and again other, and that now as it were of custom, and by a kind
of law, shall be given up.' [*Commonit.* XXIII]

[e] 'Fitting it is, therefore, that the understanding, knowledge, and wisdom, as
well of every man in particular, as of all in common; as well of one alone, as of the
whole Church in general; should by the advance of ages abundantly increase and
go forward, but yet for all that, only in its own kind and nature; that is, in the same
doctrine, in the same sense, in the same judgment.' [*Commonit.* XXIII]

5. these developments are from tradition, or are[1] the work[2] of the existing[3] Church. I will quote your own passage. 'Denique quid unquam aliud conciliorum decretis enisa est, nisi ut quod antea simpliciter credebatur, hoc idem postea diligentius crederetur? . . . Hoc, inquam, semper, neque quicquam praeterea, haereticorum novitatibus excitata, Conciliorum suorum decretis Catholica perfecit Ecclesia, nisi ut, quod prius à majoribus solâ traditione susceperat, hoc deinde posteris etiam per Scripturae chirographum consignaret.'[a] Here 'traditio' is not opposed to Holy Scripture, as you wish to make out, but to the definitive sentence of the Church, per Scripturae chirographum.[b] Vincentius says what had hitherto been received on tradition *without* the Church's decision,[4] was afterwards received *with* it. To speak of Scripture in any manner,[5] would have been beside his mark. I fully allow[6] that the corpus of interpretative tradition is the main practical *teacher* of doctrine, and that[7] the text of Scripture is not such, but only[8] referred to for *proof*.

Thus, to exemplify what I mean, the *full* ecclesiastical doctrine of the Trinity, though involved in the folds of Holy Scripture, yet was delivered to Christians,[9] *in its very form*, solâ traditione.[c] This was the state of things at the time of the Nicene Council, when the Church formally recognized it as the true comment on the Apostles' Creed, and imbodied it[10] by a new symbol, of her own choosing, per Scripturae chirographum, viz the word Homoousion. Vincentius explains his meaning more fully in the words which follow: 'magnam rerum summam paucis libris comprehendendo, et plerumque propter intelligentiae lucem, non novum fidei sensum, novae appellationis proprietate signando.'[d] We consider that this or the other simi-

---

[1] from	[2] mind/intellect	[3] present
[4] authority	[5] any how	[6] He speaks [7] not
[8] which is only to be	[9] comes to us	[10] in her creed/confession of faith

[a] 'To conclude; what hath she else at any time endeavoured by the decrees of Councils, but that what before was simply credited, the same afterward should be more diligently believed; . . . This, I say, always, and nothing else, hath the Church, provoked with the novelties of heretics, effected by the decrees of her Councils, to wit, only to confirm that to posterity by writing, which before by tradition alone she had received of her forefathers.' [*Commonit*. XXIII]

[b] 'by writing' [*Commonit*. XXXII]   [c] 'by tradition alone' [*Commonit*. XXIII]

[d] . . . comprehending a great sum of things in few words, and oftentimes, for more easy understanding, marking an old article of faith by a new and appropriate name.' [*Commonit*. XXIII]

lar passages of Vincentius breath the spirit of our Reformation, which was conducted[1] on the principle of providing[2] a more exact development and adjustment than before, by the light of interpretative tradition of those doctrines which had come down to us, not on that of[3] a recommencement of Christian Faith. 'Preciosas divini dogmatis gemmas exsculpe, (O Timothee) fideliter coapta, adorna sapienter, adjice splendorem, gratiam, venustatem.'[a] We consider that in[4] the sixteenth century we *polished* those jewels which the lapse of time had bedimmed. Nay, though[5] we plainly maintained that the Church Catholic was not infallible in non-fundamentals, and therefore took upon us to undo[6] one or two[7] of the decrees of former General Councils, yet on the whole we merely settled points which had never been settled before, as the question 'of justification,' etc. You followed us at Trent, and did badly what we had done fideliter, sapienter, splendide.[b]

Such are the principles of Vincentius, agreeably with our own. On the other hand I challenge you to produce authority from him for your two peculiar tenets, from which we dissent; first, that pure Tradition is a sufficient basis on which the Church may rest in declaring a doctrine[8] necessary to salvation;[9] next, that the Church may impose consent to any article of faith as a condition of communion over and above the original fundamentals.[10] If you can, Vincentius goes further than we do; if you cannot he does not go as far as you.

A few words will now suffice, to answer the objections incidentally made in your last letter to our doctrine. You say by way of a retort on our attack upon the Church of Rome; 'L'Eglise Anglicane admet certaines choses non écrites, comme des rites

---

[1] a clear development or purifying   [2] giving   [3] as
[4] we   [5] while   [6] undid   [7] other
[8] any traditionary doctrine which cannot also be proved from Scripture is necessary to salvation
[9] fundamental
[10] *Marginal comment at this point*: 'Declaring a thing to be true' and 'declaring it to be an article of faith' are things of vast difference, &c. &c. J. Taylor's *Dissuasive*, vol. x, p. 477, etc.

[a] '. . . engrave the precious stones of God's doctrine (O Timothy), faithfully set them, wisely adorn them, give them brightness, give them grace, give them beauty.' [*Commonit.* XXII]
[b] 'faithfully, wisely, with brightness' [*adaptation of the previous phrase from Commonit.* XXII]

et des cérémonies qu'elle révère comme divins; or, Vincent n'en parle pas: donc elle viole sa règle.'[a] Not so; we never maintained that Vincent condemns[1] the reception of ceremonies, if not mentioned in Scripture,[2] or even[3] of doctrines not in Scripture;[4] but that he implies that Scripture contains all things necessary[5] for salvation, a doctrine which is inconsistent with your system, not with ours.[6]

Beveridge is quite consistent with the Anglican[7] doctrine in saying that 'il y a bien des articles qui ne se lisent pas en termes précis, dans les écritures, et qui pourtant s'en déduisent par l'assentiment universel des chrétiens.'[b] Doubtless; Scripture does not teach us the truth or draw it into system: it is but the document of ultimate appeal, the argumentative basis of the truth.

As to your argument 'Vous adoptez, d'après vos principes, les interprétations des Pères; or, . . . ces interprétations renferment souvent des vérités nécessaires au salut,'[c] we reply, we do receive those interpretations, but we consider[8] the truths they contain necessary to salvation, because[9] they *are* interpretations; not as independent documents, but simple interpretations of what actually is in Scripture, the sole authority in fundamentals.[10]

You argue, because we admit that rites and ceremonies are to be admitted on the authority of tradition, that[11] 'ils sont donc nécessaires au salut.'[d] [12]Nay; our whole question is about matters of faith, not of practice and conduct.[13] We admit Scripture is not

---

[1] Vincent opposes not   [2] nor do we; nor   [3] nay
[4] nor do we   [5] *A later note adds:* (to be believed) July 26/35
[6] as we maintain, and you deny   [7] our   [8] make   [9] not be
[10] *A later note adds:* (here fundamentals and necessary to salvation are awkwardly confused) July 26/35   [11] therefore
[12] Not so; it is pious for the Church to adopt them, not necessary (but they do not come to us with that imperativeness as to allow of our declaring them to be necessary for salvation.)   [13] discipline

[a] 'The Anglican Church admits certain things which are unwritten, such as rites and ceremonies which she reveres as divine. Now Vincent does not speak of them: therefore she violates his rule.'

[b] 'There are many articles which are not to be read in precise terms in the Scriptures and which can nevertheless be deduced from them by the universal consent of Christians.' *Newman here quotes a rendering of Beveridge by Lepappe de Trévern. Jager, pp. 61-2.*

[c] 'According to your own principles you adopt the interpretations of the Fathers. Now . . . these interpretations often contain truths necessary to salvation.'

[d] 'they are necessary to salvation'

the sole authority in matters of conduct. E.g. It does not condemn suicide, which nevertheless[1] we entirely condemn.

You proceed, 'vous enseignez avec nous et comme nous que
Jésus-Christ est descendu aux enfers, que la mère de Dieu est
restée vierge; qu'il faut sanctifier le dimanche au lieu du sabbat,
que le baptême par infusion et le baptême conféré aux enfans
est valide; qu'il peut être donné par tout le monde en cas de
nécessité, et qu'on ne peut le renouveler, même quand il est
donné par les hérétiques. Voilà de nouveaux articles non écrits
et qui sont partie de vos enseignements. Sont ils nécessaires au
salut?'[a] Some of the things here specified are matters of conduct,
not of faith; others are contained in Scripture; others are traditions which it is pious to receive. Grant that we receive them
all; yet [2]not one is an instance of a *fundamental* doctrine destitute of proof from Scripture, which is what you ought to produce,
if you would prove us inconsistent. As to the Donatists, whom
Vincentius considers[3] as lost, they openly withstood the decree
of a Council and went into schism. They did not allow the
Church to have[4] '*authority* in controversies[5] of faith', but set
up a counter-authority to it. Therefore they are condemned.
Cyprian held the same opinion as they, but in love not in the
spirit of division, therefore in spite of his mistake he 'will reign
for ever', as Vincent says, 'with Christ'. 'Dites-moi, Monsieur,
où lisez-vous que l'Ecriture Sainte contient toutes les choses
nécessaires au salut . . . ? où lisez-vous le catalogue des livres
saints . . . ? où trouvez vous que la doctrine qui pose que nous
sommes justifiés par la foi seulement est très sainte et très pleine
de consolation' &c. &c.[b] We reply to all these questions, that
the doctrines specified are not accounted fundamental by us,[6] not
subscribed by the mass of the people. They are defined by the

---

[1] is   [2] Not   [3] whom   [4] had   [5] matters   [6] articles of Faith

[a] 'You teach with us and as we do that Jesus Christ descended into hell; that
the Mother of God remained a virgin; that the Lord's Day, and not the Sabbath,
must be kept holy; that baptism by infusion and baptism conferred on infants is
valid; that it may be administered by anyone in case of necessity, and that it cannot
be renewed, even when it has been administered by heretics. These are new,
unwritten articles and they form part of your teaching. Are they necessary to
salvation?'

[b] 'Tell me, sir, where did you read that Holy Scripture contains all things necessary to salvation? Where did you read the catalogue of the sacred books . . .? Where
did you discover that the doctrine which lays down that we are justified by faith
alone is most wholesome and full of comfort?'

'authority' of the Church, and set up as a rule of teaching. The first instance, the[1] Article about the Canon of Scripture, is the only exception to this remark. Certainly[2] the belief in Holy Scripture is not injoined by our Church in the same way as the reception of the doctrine of justification etc; for its canonicity is a fundamental verity rather than a doctrine. But this question about Scripture introduces us into a large and distinct field of inquiry, into which I shall be happy to accompany you at any time, but which is foreign to our immediate purpose.

I trust I have now satisfied your demand as far as Bishop Jebb's first head is concerned; i.e. as far as stating, as[3] matters of fact, our opinions, yours, and Vincentius's. To defend our doctrine, except incidentally, would have been beside my duty, which was to compare the doctrine of the Anglican Church with that of the ancient Gallican. However, in conclusion, it may be allowed me to justify our position in one respect.

Perhaps you will ask, '*Why* is it, you Anglicans make such a difference between the written and the unwritten word? That word is to be believed, because it comes from God; not from the accident of its being committed to paper. If the belief in the one is necessary to salvation, so is belief in the other.'

[4]We answer, first of all, that on the very first face of the matter, it is clear that Scripture alone does absolutely declare belief in [5]its doctrines necessary for salvation; but Tradition does not say so of its own. Suppose me as willing as possible to believe what is put before me; Well; Scripture expressly says 'Believe and thou shalt be saved, disbelieve and thou shalt be condemned.'[a] I cannot believe Scripture without believing reception of its doctrines necessary for salvation in the case of every one who hears them. When does Tradition binds [*sic*] any such belief upon me? a doctrine comes to me through the Fathers; they are mere[6] witnesses and transmitters of it. They witness no more at most than that such a doctrine is Apostolical; they do not witness the additional doctrine that to disbelieve is damnable. Where do I learn this addition? Will you say, from the

[1] that   [2] The   [3] the
[4] We answer that we make no difference between the two; but that we deny that what you call Tradition *is* the unwritten word; i.e. we deny that even the best authenticated tradition comes with that
[5] *Note added later*: better—'certain of'   [6] merely *then* ly *deleted*
[a] John 3: 36

Church? good[1]—but this is another matter. It is enough for my purpose that Scripture and Tradition, taken per se, come to us in a different aspect. The one comes with a demand upon our faith, the other does not.

But you will reply that, if a doctrine is *Apostolical*, surely it ought to be believed, whether it bears witness to itself or not; that *revelation*, as such, involves the obligation of faith in the recipient[2] of it. I grant this; I grant the Unwritten Word claims our assent, but I[3] go on, in the next place, to deny that what you call Tradition *is* the Unwritten Word. I consider the Unwritten Word, because Unwritten, not to have come down to us in such a shape[4] as to enable us to discriminate and verify it. It is like a stream of fresh water falling into the ocean and mixing itself with it.

To this perhaps you may object that Tertullian speaks distinctly of the rule[5] of Faith being handed down through the Bishops; that we cannot conceive a surer guarantee of the truth being preserved than such a succession; and that accordingly he actually does prefer this evidence to[6] that of the written word. I answer.

1. That it does not follow because such a transmission of doctrine was safe in the episcopal succession of 100[7] years (viz. from St. John's death to Tertullian's[8] day) that therefore it may safely be trusted for an indefinite time.

2. that such tradition[9] was not unwritten but in fact written, being a formal creed, which he actually gives.

3. that this creed we do in substance receive, and call it the Apostles' Creed, and consider it to contain the fundamentals.

4. that the articles of this creed are also contained in Scripture, so that this[10] is not a case in point, i.e. you have[11] not produced

[1] good, but how does the Church gain this said additional doctrine? You will say she has an infallible discrimination between truth and falsehood and has a power of

A marginal note adds later: I see by accident the words 'but how does the Church' got transcribed and so translated into French. July 26/35

The French translation does indeed read at this point: 'Où trouverai-je cette condamnation? Direz-vous que l'Eglise l'enseigne; mais peut-elle l'enseigner? C'est une autre question.' Jager, p. 115.

[2] hearer *superscribed*   [3] but   [4] so   [5] Unw[ritten]
[6] it to   [7] 200   [8] his   [9] transmission
[10] those who believe this tradition are not believing any doctrines independent of Scripture, which is
[11] we have

a doctrine, which though not in Scripture, rests[1] on tradition so strong as to make it absurd not to receive it.

I make the same answer to any question you may raise concerning a doctrine resting on Tradition which has antiquity, universality, and consent; i.e. before[2] you inquire of me whether I should believe such a doctrine, or on the other hand reject it, because[3] it happened not to be in Scripture. I shall think right to ask you whether in matter of fact any such doctrine can be produced. E.g. should you bring the doctrine of the validity of heretical baptism, I shall ask whether there is not as much reason to suppose it the development of 'one Baptism' Eph. iv. 5 as to suppose the tradition of it universal.

Passing from these imaginary cases to those which exist, I[4] maintain that taking Tradition in that form in which it is actually found, viz. ancient but not universal, that it can[5] not come to us with the authority of the written word. We can not be certain in the same way that it[6] came from the Apostles. Litera scripta manet. Suppose[7] a doctrine came on Polycarp's authority as from the mouth of St. John, yet, if Polycarp put it on paper 40 years after he heard it, I should have *indefinitely* less evidence that St. John spoke it than if he[8] actually wrote it, evidence different in kind. Do not we write down memorandums of important occurrences, directly[9] they happen, to help our memory afterwards? and,[10] in the delicate matter of transmitting a heavenly doctrine, who does not feel the colouring which individual minds may give to their own expression of Truths which they venerate ever so much and wish to maintain? Inspiration which originally gave the Gospel Faith, is the only safeguard of it in oral tradition.

[11]You will say that all this is a very cold and unchristian kind

---

[1] resting   [2] for till   [3] if
[4] But further I go on to   [5] does
[6] 'La doctrine unanime des Pères et des écrivans [*sic*] ecclésiastiques, par la décision des conciles, les prières et les cérémonies de la liturgie, par les témoignages des héretiques mêmes,' ['the unanimous doctrine of the Fathers and ecclesiastical writers, by the decision of councils, the prayers and ceremonies of the liturgy, by the testimonies of heretics themselves,'] does not come to us with the certainty of apostolic authority which attaches to the written word. Litera scripta manet. What the Apostles have written, they have written. But though Papias witnesses that St. John told him Polycarp that there was to be a visible sign of Christ upon earth, yet if he had not set it down in writing at the time I
[7] though   [8] St John   [9] at once   [10] who
[11] But let me not be misunderstood. I do not say this

of faith; as if we were determined not to believe more than we could help; as if we were resolved not to see except in full sunshine. Let me not be misunderstood, I have not said all this as an excuse for *my* not believing a doctrine if guaranteed by Polycarp. I should think[1] myself a fool, and worse than a fool,[2] to refuse to accept it on such authority; safest and wisest to believe it. I think them perverse[3] who do not receive such traditions; but I do not see what leave the Church has to impose[4] the belief of it as necessary to salvation[5] or as a condition of Church fellowship. The blessings[6] of Christianity are a trust given us by the Church to dispense to the world.[7] It is a grave matter for the Church to impose[8] conditions not contained in the original deed; to withhold the gift of grace from sinners without clear warrant from Him who has made us trustees. I agree with our judicious Hooker, when arguing in defence of[9] the baptism of the children of[10] irreligious parents:[11] 'God hath ordained Baptism in favour of mankind. To restrain favors is an odious thing; to enlarge them, acceptable both to God and man.'[a] But if it be charitable to enlarge, as far as truth suffers it; much more is it uncharitable actually to narrow[12] the conditions on which they are committed to us to dispense.[13] The Church is set upon certain fundamentals; why should we add to them? Rather let us take the reception[14] of such traditionary doctrines,[15] not as a duty, but as a privilege: a privilege which we who receive them enjoy, which those who reject them lose through their folly.

The history of the baptismal controversy of the third century confirms the above remarks. I believe on the whole with you[16] that Stephen decided in that controversy according to the general tradition of the Church, and, if *we* of this day have reason to believe it,[17] much more would it be clear to parties who lived so near[18] the Apostolic age. Yet Cyprian acted against that tradition; now could he have acted against a plain decision[19] of

[1] say that   [2] it weak if not [worse than] weak
[3] wrong   [4] right I have to insist upon
[5] I do not see what right I have to make the belief of it   [6] gifts
[7] *A question-mark has been inserted, probably later, in the margin at this point*
[8] to with   [9] for   [10] whose   [11] are not reli
[12] withdraw them from   [13] to our (dispens)ing them   [14] knowledge
[15] as come to us on the authority of Tradition without Scripture
[16] Neither you or I deny   [17] it is clear to us now   [18] of
[19] command

[a] Hooker, *Of the Laws of Ecclesiastical Polity*, Bk. V, Cp. lxiv, 5.

Scripture on the subject? If then an Apostolic tradition did not[1] recommend itself at once to the almost Apostolic Cyprian, [2]and to Agrippinus before him, much more possible is it to[3] fail in carrying its evidence with it to every[4] individual[5] who heard it in ages far removed from the age of the Apostles, as our own[6]; much more possible is it for the Rulers of the Church in after ages to mistake between really Apostolical and spurious traditions; much more unsafe is it for the Church to attempt to enforce a doctrine as necessary to salvation on the grounds of any supposed Apostolic tradition. Hence[7] our Article says that 'whatsoever is not read in Holy Scripture, nor may be proved thereby, is not to be required [8]of any man, that it should be believed as an Article of the Faith, or be thought requisite or necessary to salvation.' And here I conclude my remarks for the present.[9]

Yr. ob[t] servant &c.

---

[1] were obscure / ineffectual for   [2] Apo   [3] would it not necessarily
[4] one   [5] men   [6] [our]selves

[7] Again, if the Traditions of the Church are as necessary to be believed as Scripture, how shall we rescue Cyprian, Saint and Martyr, from the consequences of dying in mortal sin? I conclude then in the words of

[8] to

[9] ; and thus I end my present remarks on the first head of our controversy; being ready to resume them at your wish. One more remark, and I conclude. You may ask, why do you not consider the baptism of infants necessary to salvation; now where is that to be found in Scripture? I reply I do not consider the baptism of infants necessary. I consider baptism generally necessary to salvation; and I baptize infants

3. Jager's Case against Newman

(a) *Jager's Fourth Letter*

J A G E R ' S Fourth Letter, fifth in the original newspaper sequence, was published in part in *L'Univers* on 25 December 1834, and continued on 30 January 1835, the second part of Newman's letter having appeared the previous day. In fact he continued to add to his reply at such length that it was split into several separate letters, which appeared as the Fourth, Fifth, and Sixth of his published volume and are abridged in similar sequence in the present edition. They dominated the columns of *L'Univers* well into the spring of 1835. After the appearance of the issue of Friday, 27 March 1835, the controversy was removed to another newspaper, *Le Moniteur religieux*. When writing on the controversy, Fr. Tristram declared that no numbers of the journal had been preserved among Newman's papers. Homer must have been nodding on this occasion, for Fr. Tristram, who had seen every slip of paper in the Newman archives, cannot have overlooked the copy of *Le Moniteur*, bound into a volume of tracts, which contained Jager's Seventh Letter. The draft of Newman's Second Letter ('Fourth Reply, Part One') is available in manuscript and the French text exists both in the newspaper version and in Jager's volume. The latter's three letters in answer to Newman's one mean that Jager took five times the space allotted to Newman to answer him. The reasons are not far to seek: he is rhetorical, wordy, and eager to provide a whole host of patristic quotations for every point he makes.

Jager's Fourth Letter begins with compliments to Newman whose letter he sees as the *ultimatum*, the last word of the Anglican reformation. Although he gives reassurances of continuing the debate with calm and moderation he now promises attack rather than defence.

He is surprised by the narrow limits of the first 450 years which Newman grants to the period of apostolic purity. Harrison had settled for the first six centuries. How can their views differ on this point?

This limit itself must surely be insulting to Jesus Christ who has promised *eternal* guidance with the phrase, 'And behold I am with you all days, even to the consummation of the world' [Matth. 28: 18] and to affirm that His Church has erred in dogma and discipline is to deny the truth of His religion. Nor can Newman argue that the Church remained the true church in spite of corruption. Once the Church strays from her universal beliefs, she ceases to be Catholic: the word means that which believes and teaches everywhere the same doctrine. Take the argument further, Jager concludes, that if the Church has erred since the fifth or sixth centuries, she has ceased to exist. Hence the Reformation is either nothing because it succeeds nothing, or it succeeds the true church, which makes it schismatic.

Jager admonishes Newman for not replying fully to his letter and abandoning Jebb's last two charges. No doubt Newman had realized just how absurd it would be to give the individual the onerous task of seeking out his own faith for he acknowledges in his letter the authority of the Church and, indeed, its infallibility on the main points of belief. In fact Newman goes further and claims that the Church has the right to make articles 'according to time and circumstances', a claim Jager refuses to accept, and which the Roman Church has never attributed to herself.

Newman has conceded that Scripture does not contain everything and that there are certain doctrines not found in it. But in order to avoid the consequences of this admission he has put forward the distinction between fundamental and non-fundamental articles and seems to make so much of it that to refute it would suffice to refute all Newman's arguments. Jager challenges Newman to say where he can find this distinction set out, where in the words of Jesus Christ or His Apostles, where in Scripture or the Fathers; and by what signs the Christian can recognize what *is* fundamental or not in Scripture or tradition.

Like the Catholic Church, Jager insists, Anglicans *do* admit fundamental articles which are not contained in Scripture and repeats his accusation that this applies to many of the Thirty-nine Articles: 6, 11, 13, 14, 19, 21, 22, 25, 26, 37. He is confused by Newman's reply that apart from one single Article these are *not* fundamental. If so, why are they entitled Articles of Faith?

And if unnecessary, why have they been used to exclude the Catholics in England, who reject them, from the universities and the privileges of the law? These are the actions of a tyrannical church. But the Articles *are*, Jager claims, fundamental to the Anglican faith because they deal with essential issues and if the Anglican Church has erred in setting them up, then all its other beliefs must be called into question. If questions such as justification by faith alone, or the number of the sacraments, are not fundamental, what does the word mean?

He now confronts Newman with evidence of the Anglican's acceptance as fundamental of points of belief not to be found in Scripture. The one Article cited by Newman as being fundamental, that concerning canonical books, is founded on tradition alone. The virginity of the Mother of God and the descent of Christ into Hell are fundamental because they are contained in the Apostles' Creed, but they are not in Scripture. Keeping the Lord's Day holy is necessary to salvation yet it is not contained in Scripture. The Anglicans practise baptism by infusion; it is not mentioned in Scripture but must surely be considered fundamental. Jager is amazed that Anglicans do not consider fundamental the acceptance of baptism by heretics. Anglican baptism must originally have been received from the Roman Church, which they regard as heretical. Surely this brings the validity of their baptism into question? Yet it remains nonfundamental. Article 26 declares that the effect of sacraments is independent of the worthiness of the minister. It is nowhere in Scripture, yet surely it must be fundamental as it directly concerns the legitimacy of the Anglican episcopate.

Considering that he has proved that Newman admits fundamental articles which are not contained in Scripture, and hence that the refutation of Jebb is complete, Jager moves to the next argument. Newman does not agree that tradition is sufficient basis for a fundamental doctrine, challenges Jager to adduce a single proof in his favour from Vincent, and completely rejects the Council of Trent's authority to establish, on the basis of tradition alone, the dogma of transubstantiation, the sacrifice of the Mass, and indulgences. Newman holds the decrees of the first four councils as the rule of orthodoxy against heresy. Jager decides to examine these to prove that their conduct was exactly the same as that followed at Trent.

The Council of Nicaea set against the Arians the great truths of Scripture and the ancient beliefs of the Church from the Apostles but their judgements were based on tradition alone.

The Council of Constantinople confirmed the faith of the Fathers of Nicaea.

The council of Ephesus, Vincent himself records, brought forward the opinions of Holy Fathers, 'that by their consent and verdict, the true religion of ancient doctrine might be duly and solemnly confirmed' (*Commonit.* XXIX).

At the Council of Chalcedon, faith was confirmed by the cries of the bishops: 'The definition pleases all . . . It is the faith of the Fathers' (Labbe, *Collectio Conciliorum* . . . t. iv, p. 556).

Even the Councils of Rimini and Seleucia, although their decisions are to be rejected, followed the same procedure 'to confirm the faith of the Fathers' (Socr. *Church History*, 11, c. XL).

Jager cites the councils of Jerusalem and Antioch, 'the Brigandage of Ephesus' and even later councils, to show the same procedure was always followed. In fact, all the acts, definitions, and creeds of the early Church are based on tradition. Scripture was nowhere termed the court of ultimate appeal nor was there any distinction between fundamental and non-fundamental doctrine.

That tradition is the general, perpetual, and uniform rule of the Catholic faith is borne out by the Apostles themselves. St. Paul tells Timothy, the embodiment of the Church, 'especially the body of Prelates', (Vincent, *Commonit.* XXII), to 'keep the deposit', that is, the whole doctrine of Jesus Christ communicated either by word of mouth or in writing, for it is *the pillar and ground of truth*.

The early Fathers based their struggle against heresy on the traditional teachings of the Church. St. Irenaeus says that the Apostles entrusted their perfect knowledge to the Church, particularly the Church at Rome which was founded by Peter and Paul and has her tradition from them. Had the Apostles left no Scripture, their tradition would have been enough. (Lib. 3. *Contr. Haer.*)

Tertullian says that since the Scriptures do not belong to heretics, they cannot be used as a common fighting ground and in any case no success is ever obtained by wrangling over them. It is the steadfast Christian tradition which must be used to confute heretics. The writings of St. Clement of Alexandria, Origen, Lactantius, St. Athanasius, St. Basil, St. Jerome, St. Augustine, and St. Cyril of Alexandria bear out Jager's insistence that the tradition of the Church is the rule of faith. In the third-century controversy on the repetition of baptism between Pope St. Stephen and St. Cyprian *both* sides appealed to apostolic tradition, not to Scripture, as the arbiter.

Vincent in his treatise is merely speaking in harmony with earlier authorities; and if he were not, what could he avail against the universal doctrine of the Church? To have spoken differently would have implied he was merely transmitting his own personal opinions (*Commonit.* XXVIII). At the beginning of his book he says that he is putting in writing the doctrines received from the Ancients and it is clear from what he writes that Scripture is insufficient for judging and putting an end to any dispute about faith; as Scripture can be mutilated, the tradition of the Universal Church is essential (*Commonit.* XXVII).

The doctrine of the first centuries, on which following ages based their beliefs, is quite clear. Newman cannot argue that St. Vincent put Scripture first. Certainly he refers to it, before tradition, as the Fathers do; but judgement on dogma is in accordance with tradition, which includes Scripture, its interpretation, and all Christian doctrine. The Council of Trent cannot be condemned for following the Catholic rule of antiquity. Surely Newman as a Christian also has to accept it for Vincent says 'We shall be Catholics if we follow Universality, Antiquity and Consent' (*Commonit.* II). Because the Roman Church seventeen hundred years later follows the same principle, it must be on the true path.

Protestants may hate this argument but they cannot defeat it. In fact, this basic Catholic rule exists within the Anglican Church—indeed it must if its members are to profess themselves Christians—and he gives proof of this:

(i) Many poor, unlearned people follow the word of their ministers. So a numerous class of people, in practice, form their faith on the teaching of this Church.

(ii) Those who do read the Scriptures must add the interpretation of the Fathers to avoid the hazards of individual interpretation; but are there many, even among Anglican ministers, who have read and judged all the works of all the Fathers? In fact, can any *one* of them say his Anglican faith was formed entirely on reading such a great mass of work? No—they depend on their Church's teaching and therefore follow the Catholic rule.

Why then, in the face of all this evidence, do Anglicans believe that Scripture alone contains everything necessary to salvation? Is the principle set out in Scripture or the Fathers? Where do the Sacred Writers say they have written down everything they received by oral tradition? Anglicans believe it only because they have heard it in their churches and because it is the sixth of the Thirty-nine Articles.

Jager goes on to list many other ways in which Anglicans, in spite of their protestations, *do* in fact put traditional teachings before Scripture.

(i) The figurative Anglican interpretation of the words 'This is my body, this is my blood' is not suggested by Scripture.

(ii) Anglicans prefer the words 'The Father and I are one' (John 10: 50) although Christ says elsewhere 'The Father is greater than I' (John 14: 28), the latter phrase being used by Socinians to show He was not God.

(iii) Why do Protestants believe the Roman Church has erred and been corrupt? Is this in Scripture or the Fathers? No. Their Church teaches it.

(iv) The ridiculous prejudices which Anglicans entertain about the Roman Church's supposed worship of images and relics is based on the charges of their bishops and on the twenty-second of their Articles.

(v) The primacy of Peter is shown in the words 'Thou art Peter, etc.' Anglicans do not accept this, because their Church teaches to the contrary.

(vi) When declaring himself head of the Church of England Henry VIII did not obtain his authority from the Scriptures or the Fathers.

(vii) An indifferent neutral stranger would be hard put to it to find a source for many of the Thirty-nine Articles in Scripture or the Fathers. 'Why, as a reader of them yourself', Jager concludes, 'why are you an Anglican? Because you were one before you opened a single book.'

He now turns his attention to the dissenters, Protestants who believe Scripture *alone* to be the source of faith; even they must follow the Catholic rule of tradition because their very belief does not arise in the Scriptures: it is given to them by their own sect, their Church. In fact they mutilate Scripture to preserve the traditions of their Church. Jager gives some examples:

(i)   In spite of Christ's observance of the Sabbath, witnessed to in Scripture, and the Apostles' practice, they believe the Sabbath to be a profane day, and celebrate Sunday as the Lord's Day. Why? On the authority of their Church.

(ii) Both Old and New Testaments forbid the eating of flesh with blood—but Protestants base their violation of this principle ultimately on a Catholic tradition that it was only applicable to a certain time.

(iii) Jesus bids us—'You also ought to wash one another's feet'—but Protestants believe this not to be a strictly imposed precept only on the basis of Catholic tradition.

(iv) Scripture nowhere authorizes the validity of baptism by effusion. Yet the Protestant church practises this, in accordance with Catholic tradition.

(v)   Scripture gives no sanction to the validity of baptism by heretics. This too comes from Catholic tradition, and is admitted by Protestants of all sects.

How can those Protestants who affirm that Scripture is the only source of truth be sure it is, in fact, the word of God, that it was written under divine inspiration? Only tradition asserts this for them; they return, implicitly, to the Catholic rule.

To sum up, Jager says that Protestants form their faith from their catechisms, creeds, parents, teachers, and ministers; hence ultimately from the teaching of the Church—often from the Catholic Church. They have rejected many Catholic doctrines, but have not been able to reject entirely the fundamental rule of Christianity. Although Protestants have the same rule of tradition as Catholics within their faith, instead of arriving at sound, general Catholic doctrines, they resort to private opinions and absurd inventions.

Having abandoned the true path, the Protestant Churches nevertheless expect their authority to be respected. If creeds, confessions of faith, and catechisms are not fully admitted, deposition and excommunication will inevitably result. Does not Newman's own University still exclude dissenters who will not adopt its Articles? The Protestant Churches have followed the history of all sects: first they question the mother-church, then establish their own authority which finally degenerates into tyranny. Luther provides an example of this tyranny—'I, Martin Luther, will it. I order it thus. Let my will stand in the place of reason.' Calvin, Henry VIII, and Queen Elizabeth displaced authority, but they did not destroy it.

No question, then, that the Roman Church at the Council of Trent was completely justified. Having proved his point, that tradition has served as the foundation for the Church's decisions from Apostolic times, and that even Protestant practice shows forth this principle, he considers this particular debate at an end, and declares that a new one is opened up by it: to discover whether the Protestant, in holding to his Church's teaching, is sure he possesses the doctrine of Christ and the Apostles; and whether the Roman Catholic has that certainty.

(b) *Jager's Fifth Letter*

Jager has already introduced the subject of this letter at the end of the last: can the Protestant holding to the teaching of *his* Church have certainty of faith? And can the Roman Catholic have that assurance? These questions are raised by Newman's accusation that the Roman Church has added to the fundamental beliefs.

Newman must agree, says Jager, that they can establish quite clearly what the doctrine of the Church through the ages has been: and also that faith must be based on truths beyond doubt— without this solid foundation it will lapse into mere opinion. Therefore, in order to have a Christian faith, our belief in the doctrine of Jesus Christ must be absolutely secure.

Jager feels he has already fully proved that the only way to achieve this certain truth is to follow the constant and universal teaching of the Church—an idea suggested by quotation from St. Vincent, St. Augustine, and the Anglicans Field and Leslie.

Why must we admit this faith which is based on the unanimous or almost unanimous tradition of the Church? Because by its very unanimity it must be based on the doctrines of Jesus

Christ or the Apostles. Error varies. It takes different forms, but truth alone, coming from a common origin, is one.

In order to be absolutely secure in our faith, we must be sure it is the same one professed and taught in all places in all ages. He begins by examining the Protestant faith. Can its members be assured in their faith when their present doctrine was unknown before Queen Elizabeth and opposes that followed by their ancestors for a thousand years? Can it be of all time when there was an interruption—in their own view—from the truth, beginning in the fifth century?

He anticipates the reply that the Protestant faith is that of the primitive Church. Only Protestant bishops and divines assert this and they themselves admit their fallibility. It is therefore possible they are mistaken in their interpretations of Scripture and the Fathers. In fact, some Christian scholars have maintained that Protestant bishops have ignored the Fathers' teachings and consulted heretics; and that some delved only into the works of Luther and Calvin for their confession of faith. Surely, Protestants cannot find in their Church's teaching absolute assurance? To attempt to find certainty, the Protestant's only recourse is to seek his faith in antiquity, as Jebb indicates. Did Jesus Christ prescribe such an exhaustive study? Even if it were possible, human error would creep into the interpretations; religion would degenerate into opinion.

There can therefore be no certainty in the Protestant faith. In fact, it does not even have probability on its side. Newman has claimed the Church has erred since the fifth century but, replies Jager, is it probable that Christ would have allowed this or that the entire body of Church teachers should have erred almost at once or one after the other and that He would choose Luther and Calvin and Henry VIII to restore it? It is quite improbable and the very foundations of Protestantism stand condemned by reason. All that is left is doubt, remorse, and the destruction of all truth. If there is no certainty of the truth of a faith, there can be no *necessity* for people to carry out its duties and disciplines.

What can the Anglican reply to these accusations? If he tries to say the Church is infallible in fundamentals he must submit to what the Council of Trent has declared fundamental. He might reproach the Roman Church for claiming as fundamental what is not so—but he must then ask himself if the Anglican Church is more infallible than the Roman Church; and in fact he cannot be sure whether or not she is equally in error.

Has the Roman Catholic certainty of faith? He has, Jager insists, because by adhering to the teaching of the Church, which is infallible, he is committed to a doctrine which is of all times and all places. His catechism teaches the same things all over the world. Cicero maintains that what is universal in a philosophy is essentially old and derives from common origins, so the history of the Roman Church is in agreement with human reason. The Council of Trent in opposing Luther and Calvin decided nothing new. If the Catholic Church had originally professed Anglican principles there would have been some record of their introduction. Jager challenges his opponent to produce any.

He goes on to discuss the changes which Anglicans accuse the Roman Church of making:

1. prayer for the dead
2. invocation of saints
3. the Real Presence
4. transubstantiation
5. the infallibility of the Church
6. the supremacy of the Pope
7. confession
8. the number of sacraments and the duties they create.

None of these, says Jager, are concerned with uninteresting historical fact or speculative truths but with the mysteries and duties of faith in which everyone's salvation is involved. Would not innovators introducing them have encountered opposition from people and clergy? The Fathers and bishops who cherished tradition were completely hostile to any innovation.

To indicate how completely impossible it would be to introduce anything new, Jager supposes that someone *did* manage to introduce an innovation in spite of all. All the rest of the Catholic Church would immediately rise up against it because it was opposed to the teaching of the Church. Interferences with articles of belief by Henry VIII and by the Iconoclasts caused an uproar. Could the great innovations supposed to have occurred have come about with no reaction at all? Jager supposes further that a whole country altered its faith. The problem of introducing that changed faith to the rest of the world would require a criminal conspiracy among the faithful of all churches. The nature of heresy is essentially conspicuous; but in the present case there is no evidence of councils, appeals, synods, discussions, as the history of other innovations would lead us to expect. He challenges his Anglican opponent to state when these so-called innovations occurred. It was not in the Middle Ages because the Greeks separated from Rome in the ninth and eleventh centuries and they profess all doctrines except papal supremacy and some points of discipline. The purity of the first four hundred and fifty years has already been admitted. Did the 'innovations', therefore, occur in the fifth century? But at this time the various parts of the Catholic Church were scattered and remote from each other. It would have been difficult for heresy to spread unrecorded, particularly when the Church's faith was extremely strong so soon after the Apostles. Unless it might be said that doctrines were introduced in the sixth and seventh centuries which were not found in the primitive Church. Just because they were not found, does it mean they were unknown? If the silence was absolute, which it was not, are we to think the primitive Church was Protestant? Can his opponent be sure the Fathers wrote everything down, that all their books came down to us, that none were lost? The Fathers of the sixth and seventh centuries said the Church's doctrines were not new to them and several heretical sects had already split off and taken the doctrine with them. Unless Anglicans can convince us that these changes from Anglicanism to Roman Catholicism took place in a single moment without record, they must concede to the Roman Catholic full assurance of faith.

Jager next proceeds to discuss these so-called innovations in more detail. He quotes the Anglican Bishop Beveridge to support his claim that rites and interpretations could only have been received with unanimous consent because they were derived from the Apostles and accepted by all Christians. Another Anglican bishop, Hammond, asserts the pre-eminence of bishops above priests and claims it as being Christ's will. There was no opposition to this form of government, no synod to pronounce on it, precisely because there was no change. His opponent sees this as a non-fundamental point of discipline but, says Jager, would it have been any easier to change those fundamental principles of which the Roman Church is accused: suddenly to raise the Pope's authority above that of the bishops, to set up transubstantiation, to introduce sacraments—especially confession which put such arduous duties on both priests and faithful—if contrary doctrines had been taught for the previous four hundred and fifty years? If the authorities of the Church—Fathers, councils, bishops—cannot be relied on, Anglicans must renounce their faith and tear up the New Testament, because these were its guardians.

But if Anglicans admit the integrity of Scripture, then they must admit *all* that its guardians teach. Dr. Jebb claims that the Church of England holds a middle course between Catholics and Protestants. There is no such middle course. If any foundations of the Protestant Church are to remain, they must admit everything which the Fathers taught from the Apostles. If they reject tradition on points which divide the Church, they must reject Scripture. It is all or nothing, for everything rests on the same foundation. Therefore the Protestant has two alternatives—both fearful. Ahead there opens before him an abyss of doubt. Behind him looms the Council of Trent and all the overwhelming evidence of tradition. On the other hand, the Roman Catholic finds assurance in the past and trust in the future.

Jager goes on to demonstrate in greater detail the evidence for the Church's infallibility. Because the universal teaching of the Church is infallible it follows that the bishops who are the judges of faith cannot be deceived on that teaching. Nothing new is ever allowed into the doctrine and in answer to Newman's charge that the Roman Church adds to the fundamentals of faith and draws the line of infallibility higher than Anglicans do, Jager says that the Pope, the bishops, and the councils have no right to depart from fundamentals. They are not arbiters but depositories of Christ's word. He gives examples:

1. At the Council of Nicaea, the bishops bore witness that the consubstantiality of the Word was universal and had always been the belief of their dioceses.
2. The task of the Council of Ephesus was to declare universal teaching and pronounce sentence on Nestorius.
3. At the Council of Trent the bishops bore witness that belief in the Real Presence, transubstantiation, had always been professed in their churches.

Jager points out that general councils are usually not necessary as the very universality of a doctrine proves its truth. If there is a contested point of faith, the decision of the Roman Pontiff, expressly or tacitly agreed to by the bishops, becomes an infallible judgement, because it is no longer in doubt that it is in conformity with the universal belief of the Church.

The bishops, therefore, provide human testimony of the Church's infallibility. But his belief in the infallibility of the Church also has a supernatural basis set out in Scripture. (1) Jesus Christ said to the first of the Apostles 'Thou art Peter, and upon this rock I will build my church, and the gates of hell shall not prevail against it' (Matt. 16). A Church which must exist forever is of necessity infallible. (2) Jesus Christ promised the Apostles that the Holy Ghost would abide with them forever. Can men guided by the Holy Ghost ever be deceived? (3) He says of His teaching 'he that believeth not, shall be condemned' (Luke 10). One would not be condemned for not heeding His word were it possible for that word to become corrupt. Christ's words presuppose the infallibility of the Apostles and their successors.

Jager next examines the doctrines of the primitive Church as further justification of the principle of infallibility. The Fathers have left no special treatise on the infallible authority of the Church because it was perfectly acceptable at a time so near Christ that heretics taught only in secret. Before the Reformation, Lamennais points out, there had been no attack on the right of the Church to judge on faith. Points of order were contested. but not the infallibility of her decisions (*Essai sur l'indifférence en matière de religion*, chap. VI). But if there are no direct references to the dogma, there is much evidence to suggest the universal belief in the Church's ultimate authority. Jager cites St. Irenaeus, Tertullian, Origen, St. Cyprian, St. Athanasius, the Emperor Constantine, St. Cyril of Alexandria, St. Epiphanius, St. Theophilus, St. Jerome, St. John Chrysostom, St. Augustine, Pope St. Celestine, St. Leo, the Emperor Marcian, St. Gregory the Great in a catena of patristic evidence and ends with the affirmation of Vincent of Lérins:

We said also that in ecclesiastical antiquity itself we were diligently to observe, and seriously to consider, two things, unto which all those that will not be heretics must of necessity cling fast. The first is, that which hath in old time been determined by all the Bishops of the Catholic Church, by authority of a General Council. The second is, that if any new question did arise, in which that were not to be found, we ought to have recourse to the sayings of the Holy Fathers, but yet of those only, who in this time and place were approved masters, being such as continued in the unity of the communion and faith: and whatsoever we find that they held with one mind and one consent, to judge that, without all scruple to be the true and Catholic doctrine of the Church.' (*Commonit.* XXIX)

Christ has given us a body of doctrine necessary for salvation. He foresaw disputes of faith—in fact they are part of God's plan —and therefore left to us a simple means to distinguish truth from error: the infallible voice of the Church. Scripture itself would not have been enough because it is subject to a thousand different interpretations. Tertullian even thinks that 'the Scriptures themselves were so disposed by the will of God as to supply matter for heretics' (*De Praescript.* XXXIX). The interpretations of the Fathers would not have been adequate authority of themselves because faith would then depend on learning and because their writings can be diverted from their true meaning. The living and speaking authority of the Church is necessary, and the unity of faith is impossible without it.

How will Newman reply to this? That the Church is infallible on fundamental points only and yet fallible enough not to recognize what the fundamentals are?

Jager concludes that the Roman Church has authority on its side. The Protestant Church, repudiating this, can only be a mixture of uncertain opinions.

So reason, Scripture and the Fathers, unite to demonstrate to you the infallibility of the Church. How will you answer such numerous and striking proofs? That the Church is infallible in fundamental points? That, in effect, is what you say in your letter. What a curious infallibility! She is infallible in fundamental points, and she can be deceived in the discernment she makes of what they are, and deliver to us as fundamental that which is not so! Further, by admitting this distinction, you must begin by a reconciliation among yourselves. You declare the Church to be infallible on capital points, and yet you accuse the Roman Church of having erred on dogma and on morals, of having fallen into idolatry and superstitition, of having added to the religion of Christ *strange and monstrous* dogmas, opposed to the word of God. So you have two alternatives: either these errors are fundamental, or they are not. If they are fundamental, your opinion is false. If they are not, you are schismatics, condemned by St. Vincent as the Donatists were, since, like them, you have cut yourselves off from the Church for the sake of non-fundamental articles. Besides, what is more fundamental in religion than the dogma of infallibility, since on this dogma depends the certainty or uncertainty of our faith? If therefore the Church cannot be deceived on fundamental points, she cannot have been deceived in believing herself to be infallible. The dogma of infallibility is therefore supported by your own assertion.

Moreover, why should the Church be infallible in certain points of faith and not in others? Do Scripture and the Fathers make this distinction? The Holy Spirit who must remain *eternally* with the Church must teach, not some truths, but *all truth.** The Fathers condemned any innovation opposed to universal teaching, without examining whether it were fundamental or not. I say no more, having set myself to treat this subject in a special way in my next letter.

Before I conclude, I beg you to consider once more the unshakeable foundation on which the faith of the Roman Catholic is based. He has universality, antiquity, consent, number, learning and virtue on his side, that is to say, reason, Scripture, the Fathers, the councils, the ecclesiastical writers of every age, the liturgies of the whole world, the testimony, or, what is no less significant, the silence of heretics; and above all, the authority of an infallible Church. There is no certainty like it anywhere in the world. That of the sciences comes nowhere near it. If you dare to repudiate it, then speak no more of your faith or your religion, there is none for you. Uncertain opinions alone will be your lot, shifting like the sands. May you have a happier fate!

(c) *Jager's Sixth Letter*

Turning to the main body of Newman's letter, Jager deals with the system of fundamental and non-fundamental dogma which has been of great importance in Protestant controversy— in fact, it is a serious issue for all Christians to discover whether they must believe all Christ and the Church have taught or merely certain articles; whether a sect, if it refuses to believe in the totality of dogmas, is to be excluded from the Church or tolerated. Without the system, Jager asserts, it is impossible to defend the Reformation. Nothing is therefore more fundamental than this distinction between fundamental and non-fundamental dogmas.

* John, 16: 13.

Some articles of faith, according to Newman, *are* necessary to obtain salvation; others can be rejected without any risk or fear of exclusion from the Church. Reminding him of the rule they have agreed upon—whatever has no foundation in Scripture or tradition must be rejected—Jager asks yet again, 'Where and when was the distinction made?' for he can find no reference to it in the Gospels or the writings of the Apostles or the Fathers. Had this system been in existence, it would have been in their interest to use it in order to make conversion easier; and surely in their fight against heresy they would have had cause to mention it. In addition to the silence of the primitive Church on the matter there is no written evidence for it in *later* centuries. Even heretics do not mention it, yet such a system must have been to their advantage.

In fact, claims Jager, this system was completely unknown before the Reformation. Therefore it is on Newman's own principles a false and gratuitous invention. Logically, his case could end here, but he goes further and points out that the distinction is not only without foundation in the Scriptures and the Fathers but is diametrically opposed to them.

1. Jesus Christ tells the Apostles to teach not part but the whole of what He had commanded (Matt. 28). There are no restrictions when He says 'he that believeth . . . shall be saved, he that believeth not shall be condemned.' Obviously, then, everything Christ taught is fundamental.

2. The writings of the Apostles support this: St. Paul warns against 'those who make dissensions' (Rom. 16: 17) and tells the Corinthians to 'speak the same thing' and 'be perfect in the same mind' (1 Cor. 1: 10). How could they be of the same mind if they differed on numerous points which were non-fundamental? St. John does not distinguish, says Jager, between the man who denies God and the man who denies one article of Christ's teaching (2 Epist. 1: 9).

3. St. Paul (Gal. 1: 9) and Vincent's interpretation of him (*Commonit.* VIII) shows clearly that Apostolic teaching condemned all novelties in doctrine and anathematized those who sought to introduce them. Every novelty was a fundamental error. Timothy was instructed to guard the deposit of faith and avoid profane novelties (1 Tim. 6: 20).

Do the Apostles make any acknowledgement of the system

by their actions? There is only one example in the New Testament but it proves there is no such thing as a non-fundamental error. Although Paul circumcised Timothy in order not to scandalize the Jews, who knew he had been a pagan, he spoke *against* circumcision (Gal. 5: 2) when the council of Jerusalem pronounced it unnecessary, because he believed the *slightest* error was fundamental and would entail loss of faith and salvation.

4. The distinction is contrary to the teachings of the Fathers who all insist on perfect unity of thought. Tertullian, St. Irenaeus, St. Athanasius, St. Cyprian, and St. Vincent are quoted to prove that the *whole* of Christ's doctrine is the object of faith. That doctrine, being one, must produce unity among those who profess it. That unity is incompatible with the tolerance of errors which Protestants call non-fundamental. The Fathers go further and point out that anyone who does not hold the faith in its entirety will be excluded and condemned as a heretic. Examples to prove this are drawn from St. Augustine, St. Jerome, Lactantius, Pope St. Celestine, and various Councils.

There is much evidence, affirms Jager, that the present-day practice of the Roman Church, of excluding all who do not accept complete faith, is exactly the same as in early centuries and he refers to the Councils of Nicaea, Constantinople, Laodicea, and Orléans, the latter of which decreed that in order to be readmitted heretics must accept *all* the articles of the Catholic church whole and entire (*integré*, Concil. Aurel., I, can. 10, Labb. t. iv, p. 1406).

Jager discusses the meaning of the word 'heresy', which means choice, an individual opinion opposed to universal belief. An innovation, however slight, disturbs unity of thought and constitutes heresy, involving the loss of the whole of religion. Gregory Nazianzen sees it as 'killing with a single word, as with a single drop of poison' (*De fide Orthodoxâ*). St. Vincent is persuaded that the slightest error goes on to destroy the faith in its entirety: 'If we give up any part of the Catholic faith, straightway other parts, and after that another, and again another, shall be given up . . . until the whole in like manner must be set aside' (*Commonit.* XXIII). Could anything be more exclusive of the idea of non-fundamental errors? St. Augustine lists eighty-eight heresies, some of which do not attack doctrines

called fundamental by Newman, yet they are *all* condemned.
There is no need to examine heresies in detail: the sole charac-
teristic of novelty is enough to condemn them (Tertullian, *De
Praescript.* XXXI–XXXV).

Jager next examines Newman's system in detail, in itself, and
in its consequences. Have we the right, he asks, to reshape God's
revelation and assess each part for ourselves? However Protestants categorize them, non-fundamental articles are part of the
essential truth. Why, then, do Protestants call these truths
unnecessary? Their isolation and inability to justify themselves
in terms of the Apostles' Creed as a Church One, Catholic, and
Apostolic has led to this system of fundamentals and non-fundamentals in order to bring into communion all the various sects
with their different dogmas. The truths of religion were called
non-fundamental not because they were so declared by Scripture,
but because they were repudiated by some Protestant sect. The
further sects wander from the truth, the greater the number of
essential dogmas which has to be reduced in order to appease
them. But in spite of this attempt at unity, the Protestant Church
remains divided and in conflict. The French Protestant minister
Coquerel admits the violence of hatred among the Protestant
sects and uses the notion of fundamental Christianity to find
agreement.* Jager knows that Newman considers French Protestants to be far from the truth and the reproach is mutual.

What of the consequences of the system? One error of faith
leads to thousands. If we are to accept the system of non-fundamentals, we must believe that nobody before the sixteenth century understood his creed, since it implied a Church united by
the same faith and from which heretics were excluded. But Newman has said the Church is infallible on fundamentals and that
the truths in the creed were fundamental. The Church could not
therefore have been deceived about the meaning of the Creed,
and his system was false. Another consequence was the constant
uncertainty about which dogmas are fundamental because there
are so many variations between the sects—no one Protestant is
sure of believing everything which is necessary to salvation.
When the Protestant sees his learned theologians still disputing
truths necessary to salvation, how is he to find peace of mind?

* Charles Coquerel, *Essai sur l'histoire générale du Christianisme* [Paris, 1828],
pp. 267–9.

In France, argument between sects has reduced teaching to *one* fundamental doctrine, the Redemption.* The discernment of essential articles being left to private judgement, no Protestant can condemn this view. Such is the outcome of the principles laid down in Newman's letter!

To prove this assertion, Jager asks what, in fact, are the fundamental articles? Newman himself seems confused; at times he says they are what is contained in the Apostles' Creed, at others that they are all the truths delivered by tradition and supported by Scripture. The first alternative would imply that original sin and the necessity of baptism were not fundamental; and in the second case how can Anglican theologians decide which articles *are* contained in Scripture? Furthermore, whoever rejects Scripture itself attacks no fundamental dogma, as Chillingworth has made clear: 'a man may be saved, who should not believe them [the books of Scripture] to be the word of God.'† This is deism, which springs from the womb of the Reformation.

According to Anglican theologians, schism is an enormous crime. But according to the system Newman puts forward it cannot exist, or if it does exist it is in fact a duty. He gives an example of this: Article XXXI declares the effect of the sacraments to be independent of the worthiness of the minister. This, according to Newman, is non-fundamental because otherwise it would be necessary to acknowledge the authority of tradition. Whoever disputes the power of the bishops, therefore, does not err on a fundamental article. So no such thing as schism can exist, for schism can only occur when there is a right to command and a duty to obey. There can be no separation when there is no union to start with. If bishops are not infallible it is no crime to disobey them. In fact if a minister were convinced they had made a wrong judgement it becomes his duty to oppose them. The system of non-fundamental errors leads to the total destruction of Christianity.

In conclusion, Jager examines certain details of Newman's letter.

1. Newman had written that he allowed to the Church a power to draw articles of religion from its fundamental Creed

* Ibid., p. 248.
† Chillingworth, *The Religion of Protestants a Safe Way af Salvation*, London, 1638, ch. II [cited in Milner, *End of Religious Controversy*, Letter XI].

according to time and circumstances. Where is this principle to be found? Although the Protestants left the Roman Church under the pretext that it was too despotic, she never claimed the power which the Protestant Church, or rather Parliament, attributes to itself: making articles of faith *according to time and circumstances* while admitting to being fallible and possibly erroneous. This power never extends to fundamental articles of course; but the non-fundamental articles so made are either true or false. The Anglican Church has therefore taken upon itself the power of creating truth or falsehood, a principle so absurd Jager cannot imagine how Newman wrote it. To excuse himself, Newman might try to say this kind of article must be a development of fundamental points in the Creed. Jager accepts the Church's duty to elucidate and develop points but there must be no change: *Profectus, non permutatio,* as Vincent puts it. But from what creed do so many of the Thirty-nine Articles derive? Of what scriptural text are they the consequence? None, because they are profane novelties rejected by the universal Church.

1. Article 22, in which the worship of images and relics was banned, is derived from the doctrine of the Iconoclasts and Vigilantius who were condemned by the early Church and refuted by St. Jerome. Since Roman Catholics do not worship images the article is based on falsehood.

2. Article 19 states that the Catholic Church has erred on dogma and discipline. That is the opinion of Nestorius who was refuted by Vincent, and of the Donatists, who were refuted by Augustine. The Anglicans have sometimes drawn from modern heretics.

3. Article 11, justification by faith alone, is derived from Luther, not from the primitive Church.

4. Article 28, which affirms that the words 'This is My Body . . .' must be interpreted in a figurative sense, is based on a nocturnal vision of the fanatic Zwingli. Every article in which the Church of England differs from the Church of Rome comes from old or new heretical works.

Newman has claimed that the Reformation merely clarified and polished points previously obscure. The jewels have been polished so much, declares Jager, that they have completely disappeared. Article 6 says that Scripture contains all things necessary to salvation. St. James writes: '. . . by works a man is

justified and not by faith only' (St. James, 2: 14, 17, 24). Luther
was logical enough to exclude St. James from the Canon of the
New Testament. The Anglicans both admit this book and maintain Luther's principle! Christ's own words (Matt. 19: 21, 29)
show up the falsity of Article 14, that works of supereroga-
tion cannot be taught without arrogance and impiety, and
Article 13, which states that works done before justification are
a sin, is refuted by Isaiah (1: 16–18.)

Jager has already asked Newman where he finds the principle
that Scripture contains all things necessary to salvation. Newman declares it is found in Vincent, which Jager denies, with
proofs to support him. Yet Newman without reference to these
proofs has repeated his assertion. Vincent does *not* recommend
us to believe only what is in Scripture, but what is taught by the
Universal Church. Furthermore, the Fathers of the first centuries were not content to bear witness to a Catholic doctrine;
they declared it necessary to salvation and excluded from the
Church all those who would not subscribe to it.

Jager has already discussed the authority of tradition but he
feels that some new observations are required: in refuting the
words of Blanco White,* he affirms that tradition and Scripture
are in perfect harmony; although there are apparent contradictions and difficulties, the Roman Church has never claimed
tradition to be superior. Nor is tradition purely oral, and it is
certainly not *hearsay*, because it is set down in books of Christian
antiquity. Far from being a collection of vague memories and
popular traditions it is based on the consent and unanimity of
the Fathers.

---

* 'The Romanists declare that the Scriptures alone are not sufficient for salvation; but that there is the word of God by *hearsay*, which is superior to the word
of God in writing. By this *hearsay* (for tradition is nothing else) they assure the
world that the Scripture must be explained: so that if the Scripture says *white*, and
tradition says black, a Roman Catholic is bound to say, that *white* means *black* in
God's written word.' J. Blanco White, *Poor man's preservative against the errors
of Romanism*, 1834, p. 52.

4. Newman's Second Letter[a]

Sir,

1. I am delighted to see that my letter, short as it was, has given you occupation for several months. You claim that of three points contained in Bishop Jebb's treatise, I have only examined one, and that I have abandoned the other two. I cannot agree, I have not abandoned the other two, my intention was to examine them separately. But I well foresaw that the first would by itself provide ample matter for discussion, and I am bound to congratulate myself on my foresight.

2. In our discussion I think we shall do better to concentrate on one single point rather than to include several, otherwise we should never be equal to the task. The controversy which occupies us is of too elevated a nature for us to have such confidence in ourselves. None of us has the hundred arms of Briareus. For my part, I can only play one role at a time, attacking you first on one point and then on another, and waiting patiently for each point to be clarified. That is why, in my last letter, I provoked you on two theological points. I would very much have liked to be able to fix your attention on them. They arose from my subject, they marked the critical point of the question, the very one on which we differ and which we are now discussing. That would perhaps have prevented you from being so strangely mistaken about my opinions and confusing them with those of others. For those two points clearly explained what my sentiments were. It has pleased you to give to my letter the collective title of *observations*, not of *arguments*. No, Sir, it is a collection of pieces of information. You could not have known my opinions before I had explained them to you. It was my duty to do so.

3. 'What kind of a religion,' you will say, 'is that which we know only through individuals, which each person can modify as the fancy takes him, and which lacks authoritative documents?' We have those documents, namely the three Creeds, the decisions of at least the first four general Councils, our liturgy, the

[a] Fourth Reply, Part One in the original sequence of the controversy.

office and the Thirty-Nine Articles. In other matters, we leave
to each man his freedom of thought. We grant that freedom on
the articles of which Bishop Jebb treated, and which you had
selected as points for discussion. It then became necessary to
make known to you my opinions on those points, so that you
might have some ground for controversy. These opinions, I am
glad to say, are not peculiar to myself. They belong to the most
renowned doctors of our Church, even to the ancient doctors
whose teaching, as long as it be Catholic, will always have my
allegiance.

4. Perhaps you will say, if those opinions are true, why do
you tolerate others in your Church? Doubtless you can tell me
that there are opinions received by the Protestants of the Anglican Church on the subject of tradition, which differ greatly from
mine, and you do in fact reproach me with this in your letter.
To this I answer that, in my view, it is fitting to leave the mind
a certain freedom, and I hope to prove this to you, if ever we
finish the subject upon which we are at present engaged. I will
even grant you that our Church is by no means severe enough
where religious opinions are concerned, provided you, for your
part, confess that the Church of Rome is far *too* severe. Here is
the difference between us. For myself, I can be frank; you
cannot. I can confess, if need be, that the Anglican Church is not
perfect; but *you* are obliged to maintain the infallibility of your
communion. If you manage to prove it successfully, your position is a happy one; but it is disagreeable if your doctrine is
belied by the facts.

I will say no more for the moment on such a wide topic as the
variations of Protestantism. I propose to speak of them before
the end of this letter, but their place is not here.

5. I have already referred to a number of misunderstandings
about my opinions which I have encountered in your letters.
There are some I had no cause to expect, because of the explanations which I had given. I will content myself for the moment
by quoting as an example the error, no less strange than inconceivable, into which you fall, over the meaning I attach to the
word 'fundamental', an error which prevails almost from start
to finish in your first two letters. I had said: 'Such then are
the doctrines which we consider to have been revealed as the
basis of the Church, the condition of baptism, the profession of

Churchmen.' * Further, in a previous passage, I had explained myself still more clearly: 'If we are asked,' I said, 'what we mean
by *fundamentals*, we answer that we mean such doctrines as are
necessary for Church Communion; if we are asked which these
are, we answer briefly, the articles of the Creed'.✝ Nonetheless,
in spite of these precise declarations, you make me say on almost
every page that by the word *fundamental*, I mean *any doctrine
which it is necessary to profess in order to be saved*. A very different
definition, as we shall see later.

6. In your sixth letter, you appear to have noticed your
mistake. You say: 'What, in effect, do you understand by fundamental articles? The answer is not an easy one. Your theologians consider this a thorny question, one very difficult to
resolve. And you yourself seem to be in some embarrassment
over it; for *at times you call fundamental what is contained in the
Apostles' Creed, at others all the truths delivered by tradition and
supported by Scripture.'* ‡ I was about to congratulate myself on
having been understood, but unfortunately you still make me
say things I do not say. True, I call the articles of the Apostles'
Creed fundamental; you are correct in this. But you are no
longer correct when you add the words *at times*, you should have
said *always*. Where have I given that name to another doctrine?
Where have I included under that heading *'all the truths delivered
by tradition and supported by Scripture?'* Show me the page on
which I have used this expression. Quote my expressions in
English and in French. I have never said anything like it.

You thus commit two errors. You say that at times I regard
as fundamental, 'All the truths delivered by tradition and supported by Scripture,' and that by the word fundamental I mean
necessary to salvation. Those two propositions are entirely your
own, they are not mine.

7. This misunderstanding is all the more extraordinary since
in my challenge to you, I clearly distinguished these two expressions: *condition of communion*, and *necessary to salvation*. 'On the
other hand I challenge you,' I said, 'to produce authority from
him for your two peculiar tenets from which we dissent; first,
that pure Tradition is a sufficient basis on which the Church may

---

* p. 39; Jager, p. 100.
✝ p. 36; Jager, p. 95.
‡ p. 71; Jager, p. 311.

rest in declaring a doctrine *necessary to salvation*; next, that the Church may impose consent to any article of faith as a condition of communion over and above original fundamentals.'* Please observe that not only do I contrast the expression *necessary to salvation* with that of *condition of communion*, I connect the word 'fundamental' precisely with the latter phrase.

8. But it is time to pass on to the examination of that challenge. I hasten towards it, observing only that the word *ou* is not an accurate enough translation of the word *next* which I used, and that instead of 'beyond the fundamentals', I wrote 'over and above *original* fundamentals.' I make these observations merely to prove that if I had been more literally translated, my intentions would have been more clearly shown.

I now return to that challenge. Allow me to recall what gave rise to it. Bishop Jebb's first remark was thus conceived: 'The Church of Rome maintains, not only that there are two rules of belief: but that those two rules are co-ordinate; that there is an unwritten, no less than a written word of God: and that the authority of the former, is alike definitive with the authority of the latter.'ᵃ He then proves that Vincent differs from the Church of Rome. I had to defend the Bishop's assertion as being one of the three which you had taken as the basis of our controversy, and to that end I adopted the following method which is quite simple and natural. I said first that the doctrine of the Anglican Church, relative to tradition, was a matter of fact. Next, I examined the doctrine adopted by the Roman Church. Finally I compared them both with Vincent's doctrine. From these investigations it transpired that we were in agreement on several points and that we differed on others, since you affirm that tradition is a sufficient authority either for fundamental doctrines or for those which are necessary, and that we deny this. I added next: 'If you can produce authority from Vincent for your two peculiar tenets from which we dissent . . . Vincent goes further than we do; if you cannot, he does not go as far as you.'†

9. I must here point out to you the inaccuracy of the following observation: 'So you are greatly shocked, you say, by the procedure of the Council of Trent, which *had the temerity* to establish

* p. 45; Jager, p. 108.
† p. 45; Jager, p. 109.

ᵃ Jebb, *Peculiar character of the Church of England*, p. 283.

the dogma of transubstantiation, *Juxta Apostolorum traditionem*, without having recourse to Scripture'. * My real purpose was to show clearly what was the difference between your opinions and ours in a matter of fact. I meant that the Council formally founded certain doctrines on tradition, contrary to our way of thinking. My intention was not to attack you on that subject at the moment. I thought I had explained myself sufficiently by adding, by way of precaution, to the remarks to which you allude: 'These instances are given, not by way of ascertaining your view, but that we may clearly have before us the points on which we are at issue; viz. whether or not Tradition per se is a sufficient authority for the Church to go by in settling *fundamentals?* You answer in the affirmative; we in the negative.'† But this is of little importance. Let us continue.

10. My challenge had brought our controversy to its conclusion on the first of Bishop Jebb's heads. You could have answered by a single word, *yes* or *no*, and if, after all, you had held an opinion contrary to mine, you could have quoted those passages of Vincent in support of your own. I regret that you did not do so. I will even say I am surprised you did not, for the following sentence, which is in the letter you addressed to M. H. . . ., had made a great impression on my mind. 'I need not point out to you,' you said, 'how indispensable it is, for the orderly progress of our discussion, never to leave a question once entered into before elucidating it completely.'‡

11. You say: 'You are not prepared to admit that tradition is a sufficient basis for a fundamental doctrine. Here, you challenge me to show in St. Vincent a single proof favourable to our belief.'§ After having thus defined my challenge, you abandon it completely and pass on to the proofs of the Council of Trent's definition of transubstantiation, of which I had just been speaking, and then to other matters. You refer to our challenge no more at this point. It is true that you prove, or believe you do, that all the other Fathers, the Councils, etc., think as you do. I would have been content with Vincent, since you had begun with him. Yet you return later to that challenge in these words:

---

* p. 55; Jager, p. 137.
† p. 38; Jager, p. 98.
‡ p. 22; Jager, p. 27.
§ p. 55; Jager, p. 137.

'Does St. Vincent of Lérins speak differently? But what could Vincent avail against the universal doctrine of the Church?'* Remarkable words indeed! You find that it is prudent to prepare a retreat, to place a column behind you to protect you if need arise. You say that the principles of Vincent himself are opposed to his isolated opinion being considered as a decisive authority on this subject. That principle is true and wise and I embrace it with the same enthusiasm as you do. Doubtless, a single doctor has not sufficient authority by himself. It is the agreed and unanimous voice of Catholic doctors which alone has an obligatory power upon our assent. Why then did you invoke his testimony in the first place since you reject it now? Why, instead of proving that he *does in fact say* what you would like him to say, are you content to declare that he *ought* to say it? Why do you affect to treat him as a mere individual? That is insulting to him and to you. Vincent is really an authority whom one can invoke, and each time you invoke him, you do so with reason and with judgment. He does not speak only in his own name, he has no time for personal opinions, he states the doctrine of the Fathers of his age. 'I have often inquired,' he says, 'with great desire and attention, of very many excellent, holy and learned men . . . and I had usually this answer of them all.'†

12. After having taken that precaution in case of defeat, you attempt to give a proof, that is, you quote some passages which you consider as equivalent to a proof. I fear I cannot grant them. Let us see what they are, or rather let us see *the point which you wish to prove* when you report them. You say: 'Moreover, the two quotations which I have just reproduced[a] already prove that Vincent *regards the teaching of the Church as a general rule* which will serve as a basis for his treatise.'‡

How desperate this is! I thought we were going to fight it out in a hand to hand conflict, and you escape me! Is that the point which you had to prove? You had just expressed yourself with greater exactness when you said: 'You are not prepared to admit that tradition is sufficient to *act as a basis for a fundamental doctrine*. Here, you challenge me to show you in St.

---

* p. 57; Jager, p. 161.
† *Commonit*, II.   ‡ p. 57; Jager, p. 162.

[a] From Vincent, *Commonit*. II and IX, cf. *infra*, p. 80.

Vincent a single proof favourable to our belief.'ᵃ Is the teaching
of the Church, then, the same thing as fundamental? You thought
of it as such; but that was the very point which had to be proved.
The fundamentals are the conditions of communion. The teaching of the Church is the perfect and complete development of
these conditions. It is a rule for the individual who teaches, not
a creed for all Christians. It is a privilege, but the fundamental
articles are more obligatory. It is wise and pious to receive the
whole teaching of the Church. It is necessary to receive the
fundamental articles, if one wishes to be a member of the Church.
I said all this in my last letter. It appears therefore that far from
proving the only proposition which you had to prove, and which
I had challenged you to prove, you do not even attempt it.

13. Let us now examine the passages which you adduce. Perhaps Vincent will be more favourable to you than you are to
yourself. First you quote his second and ninth chapters: 'To
believe,' he says, 'that which hath been believed everywhere,
always, and by all men, that is truly and properly Catholic, as
the very force and nature of the word doth declare.'ᵇ I admit this
principle in its entire scope. Every member of the Anglican
Church, who knowingly acts otherwise, is not truly and properly Catholic. But has the Church the right, for this purpose,
to refuse communion to those who do not wish to begin by
admitting her belief? Or, to put the question another way, is the
Church authorised to demand from us, as an indispensable condition for the reception of the sacrament of grace, that we not
only believe unhesitatingly and with a filial trust that she will
always teach sound doctrines; but also that we should swear to
receive as divine everything that she considers as coming directly
from the Apostles? I cannot find that in the words you have
quoted. I cannot persuade myself that Vincent authorizes the
Church of Rome to require Pius IV's Creed from all those who
belong to her communion. Let us suppose that I am in a French
town where there is no Anglican Church, you would not admit
me to communion. Yet I find nothing in Vincent which might
justify this refusal. You will say that consciously to reject a part
of that creed is to exclude oneself from salvation. This is some-

---

ᵃ *Supra*, p. 78.

ᵇ Vincent, *Commonit*. II. Quod ubique, quod semper, quod ab omnibus creditum
est, hoc est enim vere proprieque catholicum, quod vis nominis ratioque declarat.

thing more which I cannot find in Vincent. These are two points on which I have challenged you. Let us conclude the examination of your extracts. 'To preach unto Christian Catholic men beside that which they have received, never was lawful, nowhere is lawful, nor ever shall be lawful.'[a] Doubtless, a doctor whose teaching might not be Catholic must be expelled from the Church, for he trusts in himself and thus induces others into error. But if the man who thinks, doubts, makes mistakes or has no fixed opinion on certain developments of doctrine, firmly believes the articles of the Apostles' Creed, he must not be considered as trusting in himself, nor as inducing others into error. He is silent on that subject. Vincent does not order us to reject him as a result, and the Apostle tells us: 'Him that is weak in the faith receive ye, but not to doubtful disputations'.[b] 'Is there any man either bold enough,' continues Vincent, 'to proclaim something other than what has been proclaimed in the Church, or frivolous enough to receive something other than what he has received from the Church?'[c] A man is bold when he preaches his doctrines, silence must be impelled on him; he is frivolous when he receives them, and he must be instructed, but not excommunicated, unless he propagates his opinions.

14. After having furnished two other quotations as little relevant to the matter in hand, you say: 'Thus, in reproaching the Council of Trent for having decided in accordance with tradition alone, you reproach it for being in agreement with antiquity, for following the Catholic rule.'* I beg your pardon, I did not find fault with the Council for having established dogmas on tradition alone, but for having made them *fundamental* articles, and insisting on their reception as necessary to be in communion with the Church. I was quite right to emphasise those words strongly, although I did not manage to make myself understood. 'These three words must be clearly understood,' I said; *'ultimate appeal, doctrines,* and *fundamentals.'*†

---

* p. 57; Jager, p. 166.
† p. 35; Jager, p. 95.

[a] Vincent, *Commonit.* IX. Adnuntiare ergo aliquid christianis catholicis, praeter id quod acceperunt, nunquam licuit, nusquam licet, nunquam licebit. . . .
[b] Romans, 14: 1.
[c] Vincent, *Commonit.* IX. Quae cum ita sint, estne aliquis vel tantae audaciae qui praeter id quod apud Ecclesiam adnuntiatum est, adnuntiet, vel tantae levitatis qui, praeter id quod ab Ecclesia accepit, accipiat?

I reproach the Council of Trent not with having taught the whole truth, but with having excluded from Communion those who did not profess it in all its details. Show me that such is the Catholic rule, and then you will find me guilty of censuring it; till then I cannot subscribe to it.

15. What must we conclude from all this, other than that you have declined the challenge I offered you, a challenge which was to decide our respective attachment to Vincent's doctrine, first in relation to Bishop Jebb's charge. Our religious feelings are in agreement up to a certain point and Vincent obviously agrees with us. But you go further than he does. For my part, I stop where Vincent stops, Vincent is silent where I am silent. I challenge you to make him speak. You have tried to do so, but, may I say, not as my own individual opinion but as a fact which everyone can judge, that you have failed completely.

16. This struggle is therefore terminated. There remain two more to wage. You claim that I had the intention of renouncing them. Not at all, I am impatient to be on the field of battle; but I am hindered by an obstacle in my way. That obstacle, my dear sir, is yourself. You wish me to hasten to seek you out, and you flood the road which separates us. I mean that in your letters you commit errors, and occupy yourself with subjects which are linked, it is true, with the matter in question, but in an indirect manner, and you beg me to answer the opinions which you have on these subjects. You speak, for example, of the infallibility of the Church, of the origin of the corruption of the Popes, of the question of fundamental articles, of the variations of Protestantism, and you produce all kinds of evidence taken from the Fathers and the Councils, of which some are related to the subject and others have no connection with it at all. I said to myself: when will there be an end to all this? For I saw quite clearly that you were inexhaustible; and I still think so. I am particularly obliged to you in that you fixed limits, in my favour, the lack of which in other controversialists has engendered numerous weighty, theological volumes. Allow me then to take up once more the questions which you had begun to treat, and to defer, until they have been discussed, the examination of the second and third charges relating to Vincent in Bishop Jebb's treatise.

Fundamental Articles

17. I have already said that the *fundamental doctrines* of the Church were those upon which the Church is founded, those which all her members must admit, and on which they must take their stand, if they wish to belong to the Church. That foundation, to reduce it to its simplest expression, is contained in these words: *Thou art Christ, the Son of the Living God*, which have always been developed as a matter of fact in those Creeds which are called the Apostles' Creed and the Nicene Creed. The articles of these Creeds are fundamental articles of the Gospel and they will ever continue to be so in despite of the power of the Church, however great it be, unless it is possible to make the solidity of the foundations depend on the building which has been raised up on them.

18. You ask me next, what proofs I have that these articles are fundamental.* I answer, this is how the primitive Church considered them, and that historical proof is quite sufficient. You will tell me that in admitting that fact, there exists, on my own confession, a truth supported not on Scripture, but on history. Doubtless there are a thousand truths which are proved by history alone, the certainty of which is no less unanswerable, although they be not found in Scripture. In admitting the two Creeds as fundamental, I never said that the principle itself was fundamental. I refuse communion not to those who do not regard it as such, but to those who reject it. Provided that a man receive it, I do not ask him to explain to me its theological value. Yet if the whole truth must be told, I believe that any doctrine which is of its nature fundamental is also found in Scripture. But it is not for that reason fundamental, for all doctrines which are found in Scripture are not necessarily fundamental.

19. If you ask me where is the historical proof of which I have just spoken, I refer you to the historical evidences of Scripture, to the following authorities and to many others. Irenaeus says: 'The Church, though propagated throughout the whole world, unto the ends of the earth, has received from the Apostles and their disciples the belief in one God, the Father Almighty, Maker of heaven and earth, . . . and in Jesus Christ, the Son of God, incarnate for our salvation, . . . and in the Holy Ghost,

* p. 54; Jager, p. 131.

who proclaimed by the Prophets the divine dispensations, and
the advent, birth of a Virgin, passion, etc., of His beloved Son,
Christ Jesus Our Lord, that to Christ Jesus our Lord and God
every knee should bow, of things in heaven and things in earth,
etc., and that he may exercise just judgment upon all. This
message and this faith, which the Church has received, though
disseminated through the whole world, she diligently guards.'*
Tertullian says: 'The Rule of faith is altogether one, sole,
unalterable, unchangeable, viz. that of believing in One God
Almighty, Maker of the world, and His Son Jesus Christ, born
of the Virgin Mary, crucified under Pontius Pilate, raised from
the dead the third day,' etc., etc. †

20. Without having recourse to other examples, is it not
evident from those which we have just cited, that what the primitive Church considered as the rule of faith defined and fixed, was
agreeable in substance with the Apostles' Creed? More, it was
the profession of faith that was required of those to whom baptism was given, the necessary condition to be admitted into the
communion of the Church. This results clearly from several
passages which I am going to cite. Tertullian gives the detail
of most of the articles of the Creed, when he answers an objection that was being made, namely that Christ Himself had not
baptised his disciples. 'For whereunto should He have baptized?
Unto repentance? To what purpose then His forerunner? Unto
remission of sins? which He gave by a word! Into *Himself*? Whom
in humility He hid! Into the *Holy Ghost*? Who had not as yet
descended from the Father! Into *the Church*? which the Apostles
had not as yet founded!'‡

Cyprian says: 'Moreover the very interrogatory which is put
in Baptism, is a witness of the truth. For when we say, "Dost
thou believe in eternal life and remission of sins through the
Holy Church?" we mean, the remission of sins is not given, except
in the Church.'§

'When the Catechumen,' say the Apostolic Constitutions, 'has
gone through his preparatory course, and is about to be baptized,
let him be told how to renounce the devil, and how to dedicate
himself to Christ. . . . Thus: I renounce Satan, and his works,

---

* *Contra Haeres.* lib. I, c. X.
† *De Veland. Virginibus*, c. I.—*De Praescript.*, c. XIII, *Adv. Prax.*, c. II.
‡ *De Baptismo*, c. XI.   § *Epist.* 70 *ad Januarium.*

and his pomps. . . . After this renunciation, let him enrol himself among Christ's disciples, saying "I devote myself to Christ, and believe and am baptized into One unbegotten, the only True God Almighty, the Father of Christ, Creator and Maker of all things, of whom are all things; and in the Lord Jesus, the Christ, His Only-begotten Son, who came down from heaven, and took flesh on Him and was born of the Holy Virgin Mary, etc., and was crucified under Pontius Pilate, etc. etc. . . . I am baptized into the Holy Spirit, which is the Comforter, which has wrought in all Saints from the beginning, and at length was sent by the Father to the Apostles, &c., and after the Apostles to all who, in the Holy Catholic Church believe in the resurrection of the flesh and the life of the world to come." '*

21. Does it not follow clearly from these passages, that the terms of admission into the Church were fixed and unchangeable, that the articles of the Creed were certain articles, explained and developed under all forms in the century of the Apostles and since, and not that collection of articles defined and accumulated by the Church in the course of centuries, however true they may be? What would Tertullian have said if he had learned that the Creed of Pius IV was being required of a catechumen, in place of the Apostles' Creed? You will no doubt say that the question is out of place, as heresies have arisen, since the Apostles' Creed, which have rendered Pius IV's Creed necessary. Let us suppose that all the heresies with which you believe us to be infected had existed then, do you think the African Church would have added anything to the articles of the Creed of its communion? You are obliged to answer in the affirmative. For my part, I take no side, but St. Cyprian will maintain the negative in my place. Why was no addition made to the Creed in his day, in order to condemn the Novatians? Certainly nothing *was* added. Hear his own words: 'But if any here object and say, that Novatian holds the same rule that the Catholic Church holds, baptizes with the same Creed wherewith we also baptize, acknowledges the same God the Father, the same Son Christ, the same Holy Ghost, and therefore can claim the power of baptizing, because he seems not to differ from us in the baptismal interrogatory;—whoso thinks that this may be objected, let him know in the first place, that we and schismatics have not one rule of the Creed, nor the same

* *Const. Apost.*, lib. VII, c. XLI & XLII [*sic* for XL and XLI].

interrogatories. For when they say, "Dost thou believe remission of sins and eternal life by the Holy Church?" they lie in their interrogatory, since they have no Church.'* Observe what he does: he adds nothing to the Creed, but uses the prerogative which the Church possessed to interpret it.

22. I shall adduce another example yet more explicit, and which will present itself again later. The Semi-Arians repudiated the celebrated expression *consubstantial, Homoousion,* in the Nicene Creed, with warmth and an unaccountable violence. How did the great defenders of the faith behave towards them? Did they cut them off from communion with the Church? Far from it, St. Athanasius calls them his brethren; St. Hilary calls some of their first bishops *sanctissimi viri*; and St. Basil remained attached to their party until the age of thirty.† Do I wish to conclude from this that those holy persons considered the rejection of the *Homoousion* as a trifle? By no means, but they did not go so far as to formally exclude those who rejected it from the communion of the Church. And as for individuals, they judged them as individuals, that is, with the charity and humility with which we should always judge the servants of another.

23. Such then was the fundamental or baptismal creed of the early centuries. It corresponded, nearly enough, to that which we call the Apostles' Creed, the primitive creed of the Church of Rome. If, despite its substantial identity in the different parts of Christendom, you urge some varieties in the detail of the articles, I shall answer that *that does not concern me,* and that if holy Church, in spite of that diversity, considered it as *unalterable and unchangeable (immobilis et irreformabilis),* we can do as much; more, since those varieties are not, in their nature, more important than those which we find in the different traditions on the Lord's Prayer, as delivered to us by St. Matthew and St. Luke, which do not prevent it being the seal of the spiritual union of Christians; lastly, that these variations only concern the manner in which the dogmas it contains were developed, and (for the most part) they neither add to it nor take from it anything worthy of note. Thus, the article of the African Church, 'the forgiveness of sins, *through the holy Church,*' is only a de-

---

* *Epist. 76* [Carey trans. 69] *ad Magnum.*
† Basil., *Epist. CCXXIII.* Philostorg., IV, 12.

velopment of the Roman article, 'the forgiveness of sins.'[a] And these words of Tertullian: *who produced all things out of nothing by His Word alone*, merely develop 'Maker of heaven and earth.'[*]

24. You have raised an objection relative to that interpretation of the fundamental and primitive creed,—that if we follow it, we would be admitting Socinians, Pelagians, and others, into the communion of the Church. You say: 'If you admit as fundamental only what is contained in the Apostles' Creed, then the dogma of original sin, the necessity of baptism, the sacraments and their effects, everything that pertains to justification, or morality, all these serious and important questions of Christianity will not be fundamental; you may reject them and still be a good Anglican.'[†] At first sight, this objection seems plausible; but it disappears on reflexion, and I am convinced that you will agree, when I have explained to you the meaning of the word *reject*. For you will admit to having let an important distinction escape you, one which, if you had noticed it soon enough, would have helped you to avoid the trouble of producing a great number of quotations which, strong as they are against the dissenters from the Anglican Church, are meaningless when you address them to us. Do you understand by the word *reject*, '*to deny and profess openly the contrary*,' or do you mean simply, '*not to receive*'? There is a very great difference between the man who cannot subscribe to a certain truth, and the man who teaches a completely opposite doctrine. The following reflexion will make you sensible of this difference.

25. If the Church alone has the right to teach the truth, he who teaches without conforming himself to the Church is guilty at least of the sin of having usurped the rights of others. Hence, every time the Fathers defend the Church's privilege to explain and develop the creed, they protest against the particular interpretations which mere individuals permit themselves to give of it. But over and above all this, private teaching could not be received, because of necessity it must have been erroneous. As

---

[*] *De Praescript.*, c. XIII. [†] p. 71; Jager, p. 311.

[a] In the third edition of *Proph. Office* (*Via Media*, I, pp. 226–227), Newman adds a reference to St. Augustine (Serm. 215, fin. 5, p. 952) and observes 'The African "forgiveness *through the Church*" would surely, to a Protestant, be as much an *addition* to the creed as "Purgatory" '.

long as it produced no innovations, it could be borne; but when it produced them, it could only be false, since the faith had been given to the faithful once and for all time. New doctrines had therefore to be regarded with horror, and the primitive Church anathematized and excommunicated those who taught them, for this reason, that they were attacking Catholic doctrine and ecclesiastical authority. Such must certainly be the constant rule of the Church, today as in the past. Thus, if by the word *reject*, you mean 'openly to state and dispute', your argument loses its force; for, where have I said or led you to believe that it was possible openly to reject the doctrine of original sin, the necessity of baptism, and yet be a good Anglican? Because the confession of these doctrines is not required as a condition for spiritual communion, does it follow that one can reject them, while remaining in the spiritual communion of the Church?

26. Consider what Scripture says on the matter. Did Philip oblige the Ethiopian to believe in the doctrine of original sin, and was the latter at liberty to oppose it?[a] Did he teach him to believe as a condition of baptism everything that the Church might, at whatever time, teach him? On the other hand, did the Ethiopian have the so-called exercise of private judgment? Can we suppose he did? Was he at liberty to sift, criticize, and prove for himself the Church's teaching, before he accepted it? In short, is there no medium conceivable between confessing all truth from the first and having a right of opposing it, between Romanism and ultra-Protestantism? There is certainly, in this part of the subject, something deeper than you imagine. Allow me to shed more light on it.

27. You say that, if the Apostles' Creed is the only fundamental for communion with the Church, a man may, in conformity with our ideas, deny original sin and yet be a Christian. I answer that as I have done already. If there is any difficulty in this matter, it is for the primitive Church and not for me to explain it. I take shelter under its authority. If the articles of the Apostles' Creed have so little scope, it is not I, at any rate, who have made them fundamental. But if we consider them attentively, we shall find in them not a defect of scope but a model of charity. The Church recollected she was instituted for the sake of the poor. 'To the poor the Gospel is preached.'[b] The Church

a Acts 8: 27.   b Luke, 7: 22.

was simple and precise in her fundamentals, to include all classes, to suggest heads of belief, to assist the memory, to save the mind from perplexity. However, while thus considerate she has not forgotten her high office, as the appointed teacher of her children. She is the pillar and ground of the truth, of Christian truth in all its developments, in the interpretation of Scripture, in the exposition of doctrine, in the due appointment of ordinances and their particular application and in the code of moral laws. She is called a superstructure, as being built upon the Gospel doctrine; the pillar, the ground, as being the expounder of it. She therefore requires from her children that they subscribe not only to the words of the Apostles' Creed but also to the particular sense she attached to them.

28. You will perhaps ask me what difference there is between subscribing to all the articles of the creed of Pope Pius IV, and subscribing to the Apostles' Creed, according to the sense which the Church attaches to it; since, as you will perhaps maintain, the articles of the former are only, in one way or another, explanations of the latter, as the rise of heresies gave occasion. Yet I think that a man endowed with a judicious mind can perceive a very great practical difference between the two.

Every word of divine revelation has a deep meaning. It is the outward form of a heavenly truth, and in this sense a mystery or Sacrament. We may read it, confess it; but there is something in it which we cannot fathom, which we only, more or less as the case may be, enter into. Accordingly when a candidate for Baptism repeats the Articles of the Creed, he is confessing something incomprehensible in its depth, and indefinite in its extent. He cannot know at the time what he is binding on himself, whither he is letting himself be carried. It is the temper of reverent faith to feel that in coming to the Church, it stands before God's representative, and that, as in her Ordinances, so in her Creed, there is something supernatural. Another property of faith is the wish to conceive rightly of sacred doctrine, as far as it can conceive at all, and to look towards the Church for guidance how to conceive of it. Take the case of the Eunuch.* We shall see in his faith, a submission of the reason and will towards God, wistful and loving meditation upon His message, childlike reliance in the Church, as the interpreter of it. The

* Acts 8: 27.

Church is our mother; if you attend to this figure you will follow my meaning. A child comes to his mother for instruction; she gives it. She does not assume infallibility, nor is she infallible; yet it would argue a very unpleasant temper in the child to doubt her word, to require proof, to go needlessly to other sources of information. Sometimes, perhaps, she makes mistakes in lesser matters, and is set right by her child; yet this neither diminishes her prerogative of teaching, nor his privilege of receiving dutifully. Now this is what the Church does towards her children according to the primitive design. She puts before them, first of all, as the elements of her teaching, nothing but the original Creed; her teaching will follow in due time, as a privilege to children necessarily ignorant, not as a condition of communion; as a privilege which will be welcomed by them, and accepted joyfully, or they would be wanting in that temper of faith which the very coming for Baptism presupposes.

29. Now, the Church, in behaving in this way in relation to her children, takes care to distinguish clearly what is apostolic from what is ecclesiastical in her doctrine; what carries the sure mark of Christ, from what comes less directly from him. Next, she secures to herself the power of accommodating herself to the circumstances, ranks and ages of her children. Thus, a man with no education must receive the mysterious words: His only Son, without knowing anything more of them; the educated man, on the contrary, receives ample instruction on all the theological points of his doctrine, without the subject becoming any the less mysterious. But in any case, the rule is the same; the teaching of the Church must be proportionate to their education. Thirdly, she takes care not to demand from her children any promise whatever definitely to receive her instructions, of whatever kind they may be. She is satisfied with the intention which they express to receive them in the first place, an intention which is comprised in their state as children of the Church. She is satisfied with the purpose they have of beginning, not by doubting, by arguing and questioning, but by throwing themselves into her system, considering it as true, putting it into practice; and if, at the end, they happen to differ from that system on some point, of not giving way to private opinions out of all proportion to the means they possess of establishing one; lastly not to teach that private opinion of others, not to raise themselves up against the

Church. If I expound this theory of the Anglican Church, it is not in order to sing its praises, although I regard it as a reasonable one as being in conformity with moderation and charity; but only to show you that it is different from yours, not only in its expression, but in its substance, and in its practical effects.

30. If therefore, when you say that 'a good Anglican may reject the doctrine of original sin,'[a] you only mean that a good Anglican is not obliged to receive that doctrine in every detail, we admit that your accusation is well founded; for it amounts to nothing more than saying, it may happen that a good Anglican may be a limited man, of no education. In the same sense, a good Gallican may also reject it; for you will not say that a Roman Catholic with no education, understands it more, because he orally confesses that: '*Adae peccatum origine unum est, et propagatione, non imitatione transfusum, omnibus inest unicuique proprium.*'[b]* Thus, as you differ from us in the matter of which I have spoken, so you are equally subject to the reproach you address to me and to the primitive Church, of admitting those who reject, that is, who do not confess in a distinct manner, the doctrine of original sin. To comprehend in a single sentence everything that I have just established: the Apostles' Creed is the confession of the Christian, the Church is its legitimate interpreter. As the Christian develops the Creed, he must receive with trust, and unhesitatingly, the interpretation which the Church gives of it; and if in the end, he differs from her on some points of little importance, he must not raise himself up against her.

31. Before continuing, I will prove the rightness of this opinion, by some quotations taken from the Fathers. I refer firstly to the conduct of the Fathers at the Council of Nicaea; their Creed was exacted of the Clergy, but not of the laity, that is to say, in conformity with the opinion I have stated, the obligation to subscribe to it was not a condition necessary for communion, it was given solely as a rule of teaching. On the other hand, anathemas were levelled against those who professed any other doctrine. Here you have exactly the three steps which

* Concil. Trident., sess. V, can. 3.

a '. . . le dogme du péché originel, la nécessité du baptême, . . . ne seront pas fondamentales: on pourra les rejeter et cependant être bon anglican.' Cf. p. 71; Jager, pp. 311–12.

b 'The sin of Adam is one in origin, and transferred by propagation, not by imitation, and is present in all and proper to each and every one.'

I have established: a creed developed in precise and fixed terms, declaring the one sole truth, once and for all established for those who teach, contumacious opposers excommunicated and the mass of Christians left as before who were neither teachers, nor adversaries of the doctrinal system as it was developed.

'What has been said,' says Athanasius, 'is sufficient for the refutation of those who altogether reject the doctrine of the Council of Nicaea; but as for those who receive its whole Creed, except the word consubstantial (*Homoousion*), but doubt about it, *we must not regard them as enemies*; for our opposition to them is not as if we thought of them as Arians, and impugners of the Fathers, but we converse with them as *brothers with brothers*, who hold the same sense as we do, only hesitate about the word.'[*][a] We have here a striking example of a class of men, who do not receive the Nicene Creed, and who in spite of their resistance, were not excluded from communion with the Church. What position then were they in? In that of the laity. It is at any rate the only one which remains. But this passage tells us something more, namely: that not all ecclesiastical decisions are of equal importance. Athanasius did not want to have anything in common with those who rejected the general doctrine of the Council of Nicaea, but he tolerated those who rejected the word *consubstantial*. Moreover, the Council of Ephesus threatened to depose any bishop or priest who should dare to compose or present a new creed to any one who wished to be converted, pagan, Jew, or heretic.[†]

To the same purpose are the following passages from Vincentius: 'It is necessary that the heavenly sense of Scripture be explained according to this one rule, the Church's understanding of it, principally in those questions on which the foundations of the whole Catholic doctrine rest.'[‡] It appears, therefore, that in spite of the contempt in which you hold the distinction between fundamental and non-fundamental doctrines, Vincentius had some idea of it, as Mr. H. . . . had already pointed out to you, but to no purpose.[b] Again he says: 'The ancient consent of

---

[*] *De Synodis.* § 41.   [†] *Labb.*, t. iii, p. 690.   [‡] *Commonit.* XXIX.

[a] Cf. *Proph. Office*, 1st ed. pp. 274–5; 3rd ed. pp. 230–1.

[b] Harrison (Second Reply, in Jager, *Le Protestantisme*, etc., p. 45) had quoted Vincent as saying that his Rule should only be applied in the fundamental questions of Catholic doctrine (In his duntaxat aut praecipue questionibus, quibus totius catholici dogmatis fundamenta nituntur. *Commonit.* XXIX) (cf. p. 24).

the Holy Fathers is to be diligently ascertained and followed, not in all the lesser questions of the Divine Law, but only, or at least principally, as regards the Rule of Faith'. * And again, in the following passage, Vincent tacitly allows the right of private judgment in lesser matters, so that our conclusions be not pertinaciously urged, for then our Judgment is no longer Private. 'Whatever opinion,' he says, 'has been held beyond or against the whole Church, however holy and learned be the author of it, let it be separated from common, public and general opinions which have authority, and included among peculiar, secret and private surmises.'† Thus Vincent permits us to differ from the Church, without being excluded from communion.

32. This is quite enough, I think, for my cause. Allow me now to put a serious question to you. Athanasius calls *brothers* certain adversaries of the word *consubstantial*. You claim, according to the Creed of Pope Pius IV, that, although one does not raise oneself up against the Church, and does not preach one's error, one is outside of salvation. By what authority do you go further than Athanasius or the Council of Nicaea? Or rather by what authority do you refuse the bread of life to Protestants, however slight be the difference which separate you from them, if they do not receive in its entirety everything that your modern Church regards as necessary to salvation? I do not ask you if the early Fathers admitted the doctrine of Purgatory or not, but by what authority you deprive of the sacraments those who do not admit it. Was I not right to send you the challenge contained in my first letter? Is it not a heinous crime to refuse the means of salvation without having any authority on your side? It is criminal to kill a man, without having the mandate of authority, and shall it be permitted to kill the soul, at least as much as we have the power to do so, without being authorised! An excommunication issued by the Church of Scotland is little matter, but your crime will be in proportion to the gifts you have received. Whatever our own errors may be, Rome is certainly, in the full meaning of the term, *the cruel Church*. Let us return to our subject.

33. I must anticipate an objection which you have perhaps already prepared against the foregoing opinions. 'What do you mean,' you will say, 'when you permit private judgment in

* *Commonit.* XXVIII.   † Ibid.

matters of little moment, and what line of demarcation do you draw between one and the other?' Or else, presenting your objection in this form, you will say: 'what right have you to establish a difference between the Apostles' Creed and the general teaching of the Church? Both come to us from tradition, both are in matter of fact apostolic. The Church does not develop articles of faith on her private authority, she only proposes those which exist, and in that she does no more than follow the command she had received from the Apostles: keep the deposit, *depositum custodi*, etc.' Such are more or less the expressions you use in your sixth letter.[a]

34. To this I answer that the Apostles' Creed does not come to us by the same tradition as the corpus of theology which contains its development. The Apostles' Creed is a collection of definite articles, passing from hand to hand, rehearsed and confessed at Baptism, committed and received from Bishop to Bishop. This Creed is received on what may be called *apostolical tradition*. Its existence and its preservation in the divine office are guaranteed by the New Testament, where it is called the *Hypotyposis*, or outline of sound words, that is why we say that it is ultimately based upon Scripture; it has, moreover, as guarantees the works of Irenaeus[*] and of Tertullian.[†] I must here observe that a Tradition formally enunciated on certain occasions, and delivered from hand to hand, is of the nature of a written document, that is to say the force of the testimony which guarantees its authenticity is the same in kind with that for the Scripture. For the same reason, though it is not to the purpose here to insist on it, rites and ceremonies are something more than mere oral Tradition and carry with them a considerable presumption in behalf of the things signified by them. Such then is Apostolical Tradition. But besides this, there is what may be called Prophetical Tradition. God placed in his Church first Apostles, secondarily Prophets. Apostles rule, Prophets expound. Prophets are the interpreters of the divine law, they unfold and define its mysteries, they illuminate its documents, they harmonize its contents, they apply its promises. Their teaching is a vast system not to be comprised in a few sentences, not to be embodied in one code or treatise, but consisting of a

---

[*] *Contra Haeres.* 1. I. 3.   [†] *De Praescript.* XIII.

[a] Cf. p. 68.

certain body of truth permeating the Church like an atmosphere, irregular in its shape, from its very profusion and exuberance. That body of Truth is part written, and part unwritten, partly the interpretation, partly the supplement of Scripture; partly preserved in intellectual expressions, partly latent in the spirit and temper of Christians; poured to and fro in closets and upon housetops, in liturgies, in controversial works, in obscure fragments, in sermons. This I call Prophetical Tradition, existing primarily in the bosom of the Church itself, and recorded in such measure as Providence has determined in the writings of eminent men. This is obviously a very different kind from the Apostolic Tradition, yet it is equally primitive, and equally claims our zealous maintenance. 'Keep that which is committed to thy charge, *depositum custodi,*' is St. Paul's injunction to Timothy,[a] and for this reason; because from its vastness and indefiniteness the deposit is especially exposed to corruption if the Church fails in vigilance. This is that body of teaching which is offered to every individual according to his capacity and which, as I have already said, must be received with trust and affection, and not be said to err, although it be not necessary to submit to it without proof.

35. Now what has been said has sufficed to show, that it may easily happen that this Prophetical Tradition may have been corrupted in its details, while the Apostolical Tradition is pure and worthy of faith; that is what I suppose to be the case. In the excess of the extent of the first tradition over the second, which is, if I may so express myself, like the flesh covering a skeleton, there will be lesser points of which we have spoken, from which a person may possibly dissent, without incurring any anathema or public censure.

36. The Church has fixed and perpetuated that Prophetical Tradition, in the shape of formal articles or doctrines, as the rise of errors or other causes gave occasion. For a time the whole Church agreed together in giving one and the same account of it, but in course of centuries, love waxing cold and schisms abounding, her various branches developed them out of the existing mass for themselves; and, according to the accidental influences which prevailed at the time, the work was done well or ill, rudely or accurately. It follows that these developed and

[a] 1 Tim. 6: 20.

fixed truths are entitled to very different degrees of credit, though always to attention. Those which are recognized by the Church at an early date are of more authority. Those which are made by the joint assent of many independent Churches, or those that are sanctioned dispassionately, are more deserving of credit than those which are the result of some preponderating influence and are done in fear. Accordingly we accept the decisions of some Councils, and reject the decrees of some others. By explanations of this kind, I am preparing the way for two questions which we will discuss in due course, namely the infallibility of the Church, and the Protestant theory of the corruption of Romanism.

37. As for the Prophetical Tradition, I have only one more thing to say of it, and that is it seems to me to deserve the greatest veneration. And this view I would take even of the decrees of Trent, although I do not receive them as the body of doctrines. They are ruins of primitive antiquity, worthy of respect, although they are in my view often altered, and they introduce great corruptions into the practice of Christians who receive them. For the capital fault of that council does not consist, precisely, in the exposition of Christian doctrines (although in many points they are in opposition to antiquity), but in the right it arrogates to itself to impose its belief as being part of the fundamental dogmas of Christianity, and as a necessary condition of being received into the Church.

38. After such a dry discussion, will you allow me, my dear sir, to entertain you by a series of observations foreign to our subject: I am sure they will amuse you, although they are your own. I am going to put before you again some arguments which you have employed against my opinions on fundamental doctrines. They are perfectly well written, but they are, I am sure you will agree, more brilliant than solid and forceful in relation to the question. I will take them in order.

39. 'You grant to the Church,' you say, 'more than we desire and more than we can accept, the right *to make articles of faith*, according to times and circumstances.'*[a] I did not say that. My words were: The power *to develop its fundamental Creed* into Articles of *religion*, according to times and circumstances;† to

---

* pp. 54 and 71; Jager, pp. 139 and 318.   † p. 40; Jager, p. 100.

[a] References to the French text of Jager's Fourth and Sixth Letters, respectively.

develop is not to create. Articles of religion are not essentially fundamental articles, as articles of faith are.

40. 'You say that Mr. H. . . . maintained so stubbornly that Scripture contained everything, and that tradition was only its interpreter'.* No, Mr. H. . . . did not say at all that Scripture contained every doctrine. His words were: 'Holy Scripture contains all things necessary to salvation, so much so that whatever is not read therein, or cannot be proved by it, may not be required or imposed by anyone, to be believed as an article of faith, or regarded as necessary and indispensable to salvation.'†

41. 'I must tell you', you continue, 'that nothing surprised me so much as this distinction between fundamental and non-fundamental articles; Mr. H. . . . doubtless *did not know it* when he wrote to me, since he *kept silent* on that part of my letters in which reference to it was made.'‡ Poor Mr. H. . . . I shall quote his words to you. Speaking of Vincent, he says: 'I think, on the contrary, I see very clearly that he is speaking of the great fundamental doctrines of the Catholic faith, and that he is directing the Christian so that he may know, in times of heresy, that he is in safety. Yes, he expressly says, that his rule must only be applied in fundamental questions of Catholic dogma.'§

42. 'Above all do not forget,' you say, 'to tell us by what signs we may recognise what is fundamental from what is not in Scripture or in Tradition. This rule is extremely important. For, once there are truths necessary to salvation, etc.'‖ Here you confuse the word *fundamental* with the word *necessary* to salvation. As for the proof of the distinction between fundamental and non-fundamental doctrines, that is a purely historical question, as I have already said. But I must add that it is a point on which you seem to be very curious, for in your sixth letter you say: 'I have asked you already, and I ask you again today: Where have you found the distinction between fundamental and non-fundamental articles? Somewhere in Scripture or in the Fathers? . . . I shall be interested to read your proofs; for, to my great confusion, I confess I am utterly ignorant of them.'** My

* Jager, p. 130.
† p. 24; Jager, p. 42.
‡ p. 130.
§ p. 24; Jager, p. 45.
‖ p. 54; Jager, pp. 131–2.
** p. 68; Jager, p. 274.

proofs are taken from Tertullian, Origen and Cyprian, which
are in harmony with Scripture itself.

43. 'The extracts which I have taken from your Thirty-Nine
Articles, articles 6, 11, 13 etc., have you will agree, no foundation in Scripture'.* No, I do *not* agree. 'If these articles', you
continue, 'are not necessary, if they are numbered amongst those
pious beliefs which may be discarded, as the whim takes us, why
then do you give them the title of *Articles of faith?*'† It is you,
not I, who give them this title. I call them, as the title at their
head calls them, *Articles of religion. Faith* is concerned with what
is fundamental, religion is the Prophetical Tradition or the
general body of doctrines of which we have already spoken. We
consider the articles of religion neither as fundamental nor as
necessary to salvation. 'Why did your Church,' you ask, 'for
three centuries, exclude Roman Catholics who did not subscribe
to them from the privileges of the law?' ‡ I answer that, according to the greater or lesser power which certain persons had to
teach, the Church required *tests*, over and above belief in the
articles necessary to be in communion. The laity of the upper
classes have a great power in the Church of England; I mean,
the Privy Council, the law officers, the members of Parliament,
etc. Just as the Council of Nicaea imposed its belief on the
Clergy, so we impose our articles on certain laymen, namely on
the members of the universities. Then there is a political question involved; we cannot count on the fidelity of a Roman
Catholic towards an heretical king; take the case of Ireland at
this moment. Further you commit an error of fact. We have
never excluded Roman Catholics from the privileges of the law,
by means of our articles. It is true that Parliament, under
Charles II, imposed a particular *test* upon them: but the Church
did not view this with any pleasure.

44. 'Does faith alone justify us? . . . Does Holy Scripture contain all that is necessary to salvation? Are there only two sacraments? Can these questions not be fundamental? If questions of
this kind are not fundamental, *tell us, pray, what* you understand
by fundamental articles.'§ An important and too§ delicate question, but you have doubtless examined my last letter before

* p. 54; Jager, p. 132.   † Ibid.
‡ p. 55; Jager, p. 132.
§ p. 55; Jager, pp. 133–4.

having it printed. Fundamental doctrines are those, belief in which is necessary in order to be admitted into the Church. That faith alone justifies us, that the Scripture contains all necessary truths, that there are only two sacraments, these points are not essential for communion with the Church.

45 'You admit that one of these doctrines, that which concerns the catalogue of the Canonical Books, has this character (of being fundamental)?'* I beg your pardon, I do not admit this. In the passage to which your observation refers, I refused to enter upon this topic, as foreign to the subject which we were then discussing. It is impossible for me to give an explanation in a few words; but you can be sure I will do so fully when the subject presents itself openly before us.

46. 'The Virginity of the Mother of God, the descent of Jesus Christ into hell, are not found in Scripture. Nonetheless, these articles are fundamental, since they are recorded in the Apostles' Creed'.† I beg your pardon, these articles are found in Scripture. (Cf. Matth. 1: 23; Acts 2: 27.)

47. 'Keeping the Lord's Day holy is doubtless necessary to salvation?' ‡ Whether it be so or not, it is a point in which it is not necessary to believe, in order to be in communion with the Church; 'yet it is not contained in Scripture.'—It most certainly is. The sabbath day kept holy by the Apostles is one of the most obvious facts in the New Testament.§

48. 'The Baptism which you administer by infusion, as we do, is not in Scripture. . . . Will you dare to maintain that that point is not fundamental?'|| Yes, I dare to maintain that the point is not fundamental, that is, that the admission of the validity of baptism by infusion is not a condition for admission into the Church; the same is true of baptism by heretics. When a person comes to us to ask for baptism, we do not ask him if he has had time to reflect on heretical baptism, or to form an opinion on that subject.

49. To give you fresh examples of your misunderstandings, which are to be found everywhere in what you have written, I return to your sixth letter. For example, you compare these words of our Saviour: 'All things that I have commanded you,

* p. 55; Jager, p. 134 † Ibid. ‡ Ibid.
§ John, 20: 19–26; Acts, 2: 1; I Cor., 16: 2.
|| p. 55; Jager, p. 135.

omnia quaecumque mandavi vobis,' with those of St. Mark: *'He that believeth not shall be damned;'* and then you say: 'We must therefore believe in that sum of truths. Otherwise *no salvation*. It obviously follows from this that everything Christ taught is fundamental.'*

50. 'It is thus proved up to the hilt that you admit fundamental articles which are not contained in Scripture.'† From what I have told you, are you still disposed to maintain the same opinion?

51. Then you begin to prove that the first Councils are in agreement with the Council of Trent because they base their decisions on tradition as well as upon Scripture. That is true, but they were not in agreement with the Council of Trent when it made those decisions fundamental and necessary for admission into the Church. Therefore, permit me to say this, you wander from the point. You quote as an example of the procedure of the Council of Nicaea an author[a] who says: 'The bishops of the Council of Nicaea, say the historians of the time, set up, against the false subtleties of the Arians, the great truths of Scripture, and the ancient belief of the Church from the Apostles up to that time.'‡

52. After which you quote the Fathers, Irenaeus, Tertullian, Clement and others. For instance, Tertullian says to heretics in the name of the Church: 'Under what pretence are you removing my landmarks? What business have you with my property? the estate is mine; I have the ancient possession of it. I have the title deeds delivered to me by the original proprietors: I am the heir of the Apostles.'§ That is wonderfully well said! But that doctrine belongs to us as much as to you. We claim that the Church alone has the right to teach, that every man who teaches heresies must be anathematized. What does that profit *you*, my dear sir, who have to prove to us that the Church has the right to excommunicate whoever refuses to subscribe to the least word she teaches. I must nevertheless tell you that you

---

* p. 68; Jager, p. 278.
† p. 55; Jager, p. 136.
‡ p. 56; Jager, p. 138.
§ Jager, p. 152; Tertullian, *De Praescript.* XXXVII.

[a] Louis Maimbourg, *Histoire de l'arianisme*, quoted in Lepappe de Trévern, *Discussion amicale*, t. i, p. 138.

have an irresistible power wherever you have no antagonist. Would Cicero, in my place, not have said to you: *Utitur in re non dubia testibus non necessariis?*[a]

53. After wandering everywhere away from the point with the Councils and the Fathers, you shift your ground by a kind of argument *ad hominem*. You prove that all Protestants follow their own *opinions*, and consequently justify your Church by condemning themselves. That argument is presented under one of the following two forms: you may select the one which suits you best. The Protestant communions instruct their co-religionists. Therefore Roman Catholics are not guilty in instructing theirs. Or, the Protestant communions instruct their own members. Therefore the Roman Church has the right to refuse the sacraments to all those who doubt a single point of its teaching. Of these two things, which do you prefer? a vicious circle, or a conclusion foreign to the subject?

54. In this part of your discussion* you are invincible, when you attack our dissenters and our Bible Christians. Nothing could be stronger or clearer than your observations. You overthrow completely the so called right of private judgment, that is, the right to form opinions for oneself by means of Scripture. I listen to you then with pleasure, but do not compel me, I beg you, to reply as an adversary to opinions which I maintain as strongly as you do. As for the attack which you launch, at this point, against Bishop Jebb, I reserve the examination of it until I treat of the second head of this discussion, to which it refers.†

55. You allege the abolition of the sabbath, the permission to eat blood, and the dispensation from washing the feet‡ to prove that there are things which the Church can do. At least I suppose that that is your aim in quoting these examples; for, can they prove anything else? They certainly do not prove that the Church can excommunicate those who do not observe the sabbath day; and if the Church did so in certain circumstances, she would surely not do it for the reasons you allege, she would

* pp. 59–60; Jager, pp. 173–181.
† p. 61; Jager, p. 192.
‡ p. 59; Jager, p. 176.

[a] 'He calls in witnesses, whom he does not need, to prove a fact that no one questions.' *De officiis*, II, 16.

not rely on the sole fact of the abolition of the sabbath. For, although your conditions for communion be wider than ours, yet you do not demand, as an indispensable condition, assent to every fact considered merely as a fact.

56. Then you insist again on the canonicity of Scripture, supported by tradition alone, and you add: 'You have rejected many of the doctrines which we profess, but you have not been able to reject entirely the fundamental rule of Christianity.'* Alas! how you confuse the basis of ecclesiastical teaching with that which serves as a basis for individual admission to the Church!

To so many examples of misunderstanding, add the one I take from your sixth letter. You cite the words of St. Paul to the Romans, in which that Apostle warns his brethren to keep themselves from those 'who make dissensions',[a] and you say: 'Hence the moment we put forward anything against the received doctrine, we are outside the Communion.'† I grant you this. You also quote St. John: 'If any man come to you, and bring not this doctrine, receive him not'[b] as if St. John were not speaking here of an heretical doctor, who must be avoided and excommunicated, as I have already said.

Yet again you say, O Timothy, keep the deposit,[c] etc.; and from that you conclude that the duty of the Church is to prevent all novelties of whatever kind they may be, without examining whether they are fundamental or not. I grant you that quite willingly; but this is how you express yourself; 'Hence, according to the text of the Apostle, to err concerning the Faith, to be excluded from the bosom of the Church, it suffices to profess some novelty.'‡ The profession of a new doctrine justifies exclusion, but nothing can justify adding to the conditions of baptism. The Church of Rome errs, not in excluding those who have fixed opinions against the truth, but in excluding those who do not have fixed opinions on its details.

57. You quote in your favour the severity of St. Paul to the Galatians,§ as if it were possible to preach false doctrines more

* p. 59; Jager, p. 179.
† p. 68; Jager, p. 278.
‡ p. 68; Jager, p. 282.
§ Gal. 5: 2; p. 69; Jager, p. 284.

[a] Romans 16: 17.   [b] II John, 10.
[c] I Tim. 6: 20.

effectively, and behave in a way more worthy of censure than
by collecting them and displaying them in rites and ceremonies,
as had been done at that time.

58. After quoting various Fathers to prove that the Faith of
the Church must be *one*, you add: 'Now, that unity is incompatible with tolerance of the errors which you call non-
fundamental.'* Very well, but it is not incompatible with tolerance
of those who are silent on truths which are not inserted in the
articles which are fundamental and necessary to Communion,
or who do not know them.

59. The Council of Nicaea, you say, did not wish to receive
the Novatians before they had subscribed to *the decrees of the
Catholic Church*;† but that canon is in perfect agreement with
what I say. The Council does not speak of laymen, but only of
the clergy, as your quotation proves. Now, if it be possible to
compel even those who have never taught error to retract, then
a fortiori this must be required of the leaders of novelty and
schism.

60. The same answer applies to the other examples which
you quote;‡ to the extent that individuals found themselves
personally involved in innovations, the Church required an
abjuration of them, that is an admission not only of the fundamental articles, but also of the meaning she attached to them.
You say: 'You admit the validity of this baptism, [baptism
administered by heretics], as the Roman Church does, but you
declare St. Cyprian's error to be non-fundamental. Well, sir,
this question makes an end of you'§ and you at once hurl at me
darts which you deem to be lethal, namely, that the Donatists
were considered by the Church as excluded from salvation,
although their error was against Scripture. I answer, almost in
your own words, that to maintain an opinion against the voice
of the whole Church stubbornly and publicly is of itself without
any doubt a mortal sin, and that such was the flagrant sin of the
Donatists, as St. Augustine tells us. But, while you hurl these
darts at me, you do not try to free yourself of that arrow with
which I had pierced you through, and which I took from an

* p. 69; Jager, p. 291.
† p. 69; Jager, p. 293.
‡ p. 69; Jager, p. 294.
§ Jager, p. 302.

historic passage. I had written: 'I believe on the whole with you that Stephen decided in that controversy according to the general tradition of the Church, and, if we of this day have reason to believe (in the validity of that baptism), much more would it be clear to parties who lived so near to the Apostolic age. Yet Cyprian acted against that tradition; now could he have acted against a plain decision of Scripture on the subject?'* *Haeret lateri lethalis arundo*† and you seem content to drag it with you everywhere. You contemplate killing without perceiving the danger in which you are placed yourself. You even strengthen my argument by quoting St. Augustine on the subject. 'For if St. Cyprian appears excusable to St. Augustine, it is because in his day the question *was not yet sufficiently clarified*; it was because St. Cyprian *could still doubt the universality of the ecclesiastical teaching, since many shared his views.*'‡ I beg your pardon, my dear sir, that is precisely the situation in which we find ourselves in England. We believe that your particular points of doctrine are not yet sufficiently clarified. We are, like St. Cyprian, in that state of doubt on the *Universality of the teaching*, and *many bishops* share our views. You confess that the lack of discussion may sometimes be an obstacle to the elucidation of truth; but the distance of time from the apostles to ourselves may be one also. In considering St. Cyprian's conduct, I will add that, by a very curious effect, he did not try to settle that question by tradition, but by reasoning. Such is the main characteristic of his way of conducting controversy. I believe he was wrong in this, if I may so speak of a blessed martyr; but does it not prove that the tradition of the Church, in matters of little moment, was not then received with that profound respect which the Roman Church gives it? Do we not see in that dispute a doctrine which was only partially received, however useful and however true it may have been, and that that controversy had as its aim to elucidate and recommend? Pray observe, that I call the *principle* of deciding by tradition useful and true, and such is my way of thinking. I admire it and I greatly revere it, because of its simplicity and majesty; my only regret is that the great

---

* p. 51; Jager, p. 119.
† Virgil, *Aeneid*, IV, 73, 'Fast to her side clings the lethal shaft'.
‡ Jager, p. 302.

interval of time which has elapsed since the Apostles has rendered it inapplicable and useless in point of fact.

Here I conclude the first part of my letter. I am determined to continue, and to do complete justice to all your observations, before giving you the trouble of answering mine.

I am, etc., N. . . .

5. Jager's Case against Newman

(d) Jager's Seventh Letter

ALTHOUGH Jager feels Newman has employed every possible method to defend the Reformation in his reply, he finds his arguments weak and evasive, inevitably so because of the false nature of his cause: 'Truth alone shows itself frankly . . . error dissimulates, becomes entangled and evasive and swallowed up in details' (Jager, p. 396).

He reduces Newman's letter to its seven chief points.

1. *Newman claims that he had not abandoned the last two charges made by Jebb, that he had concentrated on the first, and that it was Jager who had wandered from the point.*

Jager replies that he looks forward to Newman's further arguments on Jebb, whose doctrine he will continue to regard, in the meanwhile, as absurd and ridiculous. He admits that he has gone into great detail on authority, tradition, and the distinction between fundamental and non-fundamental articles. The detail was required to refute Newman's charges, but he will not accept that he has wandered from the main issue. Nor has Newman shaken a single one of Jager's proofs advanced against him.

2. *Newman claims that the Roman Church is too strict and admits frankly the Anglican Church is not strict enough; but Jager cannot show the same frankness in his arguments, being obliged to maintain the infallibility of his communion.*

Jager points out that he has already replied to the subject of strictness in his letter to Harrison. But how can Newman demand greater discipline from his Church when faith depends on individual judgement? The Anglican Church cannot condemn because she declares herself subject to error. Vincent says the Catholic Church has the right to condemn, and must be perfect in terms of purity of doctrine. By admitting his Church is not perfect in this sense Newman loses all claim for her to be called Catholic.

3. *Newman says Jager has made the mistake of calling fundamental any doctrine transmitted by tradition and supported by*

Scripture and by confusing 'fundamental' with 'necessary to salvation'.

Jager admits to the first instance but, he insists, it arose from the statement in Newman's letter 'The reception of pure tradition is pious, that of doctrines conveyed to us by Tradition but proved by Scripture is *imperative*.' Surely 'imperative' means fundamental? He also admits to equating 'fundamental' and 'necessary to salvation', always synonymous in earlier controversy. Newman has given the word a new meaning and in future he will understand fundamental to mean 'the articles contained in the Creed'; the rest (Original Sin, Baptism, Penance, the Eucharist) to be inessential. He shows how Christ's own words deny this meaning* and how it brings about contradictions within the Anglican faith. Even if the Creed is fundamental, its development, i.e. its real meaning, is not.

4. *Newman claims Jager has declined the challenge to produce evidence from Vincent to support his theory that tradition is a sufficient authority to act as a foundation for fundamental truth.*

Even if it could be proved, replies Jager, that Vincent does not support this idea, how could it help Jager's cause? And Jager himself delivers a challenge: does Vincent state anywhere that tradition is *inadequate* for this purpose? In fact, Vincent's acceptance of it is implicit throughout his treatise. He not only emphasizes its importance on every page, but shows it applied by the Church in action in dealing with heretics. To convince Newman completely, Jager puts forward an example of how Vincent maintains truth not given in Scripture: the validity of baptism administered by heretics. Vincent condemns in the strongest language such heretics as the Donatists who rebaptized against the universal doctrine of the church (*Commonit.* VI).

5. *Newman insists Jager is wrong to reject the distinction between fundamental and non-fundamental articles, because it is supported by historical proofs, the testimony of the Fathers and Vincent.*

Jager admits that these testimonies are excellent for demonstrating that in the primitive Church the Apostles' Creed was

---

* 'Unless a man be born again with water and the Holy Ghost, he cannot enter into the Kingdom of Heaven'; 'Except you eat the flesh of the son of man and drink his blood, you shall not have life in you'; 'Unless you shall do penance, you shall all perish.' John 3: 5; 6: 54; Luke 13: 5.

revered and considered fundamental, that it was publicly professed and recited at baptism. But this is irrelevant. It is Newman who wanders. He should have proved that the Fathers
admitted nothing else to be necessary and fundamental. Because
the primitive Church—like the modern Church of Rome—
demanded only the profession of the Apostles' Creed at Baptism, this does not mean that it alone is fundamental. It is just
a summing up of the principal truths of religion. For when we
believe in a Church one, holy and Catholic this involves all she
teaches. The creed of Pope Pius IV is only insisted on, at the
baptism of those who return from Protestantism, to prove
retractions of Protestant errors. This was unnecessary in the
primitive Church because there were no Protestant errors, but
retraction was demanded of heresies professed at the time. Jager
refers to Newman's example of the eunuch baptised by St.
Philip: because the Ethiopian made no profession of the doctrine
of original sin, says Newman, it cannot be fundamental. Jager
would answer to this that he made no reference to the Apostles'
Creed. On Newman's showing, *that* is not fundamental either.
In fact this merely indicates that an explicit profession of all
truths was not demanded at baptism.

It does *not* prove that it is possible to deny them or 'not to
receive' them and yet remain in the Church. Newman has put
up a supposedly 'irrefutable' proof. The Fathers, St. Athanasius,
and St. Hilary, he points out, called the semi-Arians 'brothers'
and tolerated them although they rejected the theory of consubstantiality, therefore certain errors in the primitive Church
did not lead to exclusion. But this is a false argument, says
Jager. Some semi-Arians rejected the dogma outright and they
stood condemned as soon as their views were known, because
they denied the divinity of Christ; *others* hesitated over the
meaning of 'consubstantial' fearing they might become heretics
by subscribing to it. The Fathers treated them mildly because
the rejection of a word is not an error when its meaning is preserved. If Anglicans admitted the dogma of *transubstantiation*
in the sense of the Council of Trent, the Roman Church would
not make an issue over the acceptance of a word. Vincent cannot
be used to support Newman for he condemns *all* heretics, even
those who did not deny a fundamental dogma. Newman has said
it should be possible to differ from the Church without fear of

excommunication and quotes Vincent in support of this idea.* Vincent is not referring to general heresy, Jager points out, but to whatever in the writings of the Fathers is against the universal consensus and is peculiar to an individual Father. Individual peculiarities cannot be adopted without risking our eternal salvation (*Commonit.* XXVIII). Does this not, asks Jager, effectively exclude the notion of non-fundamental dogmas?

6. *The consequences of the fundamental/non-fundamental distinction drawn by Jager are not accurate, says Newman, because there is an essential difference between 'rejecting' and 'not accepting' and between the Apostles' Creed and that of Pius IV.*

Anglicans exclude from their communion all those who openly reject dogmas which have been stated, but they tolerate those who are satisfied *not to receive* certain dogmas; in this way, says Jager, a man can be a heretic in the depths of his heart and yet remain a good Anglican. Newman has tried to avoid condemnation of this absurd situation by referring to the 'limited man' who cannot be expected to understand every detail of dogma. But he is not being frank, insists Jager; they are not concerned with the 'limited man' but with a man who does not believe some part of revelation, who resists the known sentiments of the Church. Even if this man is a good Anglican he is certainly not a true Catholic, for Christ condemns not only the man who resists truth openly but also the man who does not believe. So does Vincent: 'Whosoever condemneth the ministers divinely disposed and placed in the Church of God agreeing all in one mind in Christ, doth not condemn man, but God' (*Commonit.* XXVIII). Such a man is a heretic—i.e. one who holds an opinion contrary to the universal consensus—and, if he remains hidden *within* the church, he adds to his guilt the sin of hypocrisy (cf. St. Augustine, *De Baptismo contra Donat.* I, iv).

Turning to Newman's distinction between the Creeds, Jager points out that the Creed of Pius IV is based on the same foundations as the Apostles' Creed. It is based not on hearsay or on popular and oral traditions but on irrefutable testimony.

* 'Whatever opinion has been held beyond or against the whole Church, however holy and learned be the author of it, let it be separated from the common, public and general opinions which have authority and included among peculiar, secret and private surmises' (*Commonit.* XXVIII).

Newman has pointed out that the Council of Ephesus forbids new creeds. True, agrees Jager, but it had in mind creeds which differed from that of Nicaea (Labb. *Concil.* t. iii, p. 690). He agrees that there is a difference between apostolic tradition and prophetic exposition; prophets or doctors have to define, comment on, and develop the mysteries of religion in order to reach the people while, as Vincent says, 'preserving the same doctrine, the same sense, the same judgement'. When you develop a truth you do not change it, on the contrary you give it more force, more lustre, greater scope. The Fathers did this. The Church warned those who strayed from the apostolic doctrine in their explanations, and condemned them when necessary. So apostolic tradition has remained pure and intact, and will so remain until the end of time.

7. *Newman has concluded his letter with a series of points for Jager's entertainment.*

Jager sees the subject as too serious for this. Newman's levity conceals inadequate arguments. Nevertheless, he will answer the points raised.

(i) *Newman insists that he never said the Church had the power to make articles of faith at certain times but 'the power to develop its fundamental Creed into articles of religion according to times and circumstances'.* But Jager replies, if an article is true it belongs to *all* times and places. No doubt to develop is not to create but how, he asks, are the Thirty-nine Articles developments of the Creed? When you recite the Creed, he continues, you make a profession of belief in one *Church, Holy and Catholic*, which will remain so until the end of time. And then you declare before the whole world that she can become corrupt and lost, and fall into error and idolatry! Is this a development of the Creed?

(ii) *Newman assures him that Harrison knew of the distinction between fundamental and non-fundamental articles and that he maintains with Newman that Scripture contains everything necessary to salvation.* But assertion is one thing, proof another. Jager claims he has proved the falsehood of both propositions, and that Newman has kept complete silence about the second. In the case of the first, what little testimony Newman has been able to put forward in fact strengthens Jager's own arguments.

(iii) *Jager had asserted that Articles 6, 11, 13, etc., of the Thirty-nine Articles had no foundation in Scripture. If Newman believes they have, let him adduce his proof.* Newman has said they are articles of *religion* not of faith and therefore neither fundamental nor necessary to salvation; but he seems confused here, for at the beginning of his letter he says they are *authoritative documents* on which no liberty of thought is allowed and then later admits the conclusion that the Anglican can think what he likes about them. Is *this* in harmony with the doctrine of the Fathers?

(iv) *When asked why Roman Catholics were excluded from the privileges of the law by 'unnecessary' articles, Newman replied that they were used as tests for complete loyalty.* But these unnecessary tests have been used to inflict the most barbaric punishments on Catholics in England. Newman acquits the Church of England and simultaneously accuses his government on this charge, but as the great power of the laity in the Church is a fact, these tests must belong to the Church. The Church *is* the government. On the issue of loyalty, Newman cites the case of Ireland, but Jager turns this to his own advantage: it is the vexations visited by the Protestant clergy upon it which are to blame for the revolting oppression of that country.

(v) *Jager had been surprised that Newman did not include the Article on the canon of Scripture in his list of fundamentals—particularly as at one point he said he would.* But as it is now designated a fundamental verity and not a doctrine,* the Apostles' Creed must crumble from top to bottom, it no longer has any foundation. The only principle the Anglican can hold to is the Divinity of Christ, but the consistent Protestant could go on and declare 'I believe nothing'. An individual may retreat before the consequences of a principle, but society never does. No, there is no middle course between Christianity and ultra-Protestantism. That middle course would be a logical absurdity. Jager repeats to Newman what he had said in his Fifth Letter: You must be all or nothing.

(vi) *On keeping the Lord's Day holy, Newman has said that for full communion it is not necessary to believe whether it be necessary*

---

* Cf. The Third Reply, 'We reply to all these questions, that the doctrines specified are not accounted fundamental by us, not subscribed by the mass of the people. . . . The first instance, the Article about the Canon of Scripture, is the only exception to this remark. Certainly the belief in Holy Scripture is not injoined by our Church in the same way as the reception of the doctrine of justification etc; for its canonicity is a fundamental verity rather than a doctrine' (pp. 47–8).

to salvation or not; and while agreeing that the body of truths revealed by Jesus Christ are necessary to salvation they are not fundamental. So the Anglican Church is in the extraordinary position of indicating articles necessary to salvation and denying that they are fundamental, giving its members complete freedom to believe them or not as they wish.

(vii) *Belief in the validity of different forms of baptism is non-fundamental, says Newman.* It seems possible from this, says Jager, to maintain that no one is baptised and ultimately that the Anglican Church and its episcopate are non-existent . . . and yet remain a member of it!

(viii) Jager insists that the *perpetual* virginity of the Virgin, and the descent of Christ into hell are *not* in Scripture. They are in the Apostles' Creed, and hence fundamental. So Newman accepts fundamental truths which are not contained in Scripture.

(ix) *Newman has accepted Jager's demonstration that although the Council of Trent conformed with earlier councils in basing its decisions on tradition as well as Scripture, it was not in agreement with them when it pronounced that its decisions were to be fundamental and necessary for admission to the Church.* But, says Jager, when making a decision has the Church not *always* excluded those who would not conform to it? Is this not one of the best attested facts in Christian antiquity? He uses this principle to refute Newman's claim that although the Nicene Creed was exacted of the clergy it was given merely as a rule of teaching for the laity. Truth is the same for all, insists Jager; the Church only makes more severe demands of its clergy in order that they may teach the people. Newman contradicts himself: he has already admitted the constant rule of the Church in excluding anyone who teaches heresy—and claims this right for the Anglican Church—and is now himself disputing the Church's authority by saying its decisions are not fundamental.

(x) *Newman had accused Jager of wandering from the point, and summed up Jager's argument in two forms:*

(a) *The Protestant communions instruct their co-religionists. Therefore Roman Catholics are not guilty in instructing theirs:*

or, (b) *the Protestant communions instruct their own members. Therefore the Roman Church has the right to refuse its sacraments to all who doubt a single point of its teaching.*

The first is a vicious circle, says Newman, the second has a conclusion foreign to the subject.

Jager denies that his arguments can be reduced to these two forms. He has shown that the constant and perpetual teaching of the Church is the mark of truth and Catholics were obliged to follow this rule. Newman has not answered his arguments.

(xi) Beliefs held by both Catholic and Protestant such as keeping the Lord's Day (not the Sabbath) holy, permission to eat blood, the dispensation from washing feet, do not prove that there are things which the Church itself can decide (as Newman claims) but that Protestants do not rely entirely on Scripture but on the teaching of their Church.

(xii) *How can Newman on the one hand agree that the Church is right to exclude innovators, admitting that 'the profession of a new doctrine justifies exclusion' and on the other accuse the Roman Church of cruelty for doing precisely that?* If one can be excluded for *any* novelty, is it not obvious that any novelty is a fundamental error?

Newman says the Roman Church is wrong to exclude those who have no fixed opinions on the details of truth; but Newman himself is wrong: the Roman Church casts out not those who do not understand the truths of religion but those who hold fixed opinions against Catholic truth, or who profess novelties.

(xiii) *Newman had attempted to turn Jager's reference to St. Paul's severity to the Galatians against him.* But, says Jager, this severity shows up particularly clearly the falsehood of the Anglican system of non-fundamentals, for Paul considered it essential to stamp out any error however small—it was the issue of circumcision—in order to maintain the whole truth of Catholic doctrine.

(xiv) *In an earlier letter, Jager had stated that Church unity was incompatible with the toleration of so-called 'non-fundamental' errors. Newman had replied that unity was not incompatible with toleration of those who stayed silent on non-fundamentals or who did not understand them.* Jager again points out that their debate is not about the silent or the ignorant, but about those who *do* know the truths and yet deny them. According to Newman's system it was possible to deny them and still belong to the Church of England. It was this which was completely incompatible with unity as defined by the Apostles and the Fathers.

(xv) *Jager had shown that in the first centuries, heretics had to profess the Catholic faith in its entirety in order to be readmitted into the Church and from this practice had concluded that no error was regarded as non-fundamental. In reply, Newman had claimed that this retractation was demanded only from the clergy.* On being confronted with proof that it applied to all, Newman vaguely concedes 'To the extent that individuals found themselves personally involved in innovations the Church required an abjuration of them, that is, an admission not only of the fundamental articles but also of the meaning she attached to them' (p. 103). From his own words therefore comes proof that everything the Church taught was fundamental.

(xvi) *On the validity of heretical baptism Newman agrees with Jager that 'to maintain an opinion against the voice of the whole Church stubbornly and publicly, is of itself without doubt a mortal sin, and that such was the flagrant sin of the Donatists, as St. Augustine tells us'* (ibid.). The validity of heretical baptism is a non-fundamental issue, according to Newman, but is a man committing a *mortal* sin then to be excluded from the Church of England? In Newman's system, did the Donatists not have complete liberty of thought, on a minor and immaterial proposition? What then was the real cause of this exclusion? It was that they denied an essential, Catholic, fundamental dogma.

(xvii) *Newman has tried to prove in the conflict between St. Stephen and St. Cyprian on heretical baptism that the latter resisted tradition, whereas he would not have resisted a clear decision from Scripture.* But, says Jager, both sides invoked tradition in an attempt to prove the universality of their beliefs. St. Cyprian appealed to a mistaken tradition but one widely held in Africa; as a result he believed the Pope was deciding contrary to universal tradition. He was wrong, and his African tradition was no older than the end of the second century. But he would not have resisted an instant if the universality of the true doctrine had been verified as it has been since.

Newman considers the principle of deciding by tradition as inapplicable in a time so far removed from that of the Apostles. If this were true, says Jager, we must destroy the Scriptures and the Apostles' Creed for we have both of them from tradition. The older tradition grows, the stronger it becomes—its guardians become more numerous and change becomes impossible.

Similarly a dogma which has been discussed through the ages becomes clearer—it is elucidated and its universality is established in general councils. The opposition of heresy provokes argument which leads to a greater understanding. This is why Providence has decreed it shall always exist: *Oportet haereses esse* (1 Cor. 11: 19). St. Augustine develops this: 'For by heretics hath been vindicated the Catholic church' (quoted by Bishop Jebb, *Pastoral Instructions*, p. 324). So tradition, far from being enfeebled, fortifies itself with the passing of the ages, which completely destroys Newman's objection, and the dart falls back on him who had hurled it. *Haeret lateri lethalis arundo.*

(xviii) *Newman has likened St. Cyprian, living in a time when the dogma under discussion was not universally established, and therefore excusable to St. Augustine, to the present state of the Anglican church* (p. 104): *'We are in that state of doubt on the universality of the teaching, and many bishops share our views.'* But how can Anglicans be confused when, since the sixteenth century, the Catholic Church has clearly demonstrated their beliefs to be contrary to Scripture, to the doctrine of the Fathers, and to the universal teaching of the Church? Jager asserts he has already clarified Catholic doctrine on tradition, on the Church's infallibility, on the worship of images, and on the celibacy of priests. Fresh proofs are forthcoming if Newman requires them. There can be nothing in common between St. Cyprian and the Anglicans, for whom the perpetual universality of teaching in the Catholic Church has made itself heard in a thousand different ways. When Luther began to preach his errors, every church, including the Church of England, was aroused to indignation. Was he not condemned by a general council, composed of all the bishops of the Catholic world? Newman claims many bishops support him—but in proportion with those of the Catholic Church they are that tiny minority of which Vincent speaks, which has broken with the universal Church.

To sum up. When St. Cyprian maintained his error, he did not know the universality of the ecclesiastical doctrine, and he would have yielded, had it been made clear to him by a general council. So he was not a heretic. But the Anglicans resist it, even though they know the universality of Catholic teaching. It has been made manifest by their ancestors, through the medium of all their doctors, of all the bishops in a general council, and by the Catholics who surround them. They are therefore heretics, schismatics, outside the true Church. In conclusion, Jager quotes St. Cyprian himself: 'Schism is a stain which not even blood can wash away, a crime which is purged by no suffering. He cannot be a Martyr who is not in the Church; he can never attain to the kingdom, who leaves her, with whom the kingdom shall be' (*De unit. eccles.*).

6. Newman's Third Letter[a]

SIR,

I continue my explanation of the Anglican doctrine in answer to your letter. Having discussed in my first section the question of Fundamentals I now proceed to a subject nearly connected with it, the Rule of Faith. But if, after all, my discussions do not follow each other as methodically as they ought, I excuse myself on the plea that I am following your lead, not choosing my own line of discussion.

2. The Rule of Faith

I will first say what I do not mean by this phrase. I do not mean the theological system of the Church. I do not mean that great body of doctrine which in the foregoing section I have termed Prophetical Tradition. I do not mean the Creed with its developments and supplements. The phrase is often used in this sense, and warrantably; viz as that doctrine which the Church teaches and its members receive, which is scattered without order or system in Scripture, and which is moulded, finished, harmonized by the Church. But I use it in the sense of a touchstone or test of doctrine, the authority on which doctrine is taught; and in this sense we consider that it applies solely to Scripture. We consider Scripture to be the court of ultimate appeal, which has the right of definitely settling all questions of faith.

I have not even yet explained fully what I mean. I do not at all mean, while I thus contend that Scripture is the sole test of doctrine, that it is to be contemplated barely by itself, and deductions to be made from it without reference to Tradition. I consider that Tradition is as much necessary to explain Scripture as Scripture to verify and circumscribe Tradition; so that, where possible, neither should be used by itself. I only say that Scripture

[a] Written as Fourth Reply, Part Two in the original sequence of the controversy, but never printed. Newman later added a note: 'part of controversy with the abbé Jager'. The copy is in the hand of an amanuensis.

has the prerogative of being the document of final appeal in controversies; that it is ever to be honoured with a singular honour, as the formal and authoritative basis of teaching a tradition. God has revealed a certain message, called the Gospel; belief in that Gospel of course is 'necessary to Salvation'. I hold that is contained in the New and Old Testaments, which (it therefore follows) contain that doctrine which is necessary to Salvation. This is what I mean by saying that necessary doctrine is in the Bible and not elsewhere;[1] viz that the Gospel is in it. And I lay it down as a great principle ever to be acknowledged and set forth. If, from a suspicion that this is a mere theoretical difference from your belief, you ask me in what way it *practically* operates in the controversy between us, in what point my theory is realized in contrariety to yours; I answer in this—that it opposes your notion that[2] the Gospel is in part unwritten; and consequently, that certain doctrines may be rested and enforced on Tradition only, though Scripture is silent concerning them. This is the difference between us. It is not that you use and we discard Tradition in ascertaining necessary Truth; we use it also. It is not that you deny, and we affirm, the right of individuals to ascertain the Truth for themselves, we are both speaking only of the Church's means of ascertaining it, and the Church's preaching. The simple question is, whether the Church has warrant for[3] taking mere Tradition, as a sufficient voucher for any part of the gospel i.e. salutary doctrine, *the doctrine to be solemnly enforced and imposed*: this you assert and I deny.

Before entering upon the explanation and proof of my position, a few introductory remarks may be necessary.

First, we do not deny that Tradition might have been given us as an informant in sacred truth, as seems to have been more or less the case during the long period between Adam and Moses. We do not take any antecedent objection to such an appointment of Divine Providence. We only say that in matter of fact God has limited his revelation of doctrine in the Christian Church to written documents. At the same time we do not deny that accidentally the case may have been otherwise at certain times and places even in the Christian Church. I mean the

---

[1] Here the amanuensis had written 'as when'. Newman has crossed this out and superscribed 'elsewhere'.

[2] The amanuensis has added an extra 'that'.   [3] her

preaching of Missionaries and the proselyting[1] of heathens may before now have proceeded without, nay independantly[2] of Scripture. This at least is conceivable as a possible occurrence and in that case[3] the Tradition of the Church would be the guide in matters of faith, for want of a surer. Nay to a certain point, i.e. as far as the articles of the Creed go, no guide could be surer, than that Tradition. The Apostles' Creed is a document as surely Apostolic as far as the nature of the evidence is concerned, as one of the Epistles of St. Paul's.[4] These remarks will serve to illustrate a well known passage in Irenaeus, *Haer.* iii, 4. in which he says 'Had the Apostles left us no Scripture doubtless it had been a duty to follow the course of tradition, which they prove to those whom they put in trust with the Churches. This procedure is observed in many barbarous nations, such as believe in Christ, without graven or written memorial, having salvation impressed through the Spirit in their hearts, and diligently preserving the old tradition'.

But, allowing all this, we believe that Scripture being given us, and such Scripture, full, profound, determinate, and authoritative, tradition is superseded; nay even in such respects as it would have been as sufficient a guide, as Scripture itself, the greater swallowing up the less. Even the Creed has become but a concurrent and second witness to certain truths, which, with much more besides are contained in Scripture.

The word Testament or Will, by which Holy Scripture is designated, conveys fitly our notions of its real nature. It is the document bequeathed us by Christ and His Apostles and Prophets containing the privilege and the conditions of the New Covenant, its laws and its promises. All this we profess to prove from Scripture and the Fathers; not to deduce it on à priori grounds suggested by reason or imagination.

And thus we are rid of all à priori questions about the *sufficiency* of Scripture as a document of faith. It is sometimes demanded of *us* by the Romanists, whether some one book of Scripture is sufficient as a rule of faith and, if not whether the whole can be now considered sufficient, seeing some books (e.g. the epistle to the Laodiceans)[a] are lost. We answer that any one book of Scripture would be sufficient for a rule of faith, provided

---

[1] *Sic*   [2] *Sic*   [3] Amanuensis: 'code'   [4] *Sic*
[a] Cf. Colossians 4: 16.

no one other were declared to be so; and that the whole canon, as we have received it, is enough because it is all which is first given us. There is no abstract measure of what is sufficient. Faith cannot believe more than it is told. It is saving, if it believes that, be it little or great.

Here another consequence follows; that the number of credenda[1] varies according to circumstances. Certain Churches in early times could not believe the contents of the second and third epistles of St. John before they had received them, or before they had evidence of their being inspired; they could not really admit the narrative contained in certain portions of the Old Testament, as the book of Daniel, till they had an adequate translation of it. In like manner saving faith also varies with the *capacity* and *advantages* of individuals. An uneducated peasant cannot be said to believe in that sacred portion of the doctrine of the Trinity called, περιχώρησις[a] just as one man might have some supernatural and private assurance of the truth of a certain tradition, which would make it canonical to him (to put an imaginary case), so another may have some natural defect of mind disabling him from apprehending truths clearly revealed in Scripture. Prejudices and the like are of similar importance in the question; so that we cannot determine in the case of a given individual [to] what extent and grasp faith, with reference to its objects, is saving. We can only say generally that every one must believe, so far forth as the truth is brought home to his mind, and sufficiently for his acceptance (vid Stillingfl. on Laud, part i, bks. 2 and 4).

It follows that, while taking Scripture as the formal basis and canon of the Truth, I am not determining how many and what of [*sic*] doctrines can be gained from it. One man may have the opportunity of seeing more in Scripture, another less. I only maintain that it, and nothing else, is given us as the oracle of God and the law of religious truth.

This admission however involves no disparagement of the distinctness and precision of the Scripture as a document of

---

[1] Amanuensis: 'crderda'

[a] *Perichoresis*, Lat. *circuminsessio*, the doctrine which treats of the inhesion or coinherence of one Divine Person in another, the Father being wholly in the Son, and wholly in the Holy Spirit, etc. Cf. Newman, *The Arians of the Fourth Century*, Cp. II, Sec. III.

faith;—properties of it, which it were a great error and offence to deny it. Scripture has one and but one sense, however men may differ in their views about it. That one sense is not unknown or obscure; it is the Sense in which the Church Catholic has even[1] that sense which the whole Christian world from the beginning or for many centuries maintained, and which when abandoned and so far as it was abandoned, was not superseded by any other Catholic interpretation, but by discordant opinions, the test of error, which moreover after all corruptions and losses is nevertheless held unanimously in great measure by the whole Church even now. Every individual, who does not take it in that one sense, will have to give account for his not so taking it, and will be excused only on the ground of unavoidable ignorance, whether from the want of instruction, from prejudice etc. as aforesaid.

Of this Catholic Truth, of which Scripture is the depository, a certain portion more or less immediately connected with the doctrines of the Trinity and Incarnation, has from the first, contemporarily with the existence of the New Testament, been taken as the condition of communion with the Church, and called the Creed. Some confession of faith indeed was necessary, unless open infidels were to be admitted,[2] and the articles of the Creed on these [*sic*]. But why these were taken, and no others, I am not bound to show. I receive them not on grounds of reason, but as a matter of historical fact; in like manner as a matter of history, I trace the variations in this Creed in early time in various places; the African Church, or the Church of Acquileia [*sic*] or the Syrian having in them respectively articles absent from the rest; the Eastern Churches at length settling in the use of the Nicene, the Latin in that of the ancient Roman or Apostles'. I am not bound to account either that our Creed is what it is, or others now or formerly are somewhat different; I take what I find, and in the same way I wish here to be understood as receiving the main proposition of which I am to treat, that Scripture and Scripture only is the rule and canon of faith. I receive it on historical testimony.

---

[1] The amanuensis has omitted two words and mistaken a third. Newman's later copy shows this phrase should read: the sense in which the Catholic Church has ever understood it . . .

[2] An 'x' in the MS. indicates the amanuensis may have omitted a phrase here.

As then I may impose nothing to be believed as terms of communion but the Creed, so I may impose nothing to be believed in order to Salvation, but what is founded on Scripture. And the proof I say, of each proposition is of an historical character, the authority of the early Church, that church which is a sufficient [guide?],[1] first as coming close after the Apostles, next as being unanimous in its teaching.

The 6th Article of our Church speaks thus.

'Holy Scripture containeth all things necessary to Salvation, so that whatsoever is not read therein, nor may be proved thereby, is not to be required of any man, that it should be believed as an article of the faith, or be thought requisite or necessary to[2] salvation.'

The Canons of 1571 contain the following direction;

'Preachers shall be careful not to preach aught[3] to be religiously held and believed by the people, except what is agreeable[4] to the doctrine of the[5] Old and New Testaments, and collected, as *such*, from that very teaching by the Catholic Fathers and ancient Bishops.'

To these may be added the Act of Queen Elizabeth, in which it is determined that such matter and cause only shall be adjudged to be heresy, as heretofore has been adjudged to be so by authority of the Canonical Scriptures or by some of the first four general councils, or by any *other* general council wherein the same was declared heresy by *the express and plain words of the said canonical Scriptures.*

This is the Anglican doctrine: concerning which I observe, first; that the sole question decided[6] in the 6th Article, is how Christian teachers are to teach, whence they are to prove the doctrines they advance. It has no reference to any supposed rights or duties of individuals; it gives no countenance to what is called 'the right of private judgement', that is, it says not a word on the subject either way. This is evident, first because in matter of fact there is not a word in the Articles about private judgement from beginning to end, next because the Articles are

---

[1] The amanuensis has omitted a word here.   [2] 'for' deleted here.
[3] Amanuensis: 'ought'.   [4] Amanuensis: 'agreable'.
[5] From this point, *Proph. Office*, 1st ed., p. 322, reads '. . . Old or New Testament, and collected from that very doctrine by the Catholic Fathers and ancient Bishops.'
[6] Amanuensis: 'is'.

professedly *articles for teachers*, and in the 20th Article in which the doctrine of the 6th about the Sufficiency of Holy Scripture is repeated, the Church as an authoritative body (as having 'authority in controversies of faith') is the sole subject contemplated, not individuals. Lastly, the other documents cited, the Canons of 1571 and the Act of Parliament of Elizabeth, are also comments upon the 6th Article and bring out the same meaning.— In the next place I observe that in the reference to teaching the Article in question evidently considers Scripture as the exclusive document of saving faith: the exclusive witness in things supernatural;—so that as [*sic*] no one has a right to exact from another in order to his being received as a Christian belief in any thing not directly or indirectly contained in it, and it implies that Tradition has not in matter of fact had this oracular character (as it may be called) given it by Christ and His Apostles. Further our doctrine does expressly assign to Tradition a definitive and most important office, that of explaining the text of Scripture and ascertaining its doctrines, as is more clearly expressed in the Canon and the Act. Moreover not a word is said to debar Tradition from teaching doctrines additional to those which are emphatically called the Faith, much less from inculcating matters of conduct, discipline and the like, nor from being a source of instruction, comfort, and edification to the devout mind; only that it does not come to us as an independent and sufficient informant in necessary truth, that it is not such an authority that on its sanction we may exact faith of our Brethren, threaten, anathematize, excommunicate, and the like; that, not it, but Scripture alone is the basis and bond of union between Christians as far as faith is concerned.

Let us first see what light Scripture itself will throw upon the question in dispute.

The very circumstance that the Gospel is called by St. Paul a covenant and will, and paralleled to the Mosaic Covenant, and that the Law was *written*, as in the books of Exodus, Leviticus and the rest, leads us, or at least prepares us to believe that the New Law is written also.

This analogy, however faint at first, is strengthened and sanctioned by the actual mode under which the New Law was first promulgated, viz. with an intentional resemblance to the giving of the Mosaic. God spoke the Ten Commandments from Mount

Sinai first of all, but afterwards He wrote them. So in matter of fact, our Lord first spoke His own gospel, both of promise and of precept, on the Mount, and His evangelists have recorded it. Moreover, He Himself in a measure paralleled it to the Ten Commandments when He delivered it (as when He commented on the 6th and 7th of the Decalogue) [;] there is so far, no room for mistaking about it.

Consider too His discourses all through the Gospels, and see if they do not partake of this one and the same character, the character of solemn declarations, canons, sentences, proverbs, such as legislators utter, and scribes and lawyers comment on. Surely every thing He did and said partakes of this character of depth, condensation and mystery: His emblematical actions, His typical miracles, His parables, His conclusions, all are evidence of a legislature in germ afterwards to be developed, a sacred text which was ever to be before men's eyes and to be the subject of investigation and interpretation, and the guide in controversy. 'Amen dico vobis' 'Ego autem dico vobis'[a] are the tokens of a supreme Teacher and Prophet.—And thus the Fathers speak. 'His sayings,' says St. Justin, 'were short and concise; for He was no rhetorician, but His word was the power of God.'[1] And St. Basil observes to the same effect, 'Every deed and every word of our Saviour Jesus Christ, is a Canon of piety and virtue. When then thou hearest word or deed of His, do not hear it by the way, or after a simple and casual[2] manner; but enter into the depth of His contemplations, become a partaker of truths mystically delivered to thee.' Const. Monast. c. 1.

It may be objected, you will say, that, granting this, it does not follow that His perfect Law should be written in the Gospels. I answer that it is in matter of fact recorded in the Gospels as regards the most solemn and ample enunciation of one inspired[3] part of it; I mean in the Sermon on the Mount. On the other hand Tradition does not in matter of fact hand down any sentences of the Saviour but those which are in the Gospels. If the

---

[1] *Apol.* i. 14.

[2] The corresponding text of the *Proph. Office* (1st ed., p. 349; 3rd ed., p. 293) reads 'simple and carnal manner'. This seems to have been the printer's misreading of the MS. The original Greek has no connection with 'carnal'.

[3] So the amanuensis; but Newman's copy made for Hugh James Rose reads 'especial part of it'.

[a] 'Amen I say to you' (Matt. 5: 18); 'But I say to you' (Matt. 5: 22).

New Law be conveyed in canons and precepts, it is contained
in the Gospels, or it is nowhere. The force of this argument will
be illustrated by considering the single exception to it which
is furnished in a passage of the Acts of the Apostles, where St.
Paul records a saying of Christ's which is not preserved by the
Evangelists; 'Beatius est magis dare quam accipere.'[a] *Acts XX*,
35. Now here moreover we have fresh proof that our Lord's
teaching was conveyed in canons and maxims; yet why is it that
no[1] others are preserved in the Epistles, why do we not find
a store of them in the early Church, if He had actually deigned
to speak others for its edification? I do not of course presume to
limit the abundance of His communications in the case of those
who lay upon His breast or conversed with Him for forty days
after His resurrection; nor do I deny that He communicated to
them much orally for the well ordering and the due guidance of
the Church. But I speak of what He communicated in the great
matters of the New Law of what He told them in order that they
should tell again; and I say it is remarkable to say the least that
if He did promulgate much over and above what is written in the
Gospels, no traces are left of it in the records of the early
Church. In addition to the instance from the Acts of the Apostles
may be mentioned two others, one preserved by several early
writers, the other by St. Jerome; 'Be ye approved money-
changers;' and 'Be ye never very glad, but when ye see your
brother live in charity.'[2] Surely here 'exceptio[3] probat regulam,'
as the proverb goes. I might then (for argument[']s sake) even
grant you the authority of Tradition: and then say to him, 'Now
you have permission to add to Christ's Law, adduce your Sentences.'

An inspection of our Lord's separate discourses confirms the
view I am taking, of course I do not mean to say He never
speaks but 'in proverbs'[b] (to use His own word,) yet if we take
what is recorded of His conversation with Nicodemus, we shall
find it summed up in the precise and pregnant enunciation on
which it turned. Every verse is a canon of divine Truth. His

---

[1] Amanuensis: 'none'.

[2] Origen, t. 19 *in Joan.* viii. 20; St. Jerome, quoted in Taylor, *Dissuasive*, pt. ii,
bk. i, §. 2. (Cf. *Proph Office*, 1st ed., pp. 355–7.)

[3] Amanuensis: 'except is'.

[a] 'It is more blessed to give than to receive.'   [b] John 16: 25.

discourse to the Jews in the 5th chapter of St. John's Gospel is perhaps a still more striking instance of this. To convey my meaning in other words, I should say that in the Epistles almost every thing depends on the *context*, in our Lord's discourses every thing is contained in the text itself immediately before us, as each comes. Indeed one great fallacy of heretical interpretation has been to measure the depth of the text by the context, as in John X, in the passage ending 'I and My Father are one,' which means far more than the context renders necessary.

It is further corroboration that we have actual evidence from the Gospels themselves, that our Savior in the midst of His condescension was *not* profuse in His words and actions before the people, as far as variety goes; He utters the same precepts again and again, and repeats His miracles.

Further, if the Gospels[,] as you maintain, contain so imperfect a revelation of the Christian Covenant, how is it that, even on your account,[1] almost all the rudiments of the Truth revealed in it, are in them?—By what accident does Scripture contain so much since it does not, (as they aver) contain all, nay why was it given at all, unless for some peculiar and singular purpose? If it is to be the record of the saving truths of the Gospel, a rule for tradition and teaching, this indeed is intelligible: else it seems to hold no definite position in the system. If it contains so much and not all, it seems to suggest for itself an end which it does not fulfil. You allow I believe, that Baptism and the Lord's Supper are the great ordinances of the New Law, and have a priority of rank over the other Sacraments. Now if you ground this on their being expressly ordained in Scripture, you seem to confess that the things prescribed therein are of more importance than those derived through the medium of Tradition. If you do not, it rests with you to account for the accidental coincidence of their being prescribed in Scripture and their also being the chief ordinances of the Gospel. Certainly as far as it goes, this circumstance leads to the surmise that Scripture is really the record of the great matters of the New Law. I give this instance of the Two Sacraments by way of illustration, as one out of various similar instances leading to that one conclusion. But on this subject I cannot do better than quote the words of our *famous Doctor*, Bishop Jeremy Taylor. 'Is not all that we

[1] Amanuensis: 'their showing'.

know of the life and death of Jesus, set down in the writings of
the New Testament? Is there any one miracle that ever Christ
did, the notice of which is conveyed to us by tradition? Do we
know any thing that Christ did or said but what is in Scripture?
—How is it possible that the Scriptures should not contain all
things necessary to Salvation, when of all the words of Christ,
in which certainly all necessary things to Salvation must needs
be contained, or else they were never revealed, there is not any
one saying, or miracle, or story of Christ, in any thing that is
material, preserved in any indubitable record, but in Scripture
alone?' (*Dissuasive from Popery*, part ii, book i, § 2.)

To this view of the subject, the words of St. John in the end
of his Gospel are singularly accordant. Let it be remembered
that he wrote his Gospel as supplementary to the others. Say
then whether the following passages do not show that the
inspired Apostle was sealing up the records of our Saviour's life
and of the Christian Law, after selecting from what remained
unnoticed by the other Evangelists, such additional materials
as were necessary for the strength and comfort of faith; say
whether the following passages taken together are consistent
with the notion that our faith in greater matters is in matter of
fact left to the mere information of tradition, however well
authenticated. 'Sunt autem et *alia multa* quae fecit Jesus, quae
si scribantur per singula, nec ipsum arbitror mundum capere
posse eos, qui scribendi sunt, libros.' '*Multa quidem et alia signa
fecit* Jesus in conspectu discipulorum suorum, quae non sunt
scripta in libro hoc. *Haec autem scripta sunt, ut credatis, quia Jesus
est filius Dei, et ut credentes vitam habeatis in nomine ejus.*'—'[Et]
Qui vidit, testimonium perhibuit; *et verum* est testimonium ejus.
Et ille scit quia vera dicit, *ut et* vos credatis.'[a] Here St. John,
closing the record of our Lord's life, declares that out of the
numberless things which might be added to the former Gospels,
he has added so much as is necessary for faith, and implies

---

[a] 'And there are also *many other things* which Jesus did, and which if they should
be written every one, I suppose that even the world itself could not contain the
books that should be written.'

'And *many other signs* truly did Jesus in the presence of His disciples, which are
not written in this book; *but these are written that ye might believe that Jesus is the
Christ the Son of God; and that believing ye might have life through His name.*'

'*And he that saw it bare record*; and his record is true. And he knoweth that he
sayeth true *that ye might believe*' (John 21: 25; 20: 30, 31; 19: 35).

moreover as a principle that in things supernatural the written testimony of the original witness is necessary for exacting belief in them.

Bellarmine indeed in replying to one of these passages argues, that the supernatural things attested by St. John are miracles, not doctrines; but surely this is over subtle, and little in accordance with that spirit of faith honorably displayed by the Church of Rome on very many occasions, which profitably enlarges the sense of Scripture by detecting principles in the particular instances under which they happen to be conveyed. I suppose you agree with us in interpreting our Lord's words 'Sinite parvulos et nolite eos prohibere &c'[a] (Matt. xix, 14) to be a permission of infant-baptism; yet one can fancy a grudging mind resolved to see nothing of a great principle in it, nothing more than the mere letter conveys. Surely when St. John speaks of 'believing' he does not mean 'belief' in *miracles* only; but he says that what he has written is enough for faith generally, is necessary in order that we may believe. What he says in the first instance of one kind of supernatural truth, miracles, may be said of another, doctrine.

But this view of the text may be illustrated by directing your attention to St. Augustine's comment upon it, which Bellarmine in vain attempts to explain away. Though I have not yet arrived formally at the consideration of the testimony of the Fathers on the subject, yet I may be allowed to introduce it here. St. Augustin says as follows. 'Whatever of his own deeds and words Christ wished us to read, He bade the Apostles write as though it had been with his own hand.' August. de consens. Evang. cap. ult.[1] Again he says elsewhere, 'The Holy Evangelist testifies that the Lord Christ said and did many things, which are not written. Those were selected for writing, which appeared to be sufficient for the salvation of believers.' *Tract. in Joann.* 49.

My present argument has gone on the supposition that our Lord Christ, the Lawgiver of the New Dispensation, has with His own mouth delivered the necessary matters of the Law. Against this hypothesis two objections appear to lie, which may

---

[1] Newman's note to this passage in *Proph. Office* reads 'Austin de Cons. Evang. i. 54. Tract. in Joann 49. In the former passage the text is not expressly referred to.' (1st ed., p. 359.)

[a] 'Suffer little children, and forbid them not.'

be answered both at once. You will say that I have proved too much, viz that I have excluded not only Tradition, but the Apostolic Epistles, not to say the Old Testament from the Canon of Faith, confining it to our Lord's words; which is a conclusion contradictory to our 7th Article. Next that the peculiar doctrines of the Gospel are found not in the Evangelists, but in the Epistles;[1] so that my theory of the exclusively Prophetical character of our Lord's teaching over all others does not hold. I reply that the doctrines of our faith *are* really promulgated by Christ Himself, though the Apostles declare them most frequently. He names 'the Name of the Father, the Son, and the Holy Ghost.' He announces Himself as 'the Only begotten Son, given by the Father, that whosoever believeth in Him should not perish, but have everlasting life'; 'the Son of man which is in heaven': having 'glory with the Father before the world was'; 'giving His flesh for the life of the world', 'giving His life a ransom instead of many'.[a] If we had only the Gospels, we should have in them all the great doctrines contained in the Epistles.

However God has given us the Epistles as a comment on our Lord's teaching to bring out and fix His sacred sense, that we might not miss it. Now this drift of the Apostles' writings is plainly declared by our Lord when He promised them His Holy Spirit to guide them. 'Adhuc multa habeo vobis dicere; sed non potestis portare modo. Cum autem venerit ille Spiritus veritatis, docebit vos omnem veritatem.'[b] Now so far it would seem as if a new revelation as to its matter was to have been made them; but the Divine Speaker proceeds, 'Non enim loquetur a semetipso, sed *quaecumque audiet*, loquetur; et quae ventura sunt annunciabit vobis. *Ille me clarificabit, quia de meo accipiet*, et annunciabit vobis.'[c] Again, 'Haec locutus sum vobis, apud vobis manens; Paraclitus autem, Spiritus Sanctus quem mittet Pater in nomine meo, ille vos docebit omnia, et *suggeret vobis omnia*

---

[1] So the amanuensis; but in his copy for Rose Newman wrote 'in the gospels'. *Proph. Office*, 1st ed., p. 360, reads 'next, that after all, the characteristic doctrines of Christianity are found in the Epistles, not in Our Lord's teaching'.

[a] Matt. 28:19; John 3:16; John 3:13; John 17: 5; John 6: 51; Matt. 20: 28.

[b] 'I have yet many things to say unto you, but ye cannot bear them now. Howbeit when he, the Spirit of truth, is come, he will guide you into all truth' (John 16: 12,13).

[c] '. . . for He shall not speak of himself; but *whatsoever He shall hear, that shall He speak*: and He will shew you things to come. He shall *glorify Me: for He shall take of Mine, and shall show it unto you*' (John 16: 12–14).

quaecumque dixero vobis.[a] From hence it seems that, together with imparting prophetical inspiration, the office of the Holy Ghost lay especially in illuminating the Son, in throwing lustre upon and drawing lustre from all which belonged to His person. His words and deeds, His trials and sufferings, and in particular *His words.* 'He shall speak what things soever He shall *hear.*'[b] 'He shall suggest whatever I have said to you.'[c]—Surely this is a plain intimation that the inspired teaching of the Apostles would be in its substance a comment upon the sacred words of Christ, an expansion of them, while they recorded them, not an independent revelation; except indeed so far as it was prophetic, 'quae ventura sunt annunciabit vobis',[d] which applies to the Apocalpyse and certain scattered notices in the Epistles.—The same general meaning is included in a later verse of the same chapter. 'These things have I spoken unto you in proverbs (ἐν παροιμίαις) but the time cometh when the Lord shall shew you plainly (παρρησίᾳ ἀπαγγελῶ ὑμῖν) of the Father.'[e]—now observe how remarkably our Lord's parting charge, recorded by another Evangelist, agrees with the same view I have been maintaining, 'all power is given &c. Go ye therefore and disciple all the nations etc *teaching them to keep all things whatever I have commanded you.*'[f] The revelation as regards its matter was already made, the Gospel committed to them. They had but to preach it in the power of Him who promised 'to be with them alway even unto the end.'[g]

This then is the true character of the Apostolic writings; they are comments on our Lord's words; and the more we examine, the more perhaps we shall find them answer to this character. The same conclusion is drawn from such passages of the Gospels as the following; which show clearly that during our Lord's ministry the Apostles were laying up in their minds stores of doctrine which they were not intended to understand or at least to reveal till after the Holy Spirit came. 'Haec non cognoverunt discipuli ejus primum; sed quando glorificatus est Jesus, tunc recordati sunt quia haec erant scripta de eo, et haec

---

a 'These things have I spoken unto you, being yet present with you. But the Comforter, which is the Holy Ghost, whom the Father will send in My name, He shall teach you all things, and *bring all things to your remembrance, whatsoever I have said unto you*' (John 14: 25, 26).   b John 16: 13.   c John 14: 26.

d 'He shall show you things to come' (John 16: 13).

e John 16: 25.   f Matt. 28: 18–20.   g Ibid.

facerunt ei.'[a] 'Quod ego facio, tu nescis modo; scias autem postea.'[b] 'Praecepit illis ne cuiquam quod vidissent narrarent nisi cum filius hominis à mortuis resurrexerit. Et verbum continuerunt apud se, conquirentes quid esset, Cum à mortuis resurrexerit.'[c] 'Quod dico vobis in tenebris, dicite in lumine; et quod in aure auditis, praedicate super tecta.'[d]

It has now been shown that even though Christ be the chief Prophet of the Church, yet his Apostles' writings may form part of the Rule of Faith as expounders of His divine maxims. And as for the Old Testament, He himself has settled the canonicity of that venerable portion of divine Truth, by formally appealing to it as authority; so that to receive it is but obedience to some of those very sentences or dicta, of which I have been speaking. And here by the bye let it be noted that He has nowhere pronounced any similar recognition of the Apocrypha, however He may have vouchsafed to appeal or allude to certain passages in it. But to return you will reply, I suppose, to the foregoing statement that you allow so much willingly; only you contend that, as the Apostles are interpreters of Christ's doctrine, so the Church is after them. Now it would be some sort of answer to this objection, to refer to the words with which St. John closes the Apocalypse, which certainly do seem, considering he was the last of the Apostles, not merely to apply to his own visions, but to conclude and seal up for ever what was in fact the supplement and completion of the inspired volume itself; especially since his Gospel, itself supplementary to the others, is closed as we have seen, in a similar way. It is an additional confirmation, that the Old Testament also has an ending, of parallel solemnity, however different in the expression of it, and this,

---

[a] 'These things understood not His disciples at the first; but, when Jesus was glorified, then remembered they that these things were written of Him, and that they had done these things unto Him' (John 12: 16).

[b] 'What I do, thou knowest not now; but thou shalt know hereafter' (John 13: 7).

[c] '. . . He charged them that they should tell no man what things they had seen, till the son of man were risen from the dead. And they kept that saying within themselves, questioning one with another what the rising of the dead should mean' (Mark 9: 9).

[d] 'What I tell you in darkness, that speak ye in light; what ye hear in the ear, that preach ye upon the housetops' (Matt. 10: 27). [In his copy for Rose, Newman writes 'Add a remarkable instance Acts 11: 16'. ('Then remembered I the word of the Lord, how that He said, John indeed baptized with water, but ye shall be baptized with the Holy Ghost.') This note is amplified into a page in *Proph. Office*, 1st ed., p. 365.]

though the prophecy of Malachi is in itself a complete and detached book as well as the Apocalypse. However waiving whatever argument is deducible from Scripture on this point, I prefer to come to the plain question of historical fact; whether the early Church did or did not consider the Canon of Faith closed and completed in the written word. The Fathers alone can answer this question; and I appeal to their writings. Did they consider the Canon confined to the books of the Old and New Testament, or did they not? I maintain they did.

You have urged in one of your letters that we of the English Church are inconsistent in receiving the Canon of Scripture on Tradition, and then decrying the authority of Tradition for any other purpose; and that, in order to be consistent, we should either reject Scripture, or recognize those doctrines which the Roman Catholics receive on Tradition.—Now if I prove what I am now undertaking, this difficulty vanishes.—That same Tradition of the Church, which bears witness to the Canonicity of Scripture, bears witness also to its sole canonicity. We appeal to Scripture as the word of God on the authority of the Fathers; on the same authority, we refrain from appealing to the Fathers themselves.—Tradition, like the forerunner of Christ, declares its own inferiority. 'He was not that Light, but was sent to bear witness of that Light.'[a]—Now then to proceed to the witness[1] [of] the Fathers.

The mode pursued by the early Church in deciding matters of doctrine, seems to have been as follows. When a novel doctrine was started, the first question which the neighbouring Bishops asked each other, was, 'Has this come down to us?' The answer being in the negative, they at once put it down on the just weight of this antecedent argument.—The prevailing opinion of the Church was a sufficient, an overpowering objection against it. When however the matter came before a Council, when it was discussed, when they reasoned, and proved, they never went in matters of saving faith by Tradition only, but they guided and (if I may so say) steered and studied their course by the written [word]. Tradition was no longer more than a subordinate guide, as explaining, illustrating, reconciling the Scriptures: it was in no true sense a Canon or Rule or oracle of Truth. Then as under

[1] Amanuensis: 'the witnessing the Fathers'.

[a] John 1: 8.

the old Covenant, the appeal was made, 'ad legem magis et ad testimonium'[a] to the testament of the Savior, the document of His words and doings, as commented on and developed by the inspired Apostles.[1] The name of Testament, given to the writings of the Apostles and Evangelists implies this.

Now first I appeal to our original authority Vincentius Lirinensis, who after all, you cannot deny, does make Scripture the Canon of Faith, and Tradition but interpretation. You cannot surely get over the broad statements of a principle with which he opens his work and which he nowhere retracts. I must be allowed to quote it once more. 'Saepe magno studio et summâ attentione perquirens à quamplurimis sanctitate et doctrinâ praestantibus viris, quonam modo possim certà quâdam et quasi generali ac regulari viâ, catholicae fidei veritatem ab haereticae pravitatis falsitate discernere, hujusmodi semper responsum ab omnibus fere retuli, duplici modo, munire fidem—*primo* scilicet divinae legis auctoritate, *tum deinde* Ecclesiae Catholicae traditione. Hic forsitan requirat aliquis, Cum sit perfectus scripturarum Canon, sibique ad omnia satis superque sufficiat, quid opus est, ut ei ecclesiasticae intelligentiae jungatur authoritas? quia videlicet Scripturam Sacram pro ipsâ suâ altitudine non uno eodemque sensu universi accipiunt, sed ejusdem eloquia aliter atque aliter alius atque alius interpretatur; ut paene quot homines sunt, tot illinc sententiae erui posse videantur . . . atque idcirco multum necesse est, propter tantos tam varii erroris anfractus, ut Propheticae et Apostolicae interpretationis linea secundum Ecclesiastici et Catholici sensus normam dirigatur.'[b]

---

[1] Newman's copy for Hugh James Rose made out after Harrison had criticized Newman's theory as 'ultra-Protestant' (cf. Appendix II), ended at this point, having begun at the phrase 'Let us first see what light Scripture itself will throw upon the question in dispute' (p. 123). He then adds the following note: 'N.B. Concerning the above I observe

1. as to the *argument*, it is put *as* an argument more completely in the Recapitulation, being here treated more in the way of exposition or teaching, as unfolding (what is familiarly called) the lie of the country.

2. as to the *theory* itself, the simple question is whether it is *essentially* ultra-Protestant, inconsistent in its necessary developments with our received doctrine—for that it is imperfect, one side of the Truth &c. is nihil ad rem, since it is but a few pages out of a long letter of at least 5 parts . . .' (p. 170).

[a] 'to the law and to the testimony' (Isa. 8).

[b] *Commonit.* II. 'Enquiring therefore often with great desire, and attention, of very many excellent, holy, and learned men, how and by what means I might assuredly, and as it were by some general and ordinary way, discern the true

—After this he goes on to speak of Universality, Antiquity, and Consent, in order, that is, to ascertain what is the Catholic sense of Scripture; not in order to discover any Apostolical Tradition distinct from it. Let this be well observed. In Vincentius's treatise Tradition is from beginning to end made subordinate to Scripture. Whether or not Universality, Antiquity, and Consent would or would not prove a Tradition, unsupported by Scripture, to be Apostolic; Vincentius does not enter on this question at all. He is but speaking of Interpretative[1] Tradition. According to his views then, for one may fairly argue from so emphatic a silence, Tradition is principally to be viewed as interpretation of Scripture; and all proofs of important doctrines drawn from it as an independent authority, are but perversions of its legitimate use. This is the fatal objection, which we consider to lie against some of the decrees at Trent, which are professedly drawn from Tradition only; and herein on the contrary is shewn the accurate judgement of our own Church, as expressed in the documents above quoted, in receiving in accordance with Vincent, the determinations of those Councils only which profess to draw their conclusions from the written word of God.

Now to proceed to other authorities. Tertullian. In the beginning God created the heaven and the earth. 'I adore the fullness of Scripture; in which is manifested to me a Maker and His work. The Gospel adds the Word as the Minister and Agent of Providence, but I read not a word anywhere of a pre-existing matter out of which things were made. Let the school of Her-

---

[1] Amanuensis: Interpretation.

Catholic faith from false and wicked heresy; to this question I had usually this answer of them all, that whether I or any other desired to find out the fraud of heretics, duly springing up, and to escape their snares, and willingly would continue in a sound faith, himself safe and sound, that he ought two manner of ways by God's assistance to defend and preserve his faith; that is, first, *by the authority of the law of God*; secondly, *by the tradition of the Catholic Church*. Here some man, perhaps, may ask, seeing the Canon of the Scripture is perfect, and most abundantly of itself sufficient for all things, what need we join unto it the authority of the Church's understanding and interpretation? The reason is this, because the Scripture being of itself so deep and profound, all men do not understand it in one and the same sense, but divers men diversely, this man and that man, this way and that way, expound and interpret the sayings thereof, so that to one's thinking, so many men, so many opinions almost may be gathered out of them . . . and therefore very necessary it is for the avoiding of so great windings and turnings of errors so various, that the line of expounding the Prophets and Apostles be directed and drawn, according to the rule of the Ecclesiastical and Catholic sense.'

mogenes' (who maintained its pre-existence) 'shew us that it is mentioned in Scripture; if it is not in Scripture, let him fear the woe destined for them who add or take away.' Contr. Hermog. 22.

Origen. [']We know Jesus Christ is God, and we seek to expound the words that are spoken, according to the dignity of the person. Wherefore it is necessary for us to call the Holy Scriptures as witnesses; for our notions and statements, without these witnesses, are not trustworthy.['] Bellarm. de Verb. Dei iv–II. Taylor. *Dissuasive*, pt. 2. i. 2.

Again—[']All the Scriptures, according to the Preacher, are "words of the wise as goads, and as stakes well planted, given on an understanding from One Shepherd," nor is there aught superfluous in them. The Word is the "one Shepherd of the things of the mind which to those who have not ears to hear, seem indeed to disagree with one another, but in truth are most harmonious. For as the different strings of psaltery or lyre, each of which has its own note, different as it would seem, from that of the rest, make discords together in the judgements of the unmusical and unscientific, on account of their variety, so in like manner ears unpractised in the divine harmony of sacred Scripture, set the Old Testament against the New and the Gospel against the Law, and Gospel against Gospel, and St. Paul against Evangelist, or against himself or against his brother Apostles. But when another comes well instructed in God's harmony accomplished in deed and words as a second David, "cunning in playing," he will bring out perfect tones, being instructed thence to strike the strings in season, now those of the Law, now the corresponding strings of the Gospel, now those of the Prophetical, now again, when it is fit, the Apostolic accordance, and in like manner those of Apostles with those of the Evangelists.—For he knows that Scripture as a whole is God's one Prophet and complete Instrument, giving forth to those who wish to learn its own saving music from many notes combined, stilling and restraining all stirrings of the evil one, as David's harmony in Saul's madness.['] (in Matt. tom. ii.) The main[1] drift of this passage doubtless is to show the *consistency* of Scripture, but it also bears clear and strong testimony to its completeness and independence of all other teaching.

[1] Amanuensis: mean (cf. *Proph. Office*, 1st ed., p. 375).

Would Origen have so spoken, had he put tradition on a level with it?—Cyril of Jerusalem. 'It is necessary as regards the divine and holy mysteries of faith, that not even a chance word should be delivered in our tradition without the warrant of divine Scripture, to the exclusion of mere improbabilities or skilfully arranged arguments. Neither give credence to my mere words, unless they are demonstrated from the Scriptures.—For this is the security of our faith, being derived not from our inventions, but from proofs of Holy Scriptures.' What makes this passage the stronger,[1] is, that Cyril speaks thus Cat. iv. 12[2] with reference to the creed, which, if any tradition, might depend on itself.[3]

　—Optatus argues against the repetition of Baptism as follows. 'You say it may be repeated, we say it may not; the minds of our people fluctuate between the two. Let no one trust you, or us either, we are all of us party men. Arbiters must be found; but if Christians, such are not produceable on either side, for truth suffers by our private leanings. If we go out of doors for an arbiter, he must be either a pagan, and so unacquainted with our Mysteries, or a Jew who is necessarily the enemy of Christian baptism. It follows that no human tribunal can be found for the question; we must have recourse to heaven. But why knock at heaven's gate, when we have with us a *testament* in the Gospel. We may here fitly compare earthly things to heavenly. It is like the case of a man with a large family. While the father is alive, he gives his orders to each of them; a will is not yet necessary. So Christ, during His abode on earth (may He still ever be present to our need!) laid His commands on the Apostles, as this or that was necessary. But [the case is the same as that of][4] a human father, feeling himself dying, and fearing lest after his death his sons should quarrel and go to Law, he summons witnesses and transfers his will from his breast, which is soon to fail, to ever enduring tablets, so that if afterwards a quarrel arise between the brothers, they have recourse, not to his tomb, but to his testament, so that he who rests in his tomb, should yet speak without voice from his writing. Now He whose will we

---

　[1] Amanuensis: stranger. Cf. *Proph. Office*, 1st ed., p. 378.

　[2] So the amanuensis; amended to Cat. iv. 17 in *Proph. Office*, 1st ed., p. 378.

　[3] *Proph. Office*, 1st ed., p. 378, reads here '. . . which, if any statement of doctrine, might surely depend on Tradition.'

　[4] Square brackets in MS.

speak of, is alive in heaven; therefore his purpose must be sought, for, as in a will, so in the Gospel.'—And thus he proceeds to prove his own view of baptism by the conduct and words of our Lord when He washed His disciples' feet. (vid. Austin also in Ps. 21.)

Basil. 'It is a plain fall from the faith, and a sign of pride either to annul any thing that is in Scripture, or to add what is not in Scripture; since our Blessed Saviour having said, "My sheep hear My voice," and "the voice of strangers they will not hear," and to add to the inspired Scriptures, or to withdraw from them is forbidden with especial earnestness by the Apostle, saying, "Though it be but a man's testament, 'nemo superordinat.'[1]"' de [verâ] Fide [et Moral. reg. 72. c. i.] c. i. fin.[2]

Again, elsewhere: What is the Characteristic of a Christian? faith working by love. What is the characteristic of faith? an unhesitating assurance of the truth of the inspired word, proof against all reasonings whether from natural necessity, or the pretence of piety. What is the characteristic of a believer? to repose in such assurance on the authority of that word, without venturing to take away or to add. For if 'all that is not of faith is sin' and 'faith cometh from hearing, and hearing from the word of God['] it follows that all that goes beyond inspired Scripture, not being of faith, is sin. Moral reg. 80. c. 22. Augustine. 'If any one, in matters relating to Christ, or His Church, or any other thing which belongs to faith or our life, I will not say, If we, but, (what St. Paul has added) if an angel from heaven shall preach unto you, besides (praeterquam) what ye have received in the Scriptures of the Law and the Gospel, let him be accursed.['] Contr. Lit. Petilian. iii. 7.

Again speaking to the Donatists, 'Why add ye to God's testament by saying that Christ is heir of no lands, but where He has Donatus for co-heir. We are not jealous. Read this to us out of the Law and the Prophets, out of the Psalms, out of the Gospel itself, or out of the letters of the Apostles; read it thence, and we believe it.' contr. Donatist. Ep. (de Unit. Eccl.) 11.

Chrysostom, commenting on the words, 'He who entereth not by the door into the sheepfold, but climbeth up some other way, the same is a thief, a robber'—speaks as follows. 'Behold,

---

[1] 'No man disannuleth or addeth thereto' (*Proph. Office*, 1st ed., p. 379).
[2] S uare brackets in MS.

the evidences of a robber; first, that he enters not openly; next, that he enters not by the *Scriptures*; for this is meant by not entering in at the door. Here Christ alludes to those before Him and those who were to come, Antichrist, and false Christs, Judas and Theudas, and such like. He suitably called the Scriptures the door; for they bring us to God, and open upon us the knowledge of Him. They make the sheep, guard them, and fence off the wolves. As a trusty door, it shut[s] out heretics, securing us from error, as far as we have the will to be so secure. And unless we damage it, we are unassailable by our enemies. By means of it we shall know who are pastors and who are not.'[1]

Anastatius of Antioch, speaking of the trees of life and of the knowledge of good and evil, says 'It is manifest, that those things are not to be inquired into, which Scripture hath passed over in silence. For the Holy Spirit hath dispensed and administered to us all things which conduce to our profit.' Anagog. Contempl. in Hexem. Lib. viii. init.

St. John Damascene, in the beginning of his work on the orthodox faith, says, 'God has not abandoned us in our complicated ignorance of Himself; nay He has implanted in all men by nature and knowledge that there is a God. Moreover He has directly vouchsafed to us a fellowship of His own knowledge, (as far as our weak nature can bear it) first by the Law and the Prophets; then also by His only begotten Son our Lord and Savior Jesus Christ.

All things therefore which are delivered to us by the Law and the Prophets, the Apostles and Evangelists, we receive and acknowledge and reverence; but we seek for nothing beyond them[2] For in that God is good, He is the giver of all good; He has neither jealousy nor other passion.—whatever were too great a weight, that He has buried in silence. These things then [which are given][3] let us on our part love, in these let us rest, neither overpassing the lines marked out by His eternal will, nor in any respect transgressing the divine message.' Again in the second chapter, he closes a reflection upon the most sacred doctrines of the faith thus: 'It cannot be that we should preach

---

[1] In Joann. 58, ed. Duc. [Newman later added: 'He is speaking primarily of the Old Testament' (*Proph. Office*, 3rd ed., p. 318).]

[2] Amanuensis opens inverted commas here.   [3] Square brackets in MS.

or at all know any thing about God, besides those things which
the holy oracles of the Old and New Testament have set forth,
said or manifested to us.'

These extracts however, strong as they are, give a very faint
impression of the distinct and familiar apprehension of this great
principle in the mind of the Fathers, as evinced by their writings.
It is not in one or two formal announcements, but in the spirit,
the drift, the concealed assumption of their treatises, that we
discern this fundamental doctrine of the Anglican Church. It is
by tracing the course of a controversy, and observing how
habitually present it was to the reasonings of all the contending
parties, how it guided the deliberations and decisions of Councils, how it is incidentally evolved in words in the articles of
Creeds, that we realize to ourselves the strength of our own
position.[1] This cannot be shown on paper in any adequate
manner; but I will transcribe a few passages which occur in the
documents of one not[2] the most elaborate controversies of the
early Church, the Apollinarian. St. Athanasius in the following
passage clearly distinguishes between Tradition as *teaching*,
Scripture as *proving*, *verifying* Christian doctrine. 'Our faith is
correct, and is *derived* from Apostolical teaching and the tradition of the Fathers, being authenticated out of the New and Old
Testaments.' ad Adelph. 6.

St. Cyril of Jerusalem in one or two places maintains a doctrine altogether parallel to this; one of which introduces the
passage already quoted from him. After reciting and commenting
on the Creed, he says 'Keep in thy mind this seal of faith alway,
which I have now summarily stated in its chief article. But if
the Lord permit, I will speak of them according to my power
with proofs from Scripture.' Cat. iv. 17. Again shortly after.
'Learn and hold fast thy faith in what is taught and promised,
that faith which alone is now delivered to thee by *tradition of the
Church*, and *substantiated from Scripture*. But since not all have
ability to read the Scriptures, but are hindered from knowing
them whether by want of education or of leisure, we comprehend
in a few articles the whole doctrine of faith, lest souls perish for
want of instruction.' Cat. v. 7.

Let me now compare with these passages my own statement

---

[1] Vid. Taylor's Dissuasive, vol. x, p. 428, and Laud, pp. 194–197–217–332.
[2] *Sic* for of.

in my first letter to you[a] and you will see its coincidence with
the doctrine of this great Teacher of the Church. 'Le grand
principe de l'Eglise Anglicane est que l'Ecriture est la *base* de
toute preuve le tribunal en dernier ressort pour toute doctrine
fondamentale.—Nous ne disons pas,—que la preuve de toute
doctrine fondamentale, doit sortir *directement* de l'Ecriture;
mais du moins elle doit en sortir indirectement. Nous admettons
même le dogme de la Trinité, doctrine fondamentale, *tirée
directement* de la tradition, mais finalement de l'Ecriture.'
p. 870.[b]

In the following passage Athanasius praises that very course
as a mode of acting familiar to his mind, which I have stated
above to be the Church's usual procedure towards innovations;
first to silence them by her own authority which is that of tradition, but if matters got worse and a controversy ensued, then
to have recourse to the tribunal of ultimate appeal, Scripture.
He has been recounting the Apollinarian tenets, and then chides
the Bishop to whom he is writing for not having silenced them
at once. 'For my part, I was astonished that your holiness
endured such profanities; and did not silence the authors of them,
and put before them the pious Faith of the Church, in order that
matters might be brought to an issue, either by their obeying
and keeping quiet on the one hand, or on the other by their
resisting and being[1] accordingly treated as heretics.—It is
necessary perhaps formally to impugn and convict their foolish-
ness, yet it were well could I stop here, and say not a word more.
For doctrines which are unsound as appears on the very surface
of these, ought not to be discussed and made much of, lest dis-
putatious men should take it as a proof there is no clear case
against them; they ought to receive this answer and nothing
beyond, "*It is enough, that these are not the doctrines of the Church*

[1] 'according' added.

[a] i.e. the Third Reply.

[b] 'The main principle which we of the Anglican Church maintain, is this: that
Scripture is the ultimate basis of proof, the place of final appeal, in respect to all
fundamental doctrine. Nor do we say that the proof of even fundamental doctrines
must rest immediately on Scripture, but ultimately ... we receive the doctrine of
the Trinity, a *fundamental, immediately* from tradition, *ultimately from Scripture.*'
[The amanuensis gives a reference, p. 870, not to Jager's book but to the column
of *L'Univers* (28 January 1835) in which the paragraph occurs. The reference to
Jager is pp. 94–5, and to the present edition pp. 35–6.]

nor of the Fathers." However, lest these inventors of evil things should be embodied by our continued silence, it may be well to bring to memory a few things *from the Holy Scriptures,* since this may shame them perhaps from pursuing their base imaginations.' ad. Epict. 3. fin.[1]

Again. 'Either then deny the sacred Scriptures, or, if you acknowledge them, do not speculate, besides what is written, words of irremediable mischief.' Contr. Apollin. i. 6.—Now this is one of those passages which taken by itself would stand for little; for one might easily say that it merely says that Scripture is of authority, not that Tradition is not. But when we find the same sentiment repeated again and again in various shapes, and if no instance occurs of Tradition being appealed to in order to prove a doctrine under discussion, no instance of a question being ultimately *ruled* by Tradition, the argument for the exclusive canonicity of the Scriptures becomes a strong one.

For this reason I add the following passages from the same treatise: 'If then ye are disciples of the Gospels, speak not iniquity against God, but walk by what is written, and done. But if ye desire to speak other things beyond what is written, why do you contend with us, who are determined neither to hear nor to speak beyond what is written, the Lord having said, "Si manseritis in sermone meo vere liberi eritis."[a] Contr. Apollin. 1. 8. fin. "What inconceivable abandonment of mind is this, which leads you to speak what is not in Scripture, and to entertain thoughts foreign to godliness?"—ibid. 9. "While then we confess that Christ is God and man, we do not speak this as if to imply separation in His nature, (God forbid!) but again according to the Scriptures." ' ibid. 11.

He concludes with these words, in which there is the same distinction between the Tradition of the Church, as an antecedent argument, a fair [plea][2] ordinarily superseding inquiry; and when for one reason or other the inquiry has proceeded, the Scriptures as the only basis of sound argument and conclusion. 'I have written the above, Beloved, though really it was unnecessary, *for the Evangelical Tradition is sufficient* by itself; but since

---

[1] A slightly different wording is given in *Proph. Office,* 1st ed., pp. 386–7.

[2] The word is missing from the MS. and is supplied from *Proph. Office,* 1st ed., p. 388.

[a] 'If ye abide in My word, ye shall be truly free' (John 8: 31, 36).

you asked concerning our faith, and because of those who are
desirous of trifling with their theories and do not consider that
he who speaks out of his private judgement, speaks a lie. For
neither the beauty nor the glory of the Lord's human body can
be adequately expressed by the wit of man: but so far we are
able, viz to confess what has been done, as it is in Scripture, and
to worship the true and living God, for the glory and acknowledgement of His love towards man, &c.' ibid. 22. fin.

Again in his second book against Apollinaris.[1] 'Whence you
got your notion [that the soul is of a fleshly nature][2] I cannot
understand; it is neither to be proved from the Holy Scriptures,
nor is it according to the received opinion of the world.' ii, 8.
And so I might go on, adducing passages from the 9th, 13th,
14th, 17th, 18th, and 19th chapters.

Now then let us turn Theodoret's mode of conducting the
same controversy.

In each of the three dialogues of which his Eranistes is composed, we find the following significant arrangement; the arguments from scripture come first, and then he adduces in
illustration[3] passages from the Fathers. Moreover in his first
dialogue, he introduces his authorities from the Fathers in the
following way. Eranistes, the heterodox disputant says, after
hearing his proofs from Scripture, 'You have expounded this
text well enough. But I would fain learn, how the ancient
Doctors of the Church had understood it.' Orthodox replies,
*'You ought to have been satisfied with these proofs from the Apostles
and Prophets.* However, since you desire besides to know the
expositions of the Holy Fathers, I will give you this aid also,
with God's blessing.' Again, in the second Dialogue: 'We will
endeavour to persuade Arius to confess the one substance of the
Holy Trinity, and we will bring the proofs of this from Holy
Scripture.' p. 78. [ed. Schulze vol. IV.][2]

We have passages to the same effect at pages 79, 97, 113; of
which I will only quote the last. 'How can a man dispute with
those who deny our Lord had taken flesh, or human soul, or
mind, except by adducing his proofs from divine Scripture? how
refute the frenzied men who study to disparage the divinity of

---

[1] So the amanuensis; altered to 'Apollinarius' in *Proph. Office*, 1st ed., p. 389,
'Apollinaris' in 3rd. ed., p. 326.
[2] Square brackets in MS.   [3] Amanuensis: 'illustrative'.

the Only begotten, except by showing that divine Scripture has spoken some things with reference to His divine, other things with reference to His human nature?'

Out of the third dialogue I select the following.

After Orthodox has stated the Catholic doctrine of the Passion and Resurrection, Eranistes answers, 'The doctrines of the Church should be set forth not in declaration merely, but by proof. Show me then that Holy Scripture teaches this.' p. 199 Upon which Orthodox proceeds to cite the Epistle to the Romans.

Again. *'Eranistes.* St. Peter says, "Christo igitur passo in carne."[a] *Orthodox.* Surely this is quite agreeable to our doctrine; *for we have learned our Canon of doctrines from Holy Scripture.'* p. 213.

A little further Orthodox, wishing to refute the doctrine of Eranistes alluded to [in] the last extract, that "Deus est passus,"[b] does it as follows. *Orthodox.* Would you dare call the All-holy Spirit by the name of Son, though He, as well as the Son, is from the Father?—*Eranistes.* By no means. *O.* Why? *E.* because I do not find this name in Holy Scripture.—*O.* Yet would you dare call Him ingenitus?[c] *E.* No surely. *O.* Why not? *E.* Because I have not learned this from Holy Scripture, and I have an extreme dread of saying what it is silent about. *O.* Well then, my friend, be but consistent enough to observe the same caution as regards the Salutary Passion; and whatever divine appellation Scripture has put aside, from all connexion with the passion, do you disconnect also. *E.* What are they? *O.* The notion of Passion is never joined to the titles of Almighty God.' pp. 214–215. To the same purpose I might quote from pp. 190, 195 and 224.

I cannot refrain from adding one sentence from the passage contained in the last of these. 'To add any thing to the words of Scripture is madness and audacity; but to unfold the sacred text, and to develop its hidden sense, is holy and religious.' Now from this and similar passages I do not argue any more than you, that nothing more may be added on any side to the Scripture notices of religion: this were a miserable perversion of the words of Theodoret. He is speaking of the high doctrines of Faith, the saving truths of the Gospel, and these it is which he maintains

---

a 'Christ having suffered for us in the flesh' (1 Peter 4: 1).
b 'God suffered death.' Migne, PG 83, cols. 221–2.
c 'unbegotten'.

are contained in Scripture, and nothing besides. Here then I part with Theodoret, merely reminding you of the remarkable coincidence [which] should be observed of the last sentence quoted from him with the doctrine of Vincentius's treatise as contained in any extract above given.[1]

Lastly, St. Maximus, or who[e]ver is the author of the Dialogues on the Trinity and Incarnation attributed to St. Athanasius, thus speaks to the Apollinarian. 'You have receded in your argument from inspired Scripture, and in consequence have fallen from grace.' Dial. v. 29. F. ed. Benedict.

Here I will relieve you and myself from future attention to this subject. Perhaps I have produced proofs of my position worthy your attention. I know it is sometimes objected that 'anything can be proved from the Fathers, owing to their voluminousness, and the inconsistencies incident to human nature.' You indeed, M. l'Abbé, as a Catholic[,] have too much reverence for them to make this objection; yet in the present instance it would be to your advantage to find it true. It would be to your advantage to be able to produce a number of counter passages which give that prerogative and precedence to Tradition which the foregoing attribute to Scripture. But that is impossible; you cannot be made the unwilling recipient of so opportune an accident. I know indeed they speak much in praise of Tradition, but we do the same; the point at issue is simply this, whether they consider it to be a tribunal of ultimate appeal, whether they dare to rest upon it solely as an article of saving Faith. We deny this principle, you affirm it. Till you adduce authorities from them to countenance this particular tenet of yours, and not any other, you have nothing at all.

And now for the present I conclude—intending to continue my remarks upon your letters in subsequent sections.

---

[1] *Proph. Office*, 1st ed., p. 391, shortens these last three sentences to the clinching phrase 'Here is the doctrine of the Gallic Vincentius in the mouth of a Syrian Bishop'.

Appendices

Appendix I

Newman's draft outline of the controversy

NB.
Reasons for our Lord's words being the substance of the Rev^n. The fact—that nothing can be found in the Ep^{t} but what in His words— or at least His words contain the &c.

v

Romans on

Controversy with
the abbé Jager
and Harrison's letters
1834 & 1835

Two parts. that w[e] do not exclude what we consider error
that [   ] our & according to incentive and in this
[   ]sider [?] the [   ]

corruptions of R[omanism]
On the principle of a[ntiquit]y
(NB. corruptions [aris]e 1st from definitions being taken
as points of faith
2nd from concentrating the Church
in *one* see.)
Begin by quoting the abbé's Challenge.
—

the true
State (Vincent's) doctrine
One dogma committed to the Church, in essence the whole truth, as a
seed a tree. It is, as time goes on, developed, discriminated,
fixed in its parts.
~~Accordingly the fact~~
It was intended to remain pure &c.—state *what* promises
were made to it. *how far*
The *sign* of its remaining pure was *agreement* i.e. unanimity &
concord.

as to An-
[tiqui]ty
tho' it m^t be
enough to show
a time when there
had been
perhaps no
corr w^h *came*
in recently
[a]nd there
[i]s a
strong prob^y
against any other
doctrine, as
being novel
since its rise
w^d be ascertainable

While it so remaining, there was a very strong presumption in favor
of its purity: viz catholicity. not conclusive, for there m^t be
a case when Antiquity must be referred and deferred to, but a priori.
Further the onus probandi wd lie on me of pointing out the time, when
corr arose.
Now apply this to the times of the Reformation. If I had lived then,
qu. whether the unanimity of the Church in what we Anglicans call
error does not floor me.

1. external influence, and the concentration of power
in one See not strong (?) evidence of catholicity,
or the universality of the Latin Church.
concord

1. Not ~~an unanimity~~. Greek Church separated.

2. but whether an agreement under separation not à
fortiori as images.

On the
question of the
6 centuries

3. & 4. then to ANTIQUITY and show that it did *not* come
in without notice. We can put our finger on the *time*.
So purgatory—its rise St. Austin. again contest
with Greek Church.
the very timing of introduction—

4. ~~but even~~ if not ~~antiquity~~—still if I can point to
a previous state of things. This at least holds
good in Rome, when the errors over difference of
rites & doctrines only *escapes* & practical corruptions

Appendix II

Correspondence between Newman and Harrison; with Newman's paper on the Rule of Faith, as sent to Hugh James Rose

   (i) Harrison to Newman 19 August 1835
  (ii) Newman to Harrison undated
 (iii) Harrison to Newman 28 November 1835
  (iv) Harrison to Newman 2 December 1835
   (v) Excerpts from the paper 'The Rule of Faith' (i.e. Newman's 'Fourth Reply, Part 2'), made for Hugh James Rose, 14 December 1835
  (vi) Note on the copy for Rose undated (presumably 14 December 1835)

The sequence of these letters is by no means clear, but appears to be as follows. Harrison naturally saw Newman's second letter, which appeared in the controversy in book form as 'Fourth Reply, Part One'. It was sent off to the abbé Jager in August 1835 and Harrison wrote to Newman to tell him this (19 August 1835). Harrison wrote from Christ Church, Oxford, on 28 November 1835 a letter in which, among other things, he commented on this second letter to Jager and quarrelled with some parts of it. Filing his letter, Newman inserted a heading 'note prior to all the Nos.' as if it were the first in a series of Harrison letters he was keeping, at any rate on this particular issue. It will be noted that Harrison refers to numbered paragraphs, as they are numbered in the text.

Next, in a postscript to this letter, Harrison asked for a loan of 'Your paper on the Rule of Faith'. This paper, which Newman had read to the Theological Society in Oxford, at a meeting chaired by Pusey on Friday, 22 November 1835, is the 'Fourth Reply, Part Two' of the Jager controversy. Jager did not print this, either in the *Moniteur de la Religion* or in book form. It is printed in the present edition for the first time. Newman sent it to Harrison, who replied with a long diatribe, dated 2 December 1835, also from Christ Church. In filing this, Newman has headed it 'No. 1'. The letter attacks the 'Rule of Faith', with many quotations, some approximate, some exact.

In an appeal for support to a distinguished outsider, Newman sent an excerpt from his paper, with a summary of Harrison's views upon it, to the Cambridge don and Principal of King's College, London, Hugh James Rose, who had been one of the early moving spirits among the Tractarians, having discussed the reform of the Church of England with several of them—Perceval, Froude, Palmer—at his Rectory in Hadleigh from 25 July to 29 July 1833. As editor of the *British Magazine*, he had already provided Newman and his friends with an alternative platform to the *Tracts*.

(i) *Harrison to Newman*

I had a letter from H. Wilberforce[a] the other day asking me to go and see him. I proposed going to him next month some time. He said you seemed to think we might together concoct something. Had you any definite scheme? or only a vague idea of 'making Henry work'.

C. Common

Aug. 19

[1835][1]

My dear Newman,

I fear, from what your Sister told me yesterday you had said in a letter to her, that you have been expecting your letter returned to you before this. I sent the copy with the French translation to the Abbé last Thursday, and yesterday wrote him a line begging him to let me know whether he had received them. The Abbé's last letter told me that he should be able to judge when he received your letter where it must come in the series. On looking to your letter I found that it must follow the Abbé's 7th,[b] as you refer in more places than one to it, and perhaps, though this arrangement interposes a fearful ocean between your first & second letter, it is better that the correspondence shd appear as it really took place, and that it should be seen how long it took to supply a sufficient antidote to your first letter. But since there was thus so much printing to be got through before the good Abbé could set to work on your new letter, I thought you might take things quietly, & not hurry yourself to go on with your second letter. If however you have time just now to spare, perhaps you are disposed to get through it; and when your letters are finished, the Abbé will make haste in the printing with a view to the pleasure of a reply. I should like to see him looking out the words in the English dictionary, in order to do

---

[1] Date entered later in Newman's hand. Harrison had received the draft of Newman's Fourth Letter, Part One, at the end of July (*Letters &c.*, ed. Mozley, ii. 119).

[a] Henry Wilberforce (1807–73), son of the abolitionist William Wilberforce, and brother of Samuel Wilberforce, later Bishop of Oxford, was one of Newman's most intimate friends. Cf. p. 10 and p. 14.

[b] i.e. the 6th in the numbering of this edition.

full justice to the stings which you have been so pitilessly planting in his sides, and making the most *vif* translation of what he will not now complain of, I think, as not 'frapper'ing sufficiently 'fortement'.—Rose[a] is very anxious that the Church History scheme should be kept in sight:—he says at the risk of appearing tiresome we must 'agitate'.

I saw Wood[b] on Monday: he is just going out of town. He has been reading Osborne's ('Doctrinal Errors')[c] and hopes it will be answered. He thinks it fully deserves it (as written in a good tone generally, & evincing some superiority of mind, tho' ill educated) that we 'must admit *some* exaggeration in Ignatius' language';—the doctrine of the early Church respecting Angels was new to him &c. He has just been with Manning.[d] Have you seen his Sermon? I was very glad to see it was so strong. Wood asked me whether I cd make Rivington mind the tracts better.[e] They will not *exhibit* them or put them in the way of their customers.

Bel[ve] me yrs very faithfully & affect

B. Harrison

Newman notes:
Answered Aug 20/35

(ii) *Newman to Harrison* [undated]

[Addressed to: The Revd. B. Harrison Ch. Ch.]

My dear Harrison,
    I think, if I may say it, you have misunderstood the object of my

[a] Rose wished to produce a vast collaborative ecclesiastical history or, failing that, to have Fleury's *Histoire ecclésiastique* translated, a project which Newman in part carried out, two volumes by him appearing in 1842 and 1843. (Cf. Newman to Bowden, in *Letters*, ed. Mozley, ii. 120.) It had, wrote Newman (*Apologia*, ed. Svaglic, p. 75), 'a good deal to do with unsettling me in my Anglicanism'.

[b] Samuel Francis Wood (1810–43), Newman's pupil at Oriel. He was the younger brother of Charles Wood, 1st Viscount Halifax, and Newman refers to him in the *Apologia* as 'an intimate and dear friend'.

[c] A Cambridge man, later well known as an Egyptologist, William Osburn published his *Doctrinal Errors of the Apostolical and Early Fathers* in 1835. Newman was sensitive to attacks on St. Ignatius of Antioch like that made by Osburn, since he founded his doctrine of the Episcopal system upon Ignatius's *Epistles* (*Apologia*, Ch. II). He later wrote an article, 'The Theology of St. Ignatius' (January 1839, reprinted in *Essays Critical and Historical*, i. 186–225), which contains his observations on Osburn's work. W. Cureton (1808–64), who had been Harrison's companion in Paris when he met Jager, published in 1845 a Syriac version of three of St. Ignatius's Epistles, from which certain passages to be found in the Greek text are absent. Newman reprinted his later notes on Cureton and Ignatius in *Tracts Theological and Ecclesiastical*, Ch. II (1871).

[d] Henry Edward Manning (1808–92), Archdeacon of Chichester and, after his conversion, later Cardinal Archbishop of Westminster.

[e] Francis Rivington (1805–85), publisher of the *Tracts for the Times*.

Paper—which was not to answer you, but a Memorandum for myself, a Memorandum which required in me to write, and in you to read, thoughts and inquiries not put upon paper.

My plan was to look through the Indexes of the Fathers and get together all the passages on the subject—to select out of these those which seemed to me most suitable to comment on—then to look at your list—and then at Bellarmine.[a] I examined them all, though I have put down a few. I cannot find one to the point. Basil is the nearest—but, even granting him which still I cannot, he is but one.[b] Some passages I did not quote, from disgust, if I may say it, at the unfairness of adducing them.

My view is this. If a new phrase is introduced into a Confession of Faith it may be done in two ways—first, an *invented* one, when I think it requires a general Council (when the Holy Ghost is present)—next an *hereditary* one, when it requires merely the testimony of those among whom it is hereditary. The ὁμοούσιον[c] is not an instance even of the first (viz. *invented*), as I notice, Arians p. 165 tho' in p. 163, 164 I allow that the Council might *lawfully* have done this. The sola fides[d] &c however was neither the one nor the other. It was not imposed by a general Council—it was not hereditary—nay it was not in antiquity (as I maintain). The reason, I said what I did about a *tessera*,[e] was merely to ascertain that the phrase was not a random expression, which one uses at one time for one purpose, at another for another. For the same reason I spoke of its being handed down from gener[n] to gener[n]. All I want is *to fix it* to one clear meaning. ELSE do not go to antiquity at all. I do not see how it can help us. I am not going to attempt it, but would you (I would not) admit the doctrine of sola poenitentia vita nostra est,[f] if I found it for you in a dozen passages in the Fathers?

If you put it on the ground of *expediency*, as necessary as a strong

---

[a] Robert Bellarmine (1542–1621). A Jesuit theologian frequently referred to by Newman as the authoritative voice of post-Tridentine Catholicism, 'the foremost . . . Catholic controversialist of the Reformation era' (*Via Media*, p. 74 n. 6—an addition to the 3rd ed.).

[b] St. Basil the Great (329–79) wrote against the Arians. Newman devoted three chapters of *The Church of the Fathers* to him (*British Magazine*, 1833; 1840 and reprinted 1873 in *Historical Sketches*).

[c] 'Consubstantial', from the doctrine that God the Father and God the Son are one in 'substance'.

[d] 'faith alone'; the doctrine that man is saved by faith, not by works; referred to in the next paragraph as Solifidianism. Cf. the Thirty-nine Articles, Article xi, 'That we are justified, by Faith only, is a most wholesome doctrine'.

[e] Solid cube of marble or ivory, used as a die or as a token. Newman is presumably using it as a metaphor for something hard and durable.

[f] 'Our life is nothing but penance.'

curb against Pelagianism[a] &c, and say that precedent is not needed in so urgent a case, I understand this ground, and think it an honest one— (though as to the nobleness of it, considering the influx of Solifidian- ism, on the other hand, that is another question). But when the For- mula[b] is made pretend to Antiquity, this seems to me, to speak clearly, not honest. I think neither Bull[c] nor any one else would have attempted it, but to defend what *had been* done. I do not think *he* would have done it. The defence of it by any one on the grounds of Antiquity seems to me the (unwittingly) dishonest *act* of loyal and filial minds desirous to cover their fathers' shame. I do not go and tell the world this—nor am I deciding how far Cranmer is our Father.

As to St. James &c, this Formula seems to me deliberately to con- tradict St. James,[d] which it does not coinciding with St. Paul. In the dozen passages in the Fathers there is no *deliberate* opposition; as well might Ecclus. xxiv, 21[e] be said to oppose John vi. 35.[f]

You used figurata in two senses. I do not consider the Fathers meant necessarily by justification what the article does.

I shall, if you will let me, keep your papers a little while, but shall not make any answer to them; as I had no intention, nor have, to *answer and dispute* but to make notes. So, please, we will now drop the subject, at least I—for till I see my way more clearly about the subject of divine judgement, it is no *practical* point with me.

Ever Yrs affly

John H. Newman

P.S. Will you be so good as to let me have this back at some time, as I wish to keep it as a Memorandum.

---

[a] A heresy in the early Church, the doctrine of the British monk Pelagius, who emphasized the freedom of the human will, diminishing the role of divine grace, and denying original sin: 'Everything good and everything evil . . . is done by us, not born with us.'

[b] Presumably a reference to the Nicene Formula, given the following allusion to Bull; and to Article xi.

[c] George Bull (1634–1710), Bp. of St. David's and author of *Defensio Fidei Nicaenae*, an attempt to show that the Nicene Formula conformed to the teaching of the Fathers. His French Jesuit contemporary, Petau (Petavius) had made out a case to the contrary, in *Dogmata Theologica* (1643).

[d] St. James, Ep. 2: 14–17: 'What shall it profit, my brethren, if a man say he hath faith, but hath not works? shall faith be able to save him? . . . faith also, if it have not works, is dead in itself.'

[e] 'They that eat me shall yet be hungry, And they that drink me shall yet be thirsty.'

[f] John 6: 35: 'And Jesus said unto them, I am the bread of life: he that cometh to me shall never hunger; and he that believeth on me shall never thirst.'

(iii) *Harrison to Newman*

[Newman notes: note prior to all the No^s]

My dear Newman,

[1][I send you back your letter according to your request. I am very sorry to have misunderstood in any way the object of your paper, but I gave it, I assure you, my very best and most earnest attention, and it seemed to me to have the form & character of an argument directed against that which would be drawn from the extracts which I had sent you. I could not possibly know on what other investigations your paper was grounded, as you did not send me your extracts in return, nor tell me what your plan had been. You will at least bear me witness that, in returning your paper, I did not enter into *disputation*, but simply stated why I could not admit your view, I did not argue from St. Basil —I merely put before you his words.]

I send you the Abbé's letter with the new numbers of the Controverse, which I have collated with the former copy. I find only two insertions, which I have marked. He has not, I see, at all availed himself of the permission you gave him to omit any expressions which might seem harsh. I confess after what both you & I said on the tone of our controversy in our first letters, I should like to see any expressions omitted which might *seem* at all triumphant or satirical—though I must admit my friend's longwindedness & evasions were enough to put any one who had to gather the *needles* out of his vast *bundle of hay* thoroughly out of patience.

Might it not be well, too, to look to any expressions which would give any sanction to the Abbé's favourite τόπος,[a] of representing the views we maintain against them as the opinions of *individuals* & not the *doctrines & views* of the Church of England, which as you & Bp Jebb tell him have slept in our cloisters only for a time.[b]

I have been looking to Waterland's Disc^n· of Fundamentals,[c] & cannot but think he shews solid objections to the plan of putting forward the Apostles' Creed as a complete[2] catalogue of fundamentals, in controversy with Romanists. The ground is, as the Abbé says, admitted by our Divines to be thorny, & the discussion seems to come to us from a bad quarter—Geneva—Holland—Lord Bacon: a thoroughly

---

[1] The square brackets seem to be in Newman's hand, not Harrison's.

[2] Note superscribed by Newman: I have never said, at least intentionally, 'complete'.

[a] 'Theme'.   [b] Cf. p. 34.

[c] Daniel Waterland (1683–1740), *A discourse of fundamentals, being the substance of two charges delivered to the Middlesex clergy at the Easter visitations of 1734 and 1735*, Cambridge, 1735 (Repr. in *Works*, ed. W. Van Mildert, 1823, vol. v).

ultra Protestant result of Calvinistic dogmatism. Could you not recall the Abbé from all associations with ultra Protestant controversy by setting strongly before him that by 'fundamentals' we mean simply the rock on which the Church is built,[1] that house of God which has the Scripture in its custody & authoritatively teaches & interprets it, as, in fact, you do in § 17. The question then becomes simply, as you state it in § 13[–]14, Has the Ch[ch] the right to enlarge its own foundation? to call all its own tradition the 'Catholic faith' which must be believed on pain of perfecting everlasting salvation? has it the right to require implicit faith in *itself*, instead of in *Christ*? Of *these* truly Catholic fundamentals may we not say that they are proved to be such by *Scripture* as well as tradition & history? But if there be no salvation but in the Church, and no condemnation for them that believe & are baptized in it, may we not make our 'terms of communion' identical with our 'articles of Faith', required to be believed as 'necessary to salvation'? Once within the Church, (we are agreed) we have only to sit at her feet, and receive piously whatever she has received from Our Lord and his Apostles & Prophets, searching in Scripture whether those things are so.

Must you not also make it clear that you regard the 'Symbolum Apostolicum'[a] as a baptismal confession of the great Catholic authorities: but seeing it did receive continual additions, down to the 5th Cent. & that too in consequence of heresies arising, can you maintain the absolute inadmissibility of additions to the Creed? Is it not, on the other hand, quite competent to say that the Catholic Faith which we profess in Baptism having been fully developed in the Constantinopolitan creed,[b] we are forbidden by the C. of Ephesus[c] to make any new Symbols of Church communion. Heresies which have arisen since have affected not the 'divinitas'[d] but 'creatura'[e] & 'mysteria',[f] the questions respecting the spiritual house of God, not its Divine foundation, as e.g. the Holy Catholic Church, the forgiveness of sins &c. Again, seeing that the Nicene was used as a baptismal Creed, can we argue that, because the Fathers judged charitably of individuals, they would have opened the gate of the Church to any who scrupled the ὁμοούσιον[g] because they doubted of the article [of the] Catholic faith which it declared?

[1] 'fundamenta Fidei Catholicae' as Vincentius speaks.

[a] The Apostles' Creed.
[b] Or Nicene Creed, promulgated at the Council of Constantinople, A.D. 381.
[c] The Council of Ephesus, A.D. 431, defined the Virgin Mary as the Mother of God, and condemned the heresy of Nestorius.
[d] 'Divinity.' Here, 'the divine foundation of the Christian faith'.
[e] 'That which has been produced by belief.'
[f] 'The objects of revelation.'   [g] 'Consubstantial.'

As a minor point, of mere impression, is it an inaccuracy in the[1] original, or in my translation that (in § 17?) the Roman creed is spoken of as though it were itself called 'Symbolum Apostolicum' from the very beginning of Christianity.[a]

In § 4, (you will think I am as endless as the Abbé, but as you told me when you looked over yr letter that I ought to have let you know if I saw anything to object to in it, I will tell you now every thing that strikes me) might it not be well to guard against the impression that the Church of England, in her *principles* as well as in her modern *practice,* is not strict enough against diversities of opinion within her pale?

Thus you see, I have fully stated any difficulty which I meet with in looking again over your letter. The Abbé is so fond of expatiating in the fields of Ultra-Protestant controversy, attacking Luther, Calvin & views which do not concern us, that it seems of the greatest importance to keep constantly before him the 'peculiar character of the Church of England',[b] as Bp Jebb put it before him from authoritative documents & standard writers of our Church, compared with Vincentius & his maxim.

It is rather a nuisance that he has sent only the first sheet of your letter, & says (I see) that the press is waiting to complete the 11th Livraison.

Believe me,
my dear Newman,
yrs. ever affectionately
Benj. Harrison

Ch. Ch.
Nov. 28th [1835]

Newman notes: [*Dec. 22. To this I answered at the time, that I had considered his objections, but having already taken Stillingfleet's basis with the Abbé,[c] I could not take Waterland's[d] without the chance of slipping between two stools. JHN*]

Wd. you be kind enough to lend me, if you do not want it just at present, yr. paper on the Rule of Faith. I will return it to you very soon—but I shd like to read it over more quietly than one can hear it in public.

---

[1] your *deleted*

[a] Para. 17 of Newman's Second Letter, p. 83.

[b] The title of Jebb's work which Jager was using as one of his sources on Anglican beliefs (v. Bibliography, Jebb).

[c] Newman had referred to Stillingfleet's discussion of infallibility and fundamentals in the latter's work on Laud's controversy with Fisher the Jesuit, *A Rational Account of the Grounds of Protestant Religion* etc. (v. Bibliography, Stillingfleet).

[d] Cf. p. 154, n. c.

And I shd be obliged for yg. Acland's[a] second vol. of Knox's (Remains)[b] I think you have it.

Newman notes: *Dec. 22, 1835. NB. The reason I did not allude to this letter afterwards, nor copy out in the passage for Rose any but my argument about Christ's 'Canons & Sentences', was, that I thought his next letter was about that argt and that only.*

At least, I was much puzzled & am now what else he could mean. He talks of my 'theory'? for a long time I was quite in the dark what he alluded to. I was conscious that my general line of argt was from Stillingfleet upon Laud. I talked a good deal with Rogers with a view to make this out.

At last I decided, though not satisfactorily, that by my 'theory', wh he opened his letter (No. 1) with, was my argt about Christ's Sentences wh was the only part of the whole to which I could advance any claim of property. And therefore I copied it out for Rose.

Now it seemed by H's note just received (No. 2) it is not his great subject of complaint. What then after all is my 'theory'?

(iv) *Harrison to Newman*

Newman notes:
N.B. Harrison borrowed my paper 'to look over it more calmly than he could hear it read'—without a word to prepare me,* this note came back with it(?) two days after it was returned—it had been kept some few days
JHN

* (a former letter had been returned with a letter of criticisms and objections paper.)

[No. 1][1]

My dear Newman,

I hope you found your MS. yesterday evening in your rooms. I have studied it with the deepest attention, and will most candidly and unreservedly lay before you the result.

Our object, in the Controversy with the Abbé, was to put forward

---

[1] Newman's numbering.

[a] T. D. Acland (1809–98), a close friend of Newman's until the latter's conversion. Fellow of All Souls 1831–7, M.P. 1837–47.

[b] Alexander Knox (1757–1831), a friend of John Jebb, and forerunner of the Oxford Movement. His *Remains* were published in four vols. 1834–7. His correspondence with Jebb was published in 1834: *Thirty Years' Correspondence between John Jebb, D.D., F.R.S., Bishop of Limerick, Ardfert and Aghadoe, and Alexander Knox, Esq., M.R.I.A.* (ed. C. Forster). Brilioth (*Anglican Revival*, p. 47) traces the first use of the term *medium* (i.e. *Via Media*) to Knox. Cf. his discussion of the relationship of Knox to the ideas of the Tractarians, op. cit., App. I, 330–3.

the peculiar system of the Church of England: instead of this your letter contains what you yourself speak of as a 'theory' of your own: —a theory moreover, which seems to be essentially Ultra-Protestant, & the tendency of which followed out to its consequences would be, I fear, to sweep away the teaching of the Church altogether, & bring in utter liberalism, scepticism, & infidelity, or else to give us over to enthusiasm, to Popery, or Socinian blasphemy. My words may seem harsh and passionate; but does not your argument, calmly considered in its *consequences*, bear them out? I wish to awaken your close attention. 'The Divine Message which contains what a Christian must believe in order to salvation is' laid down to be '*Scripture* & nothing else'.[1] There is no tradition in the Christian Church, as in the Patriarchal; or it is superseded. Scripture & nothing else is 'the oracle of God, claiming the joint assent of all Christians to its declarations';[2] 'the exclusive witness of things supernatural, the basis & bond of union between Christians, as far as faith is concerned'.[3] This assertion 'I receive on historical evidence'.[4]

'The number of *credenda* in' this 'Scripture varies according to circumstances':[5] 'Saving faith varies with the capacity & advantages of individuals.'[6] 'A supernatural & private assurance of the truth of a certain tradition would make it canonical to the individual' (supposing the case); 'another may have some natural defect of mind disabling him from apprehending truths clearly revealed in Scripture. Prejudice & the like are of similar importance in the question. We can only say, 'Every one must believe so far forth as the truth is brought home to his mind, and sufficiently presented for his acceptance'.[7] He must, indeed, believe in 'the name of the Father, the Son, & the Holy Ghost' (Matt. 28) & confess 'that Jesus Christ is come in the flesh' (1 John 4): 'but when we pass beyond this, there is no limit. One man may see more in Scripture; another, less.'[8]

This Scripture has, indeed, 'but one sense';[9] and men are bound to take it in this sense. But then 'there may be some natural defect of mind—prejudices & the like. We can only say every one must believe so far forth as the truth is brought home to his mind, & suffic^ly presented for his acceptance'.[10] And then he may have a 'supernatural & private assurance'[11] that the Catholic sense is false. A goodly field, surely, for private judgement and the inward light! and where is the end to be?

But 'of this Scripture truth a certain portion has been taken as the condition of communion with the Church, & called the Creed. *Some* confession of faith was necessary unless open infidels were to be ad-

[1] p. 118.   [2] p. 120.   [3] Ibid.   [4] p. 121.   [5] p. 120.   [6] Ibid.
[7] Ibid.   [8] Ibid.   [9] p. 121.   [10] p. 120.   [11] Ibid.

mitted. But why these articles were taken, & no others, why our Creed is what it is, I am not bound to shew:—it is a matter of historical fact. This Creed I may impose but nothing else'.[1] As matter of historical fact, this Creed is the Creed of the Church of Rome as it stood finally complete in the 5th cent^y; till that time it had been growing with the growth of heresy: at that period, the Romanist will say, Pagan Rome fell, and the Kingdom of Christ was established; but after the 1000 years Satan was loosed; Hildebrand recognised it in his age:—for 500 years however the Church endured it, but then Antichrist appeared, & there was an open revolt in Christendom (λουτερ[a] or some such thing being the Apocalyptic number), & were 'open infidels' to be admitted to Church communion'?[2] No: Rome returned to primitive practice: she enlarged still further her Creed; why the articles of the Creed of P. Pius were taken and no others, I am not bound to shew; why the Roman (or Apostolic) Creed is what it is:—it is matter of historical fact.

But, looking again to Scripture as our only Rule, we are told Christ is a *lawgiver*, & the Gospel is a New *Law*, like the Mosaic. God spake the ten Commandments from Mount Sinai, but afterwards He wrote them.[3] So Our Lord first spake His own Gospel, both of promise & precept, on the Mount, & His Evangelists have recorded it. His other discourses are all solemn declarations, canons, sentences, precepts, such as *Legislators* utter, & scribes & lawyers comment on, a *Sacred text*, to be the subject of investigation & interpretation. 'Christ is the Supreme Teacher & Prophet: the *Lawgiver* of the New Dispensation has with His own mouth declared the necessary matters of the Law'. 'His perfect *Law* is written in the Gospels. He names the Name of the Father, & the Son & the Holy Ghost.'[4] Are the Epistles then excluded from the canon of faith? [yes?[b] for] the doctrines of our faith are really promulgated by Christ Himself. 'The Epistles are' a comment to bring out & fix the sacred sense: a comment 'such as scribes & lawyers make'[5] on the text of a Law.) The Apostles are interpreters of Christ's doctrine & so is the Church after them. This is a question of historical fact. Councils 'always went "ad legem & ad testimonium" to the testament of Our Saviour, the document of His words & doings, as

[1] p. 121.   [2] Ibid.
[3] This sentence and the two following correspond to pp. 123–4.
[4] pp. 124, 129.   [5] Ibid.

[a] Luther. The reference is to the Apocalypse, 13. Both Greek and Hebrew use letters for numbers, and attempts were made to decipher the name of the beast of the Apocalypse from his number, 666.

[b] The question-mark appears to be in another hand, probably Newman's. The square brackets also do not appear to be Harrison's; though the bracket which follows 'of a Law') is left without an opening bracket.

commented on and developed by the Apostles'.[1] [Here I am quite perplexed: for I thought you held that it was always the main business of Councils simply to bear witness to what the members of them had themselves received,—what they had taught & heard from their youth up—I thought you accused our Reformers because (as you thought) our Articles had a *Scriptural* origin, which made them worth hardly anything, mere opinions of one set of men in one age, human interpretations, private judgements,—imposed as matters of faith for every age. But let this pass.] Christ then remains our only Lawgiver & the Apostles may be well-instructed scribes & expositors[2]—but 'ad legem & ad testimonium['] 'Christ's words were short and concise':[3]—there is no context to be examined logically:—'His words were the power of God'.[4] Our Blessed Lord thus held forth as the only Lawgiver, & the Sermon on the Mount as His Law,[5] his other discourses being taken by single verses, as so many independent oracles, we know the rest; for this is the very field of heresy: the disciples of the school of Priestley[a] will reap what we have sown—& an abundant harvest!

But St. John, let us remember, wrote his Gospel as supplementary to the others;[6] & when he says 'He that saw it &c' he 'implies that in things supernatural the written testimony of the original witness is necessary for exacting belief in them'.[7] Now he and St. Matthew were the only original witnesses, who have left us written testimony & St. Matthew in all probability did not hear the Sermon on the Mount. Christians! where is your 'new Law'? 'We know that God spake by Moses':[b] we *heard* Him speak; and He himself wrote His words on two tables of stone, & Moses received from His hands the lively oracles to give unto us. But as for Him who is *reported* to have spoken on the Mount, we know not whence He is! St. John's concluding words imply that enough for saving faith is contained in his own Gospel. This Gospel we will interpret, as a Law full of Divine oracular sentences—'My Father is greater than I'[c] &c.—And then—as matter of historical fact,—(Blanco White will tell us)[d] St. John set at nought,

---

[1] p. 133.   [2] p. 128.   [3] p. 124.
[4] Cf. p. 124.   [5] Cf. ibid.
[6] p. 127.   [7] p. 128.

[a] Joseph Priestley (1733–1804), Nonconformist minister, scientist, and theological writer.

[b] John 9: 29.   [c] John 14: 28.

[d] Joseph Blanco White (1775–1841), a Spaniard and one-time Catholic priest who apostatised and drifted into unbelief. He was one of the Oriel Noetics from 1826, and Newman and he worked together for a time. At the time Harrison was writing, Blanco White had recently published *Observations on Heresy and Orthodoxy*.

or 'excommunicated by the Church', does not refer to any rule of Scripture—to 'any fixed standard of faith'—'he refers to the judgment of each individual Christian—"Let that therefore abide in you wh^{ch} ye have *heard* (no written documents mentioned) from the beginning"^{a}— "Ye know all things" '.^{b}

And for the doctrine of the Divinity of the Holy Spirit, 'our Lord says "He shall guide you into all truth"^{c}—by a new revelation?—as though the Holy Spirit were the Divine Teacher of the Church?—no; the Divine Speaker goes on, "*whatsoever He shall hear*"^{d}—a plain intimation that the inspired teaching of the Apostles would be in its substance a comment upon the *Sacred* words of Christ, not an independent revelation'—as though the Holy Spirit '*heard*' only 'the sacred words which Christ spoke *on earth*! and the promise were, perhaps, merely one of individual guidance by means of a *secret influence called the Spirit* of Christ; of which influence it is said that it will guide the believers into all the truth?;' meaning perhaps 'reasonable motives operating upon the will', perhaps some supernatural and private assurance of the truth of certain traditions & doctrines[.]^1 As to the doctrine of the Divinity of the Holy Spirit as declared at the Council of Constantinople: Gregory Nazianzen himself tells us that it was not clearly revealed till after the Ascension but reserved for later times than those of the New Testament, saying ὁ ἀθετῶν ἀθετείτω, ὁ ἀνομῶν ἀνομείτω. ἡμεῖς ὃ νενοήκαμεν, κηρύσσομεν^e—treating the doctrine as a εὐσεβέςτερα ἔννοια^f which, under the guidance of that Holy Spirit, *he* had received, & would hold to the end of his life, endeavouring to bring others to receive it also. Doubtless 'a supernatural & private assurance' of the truth of a certain doctrine (for Gregory does not pretend that it was a tradition) would make it canonical to the individual: but shall a Council therefore impose it upon all Christians to the end of the world?

And thus we are left desolate, among the blasphemies of Unitarianism!

My dear Newman, are these things so, or not? it surely becomes us most seriously to consider, and you will thank me for recalling your attention to (what appear to me) *unguarded* statements of which the Enemy of our faith might, as it strikes me most painfully, take fearful

---

^{1} p. 120.

^{a} 1 John 2: 24. ^{b} John 15: 15.
^{c} John 16: 13. ^{d} Ibid.

^{e} Gregory of Nazianzus, *Theological Orations*, v, 'On the Holy Spirit': 'He that rejects it, let him reject it; he that does wrong, let him do wrong; we proclaim what we understood.' A reference by Gregory to Isa. 21: 2. Emphasis added by Harrison.

^{f} 'pious notion'.

advantage, in these our dangerous days. Believe me your faithful and affᵗᵉ friend

Benj. Harrison

Ch. Ch.
Dec. 2. 1835

Newman noted:

N.B. Dec. 5.

In the case of so mad a letter—(that is, a formal & violent charge urged without previous conversation or inquiry of me, or appeal to Pusey who had approved the paper, & on a man's own private judgment in most serious matters,)—a familiar explanation was out of place, and (which is a better reason) in answer to so [prejudiced] prepossessed a letter it would have been perfectly useless—so I wrote him a short note* saying that I would consider what he said attentively—that I did not know what he meant by saying I confessed to a theory—that, if I spoke of *my* theory, it was that the abbé might not confuse me with Chillingworthª &c. and that my main view was from Stillingfleet.
Dec. 5. 1835

* The note was

My dear H.
Thank you for your letter, which I will study.
It is quite a mistake in you, to suppose my view is meant to be a 'theory' of my own. I cannot conceive where you think I have said so. If in the introduction of my 2nd letter to the Abbé, I have only said so, (i.e. that I have a right to choose my own ground) that he may not bring agst me Chillingworth &c. I believe I have taken it entirely from Stillingfleet on Laud. I am not aware of anything orig¹· in it.

ever yrs
J.H.N.
(signed)

ª William Chillingworth (1602–44), Laud's spy in Oxford, who was for a time converted to Roman Catholicism, and returned to the Church of England in 1634. Scripture interpreted by reason was the basis of his religious theory. Cf. *The Religion of Protestants a Safe Way of Salvation* (1638) and *A Discussion against the Infallibility of the Roman Church*, printed as an Additional Discourse to the former in the 1704 edition (*Works*, London, 3 vols., 1820; and Oxford, 3 vols., 1838).

(v) *Extracts from Newman's paper on the Rule of Faith,*
excerpted, with comments, for Hugh James Rose

Dec. 14. 1835 The principal objection was not to the passage here
            extracted. (vid. my note on back of his first note of all.
            dated by me Dec 22   JHN)

N.B. A certain paper of mine on the Rule of Faith has had the following
judgment pronounced upon it, and (as I understand) on account principally of a particular position of it. Here follow first the judgment, the
portion *chiefly* (?) objected to. JHN
    Our object etc.
    'Your letter contains what you yourself speak of as a "theory" of
your own:—a theory, moreover, which seems to me essentially Ultra-
Protestant, and the tendency of which followed out to its consequences
would be, I fear, to sweep away the teaching of the Church altogether,
and bring in utter liberalism, scepticism, and infidelity, or else to give
us over to enthusiasm, to Popery, or Socinian blasphemy.' My words
may seem harsh and passionate, but DOES NOT your argument, calmly
considered in its *consequences*, bear them out? I wish to awaken your
close attention.
    'I know that your former letter would fully explain it etc. etc.

    Extracts from a paper in defence of Scripture being the sole Rule
    of Faith, i.e. authoritative document for proving necessary truth.

. . . Let us first see what light Scripture itself will throw upon the
question in dispute.
    The very circumstance that the Gospel is called by St. Paul a Cove-
nant and Will, and parallelled to the Mosaic Covenant, and that the
Law was *written*, as in the books of Exodus, Leviticus and the rest,
leads us, or at least prepares us, to believe that the New Law is written
also.
    This analogy, however faint at first, is strengthened and sanctioned
by the actual mode under which the New Law was first promulgated,
viz with an intentional resemblance to the giving of the Mosaic. God
spoke the Ten Commandments from Mount Sinai first of all, but afterwards He wrote them. So in matter of fact, our Lord first spoke His
own gospel, both of promise and precept, on the Mount, and His
Evangelists have recorded it. Moreover, He Himself in a measure
parallelled it to the Ten Commandments when He delivered it, as

when He commented on the 6th and 7th of the Decalogue; there is so far no room for mistaking about it.

Consider too His discourses all through the Gospels, and see if they do not partake of this one and the same character, the character of solemn declarations, canons, sentences, proverbs, such as Legislators utter and scribes and lawyers comment on. Surely every thing He did and said partakes of this character of depth, condensation, and mystery. His emblematical actions, His typical miracles, His parables, His conclusions, all are evidence of a legislation in germ afterwards to be developed, a sacred text which was ever to be before men's eyes and to be the subject of investigation and interpretation, and the guide in controversy. [']Verily, verily I say unto you,' 'But I say unto you', are the tokens of a Supreme Teacher and Prophet.

And thus the Fathers speak. 'His sayings,' says St. Justin 'were short and concise; for He was no rhetorician, but His word was the power of God.' Apol. i. 14. And St. Basil observes to the same effect, 'Every deed and every word of our Saviour Jesus Christ is a canon of piety and virtue. When then thou hearest word of deed of His, do not hear it as by the way, or after a simple and casual manner, but enter into the depth of His contemplations, become a proselyte of truths mystically delivered to thee.' Constit. Monast. c. 1.

You will say, that, granting this, it does not follow that His perfect Law should be written in the Gospels. I answer that it is in matter of fact recorded in the Gospels as regards the most solemn and ample enunciation of one especial part of it, I mean in the Sermon on the Mount. On the other hand, Tradition does not in matter of fact hand down any sentences of the Savior but those which are in the Gospels. If the New Law be conveyed in canons and precepts, it is contained in the Gospels or it is no where. The force of this argument will be illustrated by considering the single exception to it which is furnished in a passage of the Acts of the Apostles, where St. Paul records a saying of Christ's which is not preserved by the Evangelists; 'It is more blessed to give than to receive.' Act. 20. 35. Now here moreover we have fresh proof that our Lord's teaching was conveyed in canons and maxims; yet why is it that none other are preserved in the Epistles, why do we not find a store of them in the early Church, if He had actually deigned to speak others for its edification? I do not of course presume to limit the abundance of His communications in the case of those who lay upon His breast or conversed with Him for forty days after His resurrection; nor do I deny that He communicated to them much orally for the well ordering and the due guidance of the Church. But I speak of what He communicated in the great matters of the New Law, of what He told them in order that they should tell again; and

I say it is remarkable, to say the least, that, if He did promulgate much over and above what is written in the Gospels, no traces are left of it in the records of the early Church. In addition to the instance from the Acts of the Apostles, may be mentioned two others, one preserved by several early writers, the other by St. Jerome;—'Be ye approved money-changers—'[a] and 'Be ye never very glad, but when ye see your brother live in charity.'[b] Surely here 'exceptio probat regulam', as the proverb goes. I might then (for argument's sake) grant to the Romanist the authority of Tradition; and then say to him, 'Now you have permission to add to Christ's Law, adduce your Sentences.'

An inspection of our Lord's separate discourses confirms the view I am taking. Of course I do not mean to say He never speaks but 'in proverbs' (to use His own words) yet if we take what is recorded of His conversation with Nicodemus, we shall find it summed up in the concise and pregnant enunciations on which it turned. Every verse is a canon of Divine Truth. His discourse to the Jews in the 5th chapter of St. John's Gospel is perhaps a still more striking instance of this. To convey my meaning in other words, I should say that in the Epistles almost every thing is contained in the text itself immediately before us, as it comes. Indeed one great fallacy of heretical interpretation has been to measure the depth of the text by the context, as in John. x. in the passage ending 'I and My Father are one—' (which means far more than the context renders necessary.)

It is a further corroboration that we have actual evidence from the gospels themselves, that our Saviour, in the midst of His condescension, was *not* profuse in His words and actions, as far as *variety* goes. He utters the same precepts again and again, and repeats His miracles.

Further, if the gospels, as you maintain, contain so imperfect a revelation of the Christian Covenant, how it is that even in your account, almost all the rudiments of the Truth revealed in it are in them? By what accident does Scripture contain so much, since it does not (as they aver) contain all. Nay, why was it given at all, unless for some peculiar and singular purpose? If it is to be the record of the saving truths of the gospel, a rule of [for] Tradition and teaching, this indeed is intelligible; else it seems to hold no definite position in the system. If it contains so much and not all, it seems to suggest for itself an end which it does not fulfil. You allow that Baptism and the Lord's Supper are the great ordinances of the New Law, and have a priority of rank over the other Sacraments. Now if you ground this on their being expressly ordained in Scripture, you seem to confess that the things prescribed therein are of more importance than those

[a] Origen, *in Joh*: xix; Clem. Alex. *Strom.*, i. 28. 177.
[b] Jerome, *in Ephes.* 5[3f].

derived through the medium of Tradition. If you do not, it rests with you to account for the accidental coincidence of their being prescribed in Scripture and their also being the chief ordinances of the gospel. Certainly, as far as it goes, this circumstance leads to the surmise that Scripture is really the record of the great matters of the New Law. I give this instance of the (Two) Sacraments by way of illustration, as one out of various similar instances leading to that one conclusion. But on this subject I cannot do better than quote the words of our celebrated Divine, Bp Jeremy Taylor. 'Is not all that we know of the life and death of Jesus, set down in the writings of the New Testament? Is there any one miracle that ever Christ did, the notice of which is conveyed to us by Tradition? Do we know any thing that Christ did or said but what is in Scripture? . . . How is it possible that the Scriptures should not contain all things necessary to salvation, when of all the words of Christ,—in which certainly all necessary things to salvation must needs be contained, or else they were never revealed,—there is not any one saying, or miracle, or story of Christ, in any thing that is material, preserved in any undubitable record, but in Scripture alone?' (*Dissuasive from Popery* part 2. book i § 2.)

To this view of the subject the words of St. John in the end of his gospel are singularly accordant. Let it be remembered that he wrote his gospel as supplementary to the others. Say then whether the following passages do not show that the inspired Apostle was sealing up the records of our Savior's life and of the Christian Law, after selecting from what remained unnoticed by the other Evangelists, such additional materials as were necessary for the strength and comfort of faith; say whether the following passages, taken together, are consistent with the notion that our faith in greater matters is in matter of fact left to the mere information of Tradition, however well authenticated. 'There are also *many other things* which Jesus did, the which, if they should be written every one, I suppose that even the world itself could not contain the books that should be written.' 'Many other signs truly did Jesus in the presence of His disciples, which are not written in this book: but these are written that ye might believe that Jesus is the Christ the Son of God, and that believing ye might have life through His name.' 'He that saw it bear(s) record and His record is true; and he knoweth that he saith true, *that ye might believe.*' John xxi. 25. xx. 30–31. xix. 35. Here St. John, closing the record of our Lord's life, declares that out of the numberless things which might be added to the former gospels, he has added so much as is necessary for faith, and implies moreover (as a principle) that in things supernatural the written testimony of the original witness is necessary for exacting belief in them.

I know that Bellarmine, in replying to one of these passages, argues, that the supernatural things attested by St. John are miracles, not doctrines; but surely this is over subtle, and little in accordance with that spirit of faith honorably displayed by the Church of Rome on very many occasions, which profitably enlarges the sense of Scripture by detecting principles in the particular instances under which they happen to be conveyed. I suppose you agree with us in interpreting our Lord's words 'Suffer the little children etc.' (Matt. xix. 14) to be a permission of infant baptism, yet one can fancy a grudging mind resolved to see nothing of a great principle in it, nothing more than the mere letter conveys. Surely, when St. John speaks of 'believing' he does not mean 'belief' in *miracles* only, but he says that what he has written is enough for faith generally, is necessary in order that we may believe. What he says in the first instance of one kind of supernatural truth, miracles, may be said of another doctrine.

But this view of the text may be illustrated by directing your attention to St. Augustine's comment upon it, which Bellarmine in vain attempts to explain away. Though I have not yet formally arrived at the consideration of the testimony of the Fathers on the subject, I am sure you will excuse the irregularity. St. Augustine says as follows; 'Whatever of His own deeds and words Christ wished us to read, He bade the Apostles write as though it had been with His own hand.' (Austin. de consens. Evang. cap. ult.) Again he says elsewhere 'The Holy Evangelist testifies that the Lord Christ said and did many things, which are not written. Those were selected for writing, which appeared to be sufficient for the salvation of believers.' tract. in Joann. 49.

My present argument has gone on the supposition that our Lord Christ, the Lawgiver of the New Dispensation, has with His own mouth delivered the necessary matters of the Law. Against this hypothesis, you will make two objections, which I will answer both at once. You will say that I have proved too much, viz that I have excluded, not only Tradition, but the Apostolic Epistles, not to say the Old Testament, from the Canon of faith, confining it to our Lord's words,—which is a conclusion contradictory of our 7th Article;—next that the peculiar doctrines of the gospel are found not in the Evangelists; but in the gospels; so that my theory of the exclusively prophetical character of our Lord's teaching over all other does not hold.

I reply that the doctrines of our faith *are* really promulgated by Christ Himself, though the Apostles declare them more frequently. He names 'the Name of the Father, the Son, and the Holy Ghost.' He announces Himself as 'the Only Begotten Son, given by the Father, that whosoever believeth in Him should not perish, but have everlasting life;' 'the Son of man which is in heaven;' 'having glory with the Father before the world was;' 'giving His flesh for the life of the world,' 'giving His life a ransom instead of many.' If we had only the gospels, we should have in them all the great doctrines contained in the Epistles.

However, God has given us the Epistles as a comment on our Lord's teaching, to bring out and fix His sacred sense, that we might not miss it. Now this drift of the Apostle's writings is plainly declared by our Lord when He promised them His Holy Spirit to guide them. 'I have yet many things to say unto you, but ye cannot bear them now. Howbeit when He, the Spirit of truth is come, He will guide you into all truth.' Now so far it would seem as if a new revelation (as to its matter) was to have been made them; but the Divine Speaker proceeds; 'for He shall not speak of Himself, but *whatsoever He shall hear*, that shall He speak, and He will show you things to come. *He shall glorify Me; for He shall receive of Mine*, and shall show it unto you.' John xvi 12–14. Again—'These things have I spoken unto you, being yet present with you. But the Comforter, which is the Holy Ghost, whom the Father will send in My name, He shall teach you all things, and *bring all things to your remembrance, whatsoever I have said unto you.*' John xiv. 25. 26. From hence it seems that, together with imparting prophetical inspiration, the office of the Holy Ghost lay especially in illuminating the Son, in throwing luster upon and drawing luster from all which belonged to His person, His words and deeds, His trials and sufferings, and especially (in particular) *His words.* 'He shall speak what things soever He shall *hear'*, 'He shall suggest whatever I have said to you.' Surely this is a plain intimation that the inspired teaching of the Apostles would be in its substance a comment upon the sacred words of Christ, an expansion of them, while they recorded them, not an independent revelation; except indeed so far as it was prophetic, 'He shall show you things to come,' which applies to the Apocalypse and certain scattered notices in the Epistles.

The same general meaning is included in a later verse of the same chapter. 'These things have I spoken with you in proverbs, but the time cometh when I shall no more speak unto you in proverbs, but I shall show you plainly of the Father.'

Now observe how remarkably our Lord's parting charge recorded by another Evangelist, agrees with the view I have been maintaining. 'All power is given unto Me etc . . . Go ye therefore and disciple all the nations etc. *teaching them to keep all things whatever I have commanded you.*' The revelation (as regards its matter) was already made, the gospel committed to them. They had but to preach it in the power of Him who promised to be with them alway even unto the end.

This then is the true character of the Apostolic writings; they are comments on our Lord's words; and the more we examine, the more perhaps we shall find them answer to this character. The same conclusion is drawn from such passages of the Gospels as the following; which show clearly that during our Lord's ministry the Apostles were laying up in their minds stores of doctrines which they were not intended to understand or at least to reveal till after the Holy Spirit came. 'These things understood not His disciples at the first; but, when Jesus was glorified, then remembered they that these things were written of Him, and that they had done these things into Him.' 'What I do, thou knowest not now, but thou shalt know hereafter.' 'He charged them that they should tell no man what things they had seen, till the Son of man were risen from the dead. And they kept that saying with themselves, questioning one with another what the rising from the dead should mean.' 'What I tell you in darkness, that speak ye in light; and what ye hear in the ear, that preach ye upon the house-tops.' John xii. 16. xiii. 7. Mark. ix. 9. 10. Matt. x. 27. (add a remarkable instance Acts xi. 16.)

I think I have shown that, though Christ be the chief Prophet of the Church, yet His Apostles' writings may form part of the Rule of Faith, as expounders of His divine maxims.

And as for the Old Testament, He Himself has settled the canonicity of that venerable portion of Divine Truth, by formally appealing to it as authority; so that to receive it is but obedience to some of those very sentences or dicta, of which I have been speaking. And here by the bye let it be noted that He has no where pronounced any similar recognition of the Apocrypha, however He may have vouchsafed to appeal or allude to certain passages in it. But to return.

You will reply, I suppose, to the foregoing statement, that you allow so much willingly; only you contend, that, as the Apostles are interpreters of Christ's doctrine, so the Church is after them.

Now it would be some sort of answer to this objection to refer to the words with which St. John closes the Apocalypse, which certainly do seem, considering He was the last of the Apostles, not merely to apply to his own visions, but to conclude and seal up for ever what was in fact the supplement and compilation of the inspired volume itself; especially since his gospel, itself supplementary to the others, is closed, as we have been, in a similar way. It is an additional confirmation, that the Old Testament also has an ending of parallel solemnity, however different in the expression of it; and this, though the prophecy of Malachi is in itself a complete and detached book as well as the Apocalypse. However, waiving whatever argument is deducible from Scripture on this point, I prefer to come to the plain question of historical fact; whether the early Church did or did not consider the Canon of Faith closed and completed in the written word. The Fathers alone can answer this question; and I appeal to their writings. Did they consider the Canon confined to the books of the Old and New Testament, or did they not? I maintain they did.

The mode pursued by the early Church in deciding matters of doctrine seems to have been as follows. When a novel doctrine was started, the first question which the neighbouring Bishops asked each other, was, 'Has this come down to us?' The answer being in the negative, they at once put it down on the just principle of this antecedent argument. The prevailing opinion of the Church was a sufficient, an overpowering objection against it. When however the matter came before a Council, when it was discussed, when they reasoned, and proved, they never went in matters of saving faith by Tradition only, but they guided and (if I may say so) steered and steadied their course by the written word. Tradition was no longer more than a subordinate guide, as explaining, illustrating, reconciling the Scriptures; it was in no true sense a Canon or Rule, an oracle of Truth. Then, as under the Old Covenant, the appeal was made 'To the Law and the Testimony,' Is. viii, to the Testament of the Savior, the document of His words and doings, as commented on and developed by the inspired Apostles.

etc.

(Then follows a number of citations from the Fathers in proof of this.)

(vi) (undated note by Newman; clearly meant to accompany the copy for Rose)

N.B.

Concerning the above I observe

1. as to the *argument*, it is put *as* an argument more completely in the Recapitulation, being here treated more in the way of exposition or teaching, as unfolding (what is familiarly called) the lie of the country.

2. as to the *theory* itself, the simple question is whether it is *essentially* ultra Protestant, inconsistent in its necessary developments with our received doctrine—for that it is imperfect, one side of the Truth &c is nihil ad rem, since it is but a few pages out of a long letter of at least 5 parts. e.g. shortly before the above extract, I have the following passage—'Scripture has one and but one sense, however men may differ in their views about it. That one sense is not unknown or obscure, it is the sense in which the Church Catholic has ever understood it, the sense in which the whole Christian world from the

beginning or for many centuries maintained, & which when abandoned, and so far as it was abandoned, was not superseded by another Catholic interpretation, but by discordant opinions, the test of error—which moreover, after all corruptions & losses is nevertheless held unanimously in great measure by the whole Church even now. Every individual, who does not take it in that one sense, will be excused only on the ground of unavoidable ignorance, whether from want of instruction &c

Appendix III

Correspondence between Newman and Richard Hurrell Froude on the controversy

There are occasional references to the Jager controversy in the letters to and from Froude printed in *Letters and Correspondence of John Henry Newman*, ed. Anne Mozley, London, Longmans, 1891, vol. ii. The text has been doctored here and there, as also has the text of Froude's letters to Newman which appear in Froude's *Remains* (Vol. i, London, Rivington, 1838). The letter printed on p. 417 of the first volume of the *Remains* rehearses a supposed dialogue between Newman and a 'Romanist'. In the manuscript, the term 'Romanist' is not used, and it is the abbé Jager who is named. The arguments are, of course, Froude's own, based on his idea of what Jager is about; Newman wrote in similar vein to Froude, as the following correspondence will show.

(i) *Froude to Newman*

[*Newman notes*: answered July 20/35]

Carissime N.

My Father has set me to write to you to say that as I have been recommended sea bathing we are at present in a large house in Torbay close on the shore—also that the fare from Oxford to Southampton is one pound—2nd that a steamer leaves Southampton 20 minutes after the Oxford coach gets there, and will take you to Cowes for 3d; 3rd that every Tuesday and Friday at ½ past 6 in the evening the Brunswick Steamer passes Cowes and lands passengers as you know at Torquay at six next morning for 25s. so that from Oxford to Torquay is 22 hours, £2 8s. which with coachmen porters &c may amount to £2 15s.

If you can but get someone to take your duty one Sunday, I am sure the lark will do you good and that the money will not be grossly miss-spent. Please to think of it, and if you will write a line our boat will meet you at Torquay when the Brunswick comes in. My F[ather] will think it a great favour if you come. And you can go back the same way. I am afraid I shall not be much at Oxford myself—much as I wish it; For if there is any chance of the sea doing me good I should give it fair play. We are only just arrived here, i.e. yesterday morning—and I have not yet bathed, but hope to do so tomorrow—My cough is just where it was when I wrote last to you, i.e. just at the standard where it has been stationary so long—and I doubt the power of physic to move me much farther.

[1]And now I will have another go at you about your rule of faith in fundamentals. This is a supposed dialogue between you and the Abbé J.H.N. I deny it. M. l'Abbé. Why? J.H.N. Because it cannot be proved from Scripture. M. l'Abbé. Do you think this (supposing it granted) a sufficient argument—i.e. do you think it certain that no Doctrine is fundamental which cannot be proved from Scripture? J.H.N. Yes. M. l'Abbé. Supposing I could show that the early Christians (say of the 2nd and 3rd centuries) regarded the Doctrine of the Eucharist as fundamental should you still say that it was not so, because it cannot be proved from Scripture? J.H.N. No, in that case I should admit that it was fundamental; but you cannot show it. M. l'Abbé. Then you admit your reason for not thinking this Doctrine fundamental is not that it is not proved by Scripture but that it was not held such by the early Xtians. J.H.N. My reason for not thinking it fundamental is that it is not proved by Scripture. M. l'Abbé. But in spite of this reason you would think it fundamental if the Fathers thought so—i.e. you admit your own reason to be inconclusive. You admit that even after you had made good your assertion that the Doctrine cannot be proved from Scripture you would also have to make good that the Fathers did not think it fundamental. J.H.N. I admit this but still adhere to my original proposition.

M. l'Abbé. You have admitted that it is not enough to show that a Doctrine cannot be proved by Scripture in order to prove it not fundamental. Do you think it enough to show that a Doctrine can be proved from Scripture in order to prove it fundamental? N. No I do not think that. M. l'Abbé. Then you have proposed as a test of fundamentality one which being complied with does not prove Doctrines fundamental and being not complied with does not prove them not so.

I will not write any more about this, as I suspect you will skip; but to recur to myself—I don't think I gain flesh and am certainly not so strong as I might be, and I make my ailments an excuse for idleness. I have not yet got the O[xford] Tracts for this year. Rivington[a] is very provoking—The collection of Pamphlets is come—and I much desiderate the foundations [of] the faith—it would weigh down Sewell[b]

---

[1] From this point, up to the phrase 'excuse for idleness', the text is that of *Remains of the late Reverend Richard Hurrell Froude* [ed. J. H. Newman], London, Rivington, 1838. 2 vols., vol. i, pp. 417–18, with minor alterations.

[a] Francis Rivington, the publisher of *Tracts for the Times*.
[b] William Sewell (1804–74), Fellow of Exeter College from 1827, who broke with the Tractarians on the publication of *Tract XC*. He later founded Radley College (1847).

and Oakeley[a] together. Morris[b] has more in him than the first place I opened it led me to think. But what has most delighted me of any thing in the Vol. is Pusey's note on Question 19.[c]

Willy[d] is a great deal stronger and better than when I wrote to you last, and I hope will soon be allowed to return to his work. I have been thinking a good deal about Tony Buller's case[e]—I have come to a conclusion that he must not give up his living till he can get something to make him permanently independent of his Father. My Father does not despair of getting Phillpots[f] to let him put a curate there and take duty himself elsewhere for some time. If this could be managed it would do best. For the present I think he had better $\dot{a}\nu\delta\rho\alpha\gamma\alpha\theta\dot{\iota}\zeta\epsilon\iota\nu$[g] as well as he can—letting his Father know that he is on a lookout to change his abode. It is a very melancholy business—for poor Sir A., if left to himself, has a genuine good $\mathring{\eta}\theta$os[h] as anyone I know.

I will write to Rogers to tell him I despair of getting to Oxford yet a while.

Yours ever most affectionately,

RHF

Paignton

July 17—You may direct to Dartington as usual.

[ADDRESSED: Revd. J. H. Newman, Oriel College, Oxford.]

[a] Frederick Oakeley (1802–80), Fellow of Balliol from 1827; after his conversion in 1845, he became a Canon of Westminster, and wrote *Historical Notes on the Tractarian Movement* (1965).

[b] John Brande Morris (1812–80), Fellow of Exeter College from 1837.

[c] During the controversy on the substitution of a declaration of conformity for subscription to the Thirty-nine Articles, as necessary for Matriculation at Oxford, Pusey issued a fly-leaf of twenty-three questions in 1834 and a larger one on 3 April 1835, containing twenty-seven questions. A majority in Convocation defeated the proposed substitution on 20 May 1835. In addition to the other authors Froude mentions, H. W. Wilberforce issued anonymously a pamphlet entitled *The foundations of the Faith assailed in Oxford; a letter to His Grace the Archbishop of Canterbury, by a Clerical Member of Convocation* (London, Rivington, 1835). On the details of the controversy cf. Liddon, *Life of E. B. Pusey*, i. 303–5.

[d] William Froude (1810–79), R. H. Froude's younger brother, became an engineer, and continued to correspond with Newman on religious matters to the end of his life.

[e] Anthony Buller (1819–81), Rector of St. Tavy, Devon, 1833–76, had published a short Tract entitled 'The Catholic Church a Witness against Illiberality' (*Tracts for the Times*, No, 61, 1 May 1835). Cf. T. Mozley, *Reminiscences*, (London, 1882), ii. 121–2.

[f] Henry Phillpotts, Bishop of Exeter (1778–1869).

[g] Presumably 'play the man'. The Greek of the Septuagint (1 Macc. 5: 61, 67, and 2 Macc. 2: 21) uses the verb $\dot{a}\nu\delta\rho\alpha\gamma\alpha\theta\epsilon\hat{\iota}\nu$.

[h] 'disposition.'

(ii) *Newman to Froude*

Oriel College, July 20. 1835

Ricarde Frater,

You must not be impatient that you do not see improvement in you week by week. A complaint of such long standing as yours of course will not yield in an instant. Think how great a thing it is to know, as we trust, that your lungs are all right, and how much it tells for the strength of your constitution that the ailment, whatever it is, has been stationary so long. I should like of all things to come and see you but can say nothing to the proposal at present—being very busy here, and (to my great anxiety) being in point of finances in a very unsatisfactory state.

But as to the Abbé. I have not yet read your dialogue, as you conjecture, wishing first to set down my own sense, and then to consider it. Now this is what I mean. *N.* Scripture forbids admission into the Church to those who disbelieve its doctrines, Tradition does not. *Abbé.* What? does Scripture forbid it to those who do not receive (e.g.) that David reigned 7 years in Hebron? *N.* No. I mean there are *certain doctrines* in Scripture to which it attaches this sanction, i.e. fundamental doctrines. *Abbé.* True but Tradition also has such, e.g. the Apostles' Creed. *N.* You are using Tradition in two senses. *Abbé.* I do not see it. *N.* Still so it is. The popular sense of Tradition is the voice of the body of the Church, the received system in the Church, the spirit circulating through it and poured out through the channels of its doctors and writers. Is it not so? *Abbé.* Granted. *N.* Which I may call *prophetical Tradition*, or the system taught, interpretative, supplementary, illustrative, applicative of the Scripture doctrine. Now I maintain that Tradition in this sense, and this is the sense in which I contrasted it to Scripture, does not carry with it any witness of its reception being necessary for Church Communion. Its reception is the privilege of the Christian when admitted, not a condition of his admission. (Disciplina arc[ani] comes in here) Even were the Tradition semper, ubique et ab omnibus, nothing short of his public disavowal of it and teaching openly contrary to it, would justify his rejection or exclusion from the Church. All I have said then that at the first blush of the matter, if any fundamentals are to be found any where *over and above the Apostles' Creed* (which both of us agree in holding fundamental for communion and about which there is no question) Scripture is *likely* to be the depositary, not tradition—Scripture being an authoritative depositary, i.e. speaking by inspiration, Tradition not. I did not use the argument for more than a primâ faciê one and hastened on to others stronger. *Abbé.* But you seem to forget that the Apostles' Creed, to which you have alluded, i.e. the very series of articles which you consider to *be* the fundamentals, is received on Tradition not on Scripture. *N.* To this I answer, first it is in Scripture too, so that it is not a case in point. And if you wish me to consider the hypothetical case, I will freely confess that were the Apostles' Creed not in Scripture and only conveyed to us by the Prophetical Tradition just described, I do not see there would be any reason for considering its articles *the* foundation of Church communion. But here we come to the other sense of Tradition, viz that strict Traditio from one hand to another, from definite person to definite person, official and exact, which I may call *Apostolical* or *Episcopal.* I will allow to you that such a Tradition does carry the sanction with it as fully as Scripture does. I will receive as necessary for Church Communion all the articles conveyed by it. *But I do already.* They are the Apostles' Creed, which are the fundamentals even if Scripture said nothing about them. And if the Scripture mentioned others, there would be two sets of fundamentals; but this is impossible, else the Scripture and Church would be at variance. Therefore *no wonder* Scripture *agrees* with this Apostolical Tradition.

Abbé. But in your letter to me, you were speaking not of the *terms of communion,* but of doctrines necessary to salvation. True—but it was you began speaking of fundamentals which to me mean *nothing* else than terms of communion. Drop the word f[t.a] and take the latter, and see what I have said. I quote my words 'Perhaps you will ask, Why do you Anglicans make such a difference between the written and the unwritten word? If the belief in the one is nec. to salv.[b] so is belief in the other. We answer, first of all, that on the very first face of the matter, it is clear that Scripture does absolutely declare belief in its doctrines nec. to salv., but Trad. (i.e. Prophetical) does not say so of its own . . . Scripture and Tradition, taken per se, come to us in a different aspect; the one with a demand upon our faith, the other not.'

Froude. But hark back. You said just now that the articles necessary for *Church communion* could not be conveyed by Prophetical Tradition; *need they be contained in Scripture? N.* Why certainly our articles say nothing on the subject; they only speak of necessary to salvation. *F.* Then why not at once maintain that Scripture warrant is not necessary for an article being in your sense (i.e. Laud's &c) fundamental?

I am reading your dialogue. First I observe that I *start* with this defn. of Tradition (i.e. Prophetical) 'that which comes without sanction of its necessary importance' and fairly, *for it is a matter of fact;* therefore for the abbé to put the question '*Supposing* I could show that the

---

a 'fundamental'   b 'necessary to salvation'

early Xtians regarded the doctrine of the Eucharist as fundamental?' is quite out of place. My answer would be, not 'No—in that case I should admit that it was fundamental, but you cannot show it'—but 'if so, Tradition would not be what *by nature* it is.' I deny that 'after I have made good my assertion that the doctrine cannot be proved from Scripture, I should *also* have to make good that the Fathers did not think it fundamental—' rather, '*since* all tradition is in a matter of fact of an unauthoritative nature, an *instruction* not a *command*, I am *driven* to Scripture as a *DENIER*[1] resource, to find there *if anywhere*, fundamentals.'

Please to keep this letter—that I may think over it; and help me out of a puzzle, I may have got into. I cannot help thinking you have perverted my meaning in turning a primâ faciê argument into a (supposed) conclusive one.

Let me hear from you soon. Thank your Father for his kindness in wishing me to come down. I am at present at the Abbé and Dionysius[a] whom oh that I could despatch this vacation. Acland has sent a *fifth* Cambridge man to me, but he has not yet called.[b] I am somewhat anxious lest I have gone to[o] far in confessing Monastic doctrines.[2]

Ever yours amantissime
JHN

[*Addressed to*: The Revd. Richard H. Froude
    Torbay House
    Devon
    Paington [*sic*]
Postmarked Oxford Jy 20 1835]

(iii) Froude to Newman

[Newman notes: answered Aug 9/35]

N. 'since all tradition is *in matter of fact*, of an unauthoritative nature &c.' *Abbé.* A large assertion, and doubtless if true sufficient for your purpose! but you surely cannot expect me to assent to it, since the

---

[1] *Sic* for *dernière.*

[2] Part of this final paragraph appears in *Letters and Correspondence of John Henry Newman*, ed. Mozley, ii. 114. In the last sentence, Newman refers to his series of articles 'Letters on the Church of the Fathers' which appeared in the *British Magazine* from 1833 to 1836; cf. June 1835, pp. 662–8 and July 1835, pp. 41–5. He was worried about the unfavourable impression they might produce (cf. *Letters*, ed. Mozley, ii. 112).

[a] Bishop of Alexandria between 248 and 265 (? 160–265).

[b] Anne Mozley's insertion at this point suggests that John Sterling is the Cambridge man referred to (*Letters*, ii. 114).

very thing I am maintaining is that the traditionary doctrine of the
Eucharist is *in matter of fact* authoritative i.e. that the Fathers not
merely assert it but 'regard it as fundamental.' In maintaining this
I may doubtless be wrong—but you can hardly expect to convince me
that the Fathers do not insist on *one particular* traditionary doctrine as
fundamental by asserting that they do not insist on *any* as fundamental.
Your way will be first to prove from the fathers that I misrepresent
them in this particular case, which will be enough for the present argument. If however you are anxious to prove your general proof, you
may then proceed step by step to prove that I misrepresent them in
sundry other cases in which I conceive them to state doctrines, not in
Scripture, authoritatively. Nor shall I admit that you have succeeded,
till you have refuted me in all the points where I differ from you. When
you have done this I shall of course succumbe[1] and you will have satisfied me 'that *all* tradition is in matter of fact of an unauthoritative
nature'. But your success will then be of little avail for any controversial purpose since as far as you and I are concerned all controversy
will be at an end. And in your controversies with other people you
will have to go over all the same ground again—nor will you convince
any one of the principle for which you are contending, till you have
convinced them of every particular point for the sake of which you
contend for it.

Now the abbé has said out his say so I shall begin.

[2]Frater desiderate—speak not of finances since all the people here
are ready to subscribe for you—and as for the Abbé you can work him
here as well as anywhere. Remember every Tuesday and every Friday
at $\frac{1}{2}$ past six in the evening the Brunswick passes Cowes downwards.
Also how can you accuse me of having passed by your question about
the Laity in convocation. I told you I had tried hard to think it admis-
sible. But the Bp. Hickes in his 'constitution of the Xtian Ch' had convinced me that in spirituals each Bp was absolute in his own diocese
except so far as he may have bound himself by ordination oaths to his
Primate.[a] So that not only the Laity but presbyters are cut out. Next
as to the Bible Xtians. I said that I thought schools confined to Scripture teaching could not answer, for that their system implied a principle which must nullify all the mere intimations of Scripture itself,
i.e. the principle that Scripture is sufficient. N.B. [3]What does the article

---

[1] *Sic.*   [2] Quoted in Newman, *Letters*, ed. Mozley, ii. 116–17.
[3] From this point to 'understand the assertion' is quoted in Froude, *Remains*,
1838, ii. 419.

[a] George Hickes (1642–1715), nonjuror and theological writer, author of *The
Constitution of the Catholic Church, and the nature and consequences of Schism, set forth
in a collection of papers* . . . London, 1716.

mean by 'doctrines necessary to salvation'?[a] No doctrine is necessary
to salvation to those who have not rejected it wilfully—and every true
doctrine is necessary to salvation to those who if they reject it must
reject wilfully? If indeed by 'doctrines necessary to salvation' is meant
'terms of communion' i.e. necessary to *covenanted* salvation; I quite
understand the assertion. But if they mean necessary ἁπλῶς[b] I think
no doctrine necessary except under circumstances which will make
every religious truth necessary—i.e. circumstances which would make
its rejection an act of wilful sin. 2. Are we bound to give all the articles
an intelligible meaning? I think I understand you to say that you conceived some of them framed with a different view.

While I think of it—my Father has an indistinct notion that some
time ago he asked you to put down my Brother Anthony's name on
Hawkins' list for Oriel.[c] Is this a fancy or a fact? if the former no matter
—as he will try somewhere else.

July 30. I wrote the rest some days ago I forget exactly when and
stopped for want of matter. Since that I have thought of many things
to say and let them slip again. One thing comes into my head now.
Viz: the relapse of Pusey's brother into Whiggery.[d] I fancy I remember your telling me that the first and chief point on which he originally
detached himself from the μισητὸς στάσις[e] had been the Irish Church,
and that he had been a long time in Ireland making up his opinion.

About Arnold I have as yet taken no steps. I have not been able to
borrow his works and don't like to buy them—yet I think I must, as
I should like to have a hand in the indictment.[f]

I hear that K's ἀποστασία[g] has been announced in the papers—I do
verily believe that 9 tenths of the people[1] who hear of it will be a little
shocked. As to your monasticism articles in the B.M.[h] my father read
the offensive part of the June one and could see nothing in it that any
reasonable person could object to. And some people I know have been
struck by them. I cannot see the harm of losing influence with people,
when you can only retain it with by [*sic*] sinking the points on which
you differ from them—surely that would be propter vitam vivendi

[1] MS. people of who

[a] Article vi, 'Holy Scripture containeth all things necessary to salvation . . .'.
[b] 'Purely and simply.'
[c] J. A. Froude, the future historian. See the final para. of Newman's reply,
p. 183.
[d] Philip Pusey (1799–1855), E. B. Pusey's elder brother.
[e] 'Hateful position.'
[f] Thomas Arnold (1795–1842), Headmaster of Rugby and later Regius Professor of History at Oxford. He had published the liberal *Principles of Church Reform*
in 1833, and attacked the Tractarians in 1836 in the *Edinburgh Review*
[g] 'Apostasy.' The reference is to Keble's recent marriage.
[h] *British Magazine.*

perdere &c.ᵃ What is the good of influence, except to influence people?

¹My Brother W.ᵇ is getting well rapidly. After the rub you gave me, for saying in my last that I was stationary, I will not repeat the offence. It is exquisitely pleasant here—a hot sun with a fresh air is a luxury to which I have long been a stranger and enjoy [*illegible*] I would give much to have you here for a day or two of such weather as yesterday and today, it would almost pay for the journey—If you were to stay a fortnight you might get on with your controversy as well as at Oxford and would be inspired for the novel—I give out in all directions that you mean to write it, & divulge the plot.

I forget whether I mentioned in my last how much my F[ather] was taken with the historical part of your Ariansᶜ—& particularly its bearing on the present times. I really think he is getting to look on our projects more favourably, i.e. as practical and practicable, than he used—In his last charge he put in a good deal against the existing relations of Church & State, & couched in a kind of mystified language that seemed to imply much more than was said. One of the Church reforming Clergy in this Diocese alluded to it afterwards in conversation [with] him, and said it had put things to him & others of his friends [in a] light which had not before presented itself to them—& that it did [seem] as if the root of the evil lay deeper than was generally thought. I [do not] know what the man meant—but it is something to make them think and now I shall send off this stupid affair—which has laid on the [table?] till it is rusty—

Love amicis omnibus
Yours affectly. RHF
B.M.S.V.

please to direct. Torbay House Paignton.

[*addressed*:

Revd. J. H. Newman
Oriel College,
OXFORD]

¹ From here to 'offence' appears in Froude, *Remains*, 1838, ii. 419; the name William is omitted.

ᵃ 'for the sake of life to lose the reason for living.' Juvenal, *Sat.* viii. 83.
ᵇ William Froude.
ᶜ *The Arians of the Fourth Century* (1833).

(iv) *Newman to Froude*

Ἀδελφὲ φιλοκαθολικώτατε[1]   Oriel College. Aug. 9. 1835

Let me first say what I have forgotten these many last letters—that Rogers,[a] and another friend by way of supplement, have offered to your acceptance Du Cange's Glossary, both parts—and that the book is now in your room, or rather has been there above a month.—As to my coming to you I have made up my mind to so do, since you hope it, (though I think it a weakness in me) in the following way. Poor H. W.[b] has the responsibility of a son born to him—and, as if that were not enough, he wishes me to share it without relieving him (ut flammam a flammâ as Ennius says)[c] by being godfather. So I shall set off (I expect) for his abode at the end of August, (the 28th) and shall take the Brunswick on Tuesday Sept 1 for Torbay. This is my present plan. I shall bring with me a lot of sermons to try to put together a third volume; and shall get you to help me. At present I am hard at Dionysius—i.e. at the Apollinarian controversy. After-wards will follow the Nestorian, and by the time I have finished, I shall have materials (I suppose) for a volume on the Incarnation to accompany the Arians. Nothing but some object would enable me to rouse myself to such subtle speculations as I have to submit to—(though in these times surely most necessary, unless we are to be swept away, Creeds, Church and all,) and Dionysius answers this purpose. E.g. in a certain Creed given to the Council of Antioch A.D. 264 occurs the word προσῶπον[d] as applied to the σύνθετον or union of the δύο φύσεες[e] in our Lord. Now I think to be able to prove it was not so used till A.D. (say) 390. You see what investigations this must lead to. Poor

---

[1] 'Most Catholic-loving brother.' Passages from this letter appear in *Letters & correspondence of J. H. Newman*, ed. Mozley, ii. 123.

[a] Frederick Rogers (1811–1889), later Lord Blachford, Fellow of Oriel from 1833.   [b] Henry Wilberforce.

[c] Newman is presumably paraphrasing some lines from Ennius quoted by Cicero in *de Officiis* (Bk. I, xvi):

> Homo, qui erranti comiter monstrat viam
> Quasi lumen de suo lumine accendat, facit
> Nihilo minus ipsi lucet, cum illi accenderit.

> Who kindly sets a wand'rer in his way
> Does e'en as if he lit another's lamp by his.
> No less shines his, when he his friend's hath lit.

(Tr. W. Miller, Loeb Classics, Harvard U.P. and Heinemann, London, 1961.) Cicero then quotes a maxim 'let anyone who will, take fire from our fire' *pati ab igne ignem capere, si qui velit.*

[d] 'face', 'mask', 'person', 'manifestation'.   [e] 'two natures.'

Blanco[a] has published his book—and it is as bad as can be. He evidently hopes to be attacked. It strikes me his work might be very usefully turned as a *witness* of the tendency of certain opinions—He says in the preface, that for several years he has been a Sabellian, but he now finds Sabellianism[b] is Unitarianism in disguise—and therefore he professes himself to be what he is really.

Rose[c] is set upon having a standard history to supplant Mosheim.[d] He has pitched upon Fleury[e] which about a dozen men are to abridge or retrench, translate, prove references of, put notes to, etc. It is a good plan you shall hear more of it (so be it) when we meet.

The Tracts are defunct, or in extremis. Rivington has written to say they do not answer. Pusey has written one on Baptism, very good, of 90 pages, which is to be printed at his risk[f]—that, and one or two to finish imperfect series (or particular subjects) will conclude the whole. I am not sorry—as I am tired of being Editor.

I conceive that I have entirely beaten you as regards the Abbé—for you have brought the matter to an issue—the Abbé, so far from contesting the point, I think would be obliged to grant that Tradition (Prophetical) had no innate self-sanction—for (in the Latin Theory) *the Church in Council* (or otherwise) gives that sanction—*till then* this or that tradition has no authority at all. The Bible then has a sanction independent of the Church, the (Prophetical) Tradition has none—therefore when asked why I make a distinction between the Word Written and Unwritten, I answer, that *first* on the face of the matter the Scriptures come with a claim, Tradition does not. By the bye I am surprised more and more to see how the Fathers insist *on the Scriptures* as the rule of faith—even in proving the most subtle part of the doctrine of the Incarnation. As to Vincentius Lirinensis he *starts* by making Tradition only interpretation.

Palmer[g] will finish his work in two volumes by the Spring. It is to

a Joseph Blanco White, a former Roman Catholic priest, had published *Observations on Heresy and Orthodoxy*, London, 1835. Cf. J. H. Thom, ed. *The Life of the Rev. Joseph Blanco White, written by himself*, etc. 3 vols., London, 1845. Cf. p. 160, n. d.

b Sabellianism, a fourth-century heresy, diminished the reality of the Trinity by supposing it to be a notion of God in three temporary manifestations or πρόσωπα.

c Hugh James Rose (1795–1841), Cambridge theologian and founder of the *British Magazine*. Cf. p. 150.

d Johann Lorenz von Mosheim (1694–1755), author of *Institutionum Historiae ecclesiasticae antiquioris et recentioris Libri 11*, 1726.

e On the Fleury project, cf. p. 151, n. a.

f Published as *Tracts for the Times*, Nos. 67–9.

g William Palmer (1803–1885) of Trinity College, Dublin, and Worcester College, Oxford, published his *Treatise on the Church of Christ* in 1838. It puts forward a case for the 'Branch Theory', that the Church of England, the Church of Rome, and the Greek Church are all branches of one Catholic Church. For New-be a book of *Law*, i.e. the rules of the Church, with proofs, answers to objections, examples, cases of casuistry etc.; in fact one of the very things we want. Keble is going to introduce into his own Prolegomena a sketch of Hooker's doctrine, which will do the same service in another way.[a] It would be much, if we could cram all our men in one and the same way of talking on various points. E.g. what the Church holds about heretical baptism, about ordination before baptism, about the power of bishops etc. etc. This is one strong point of Romanism; they have their system so well up. A Mr. Maguire,[b] a Roman Priest, dined with us the other day, who was an instance of this—and astonished people so. By the bye he was avant-courier[1] to Dr. Wiseman,[c] who is now in London, and is to be here (to consult the libraries) in a week or two. Dr. W. sent a message about you as well as myself. What disgusted us in Mr. M. was his defending, not only O Connell,[d] but Hume—in fact, I suppose, he does not see the difference between the dog and the hog—and we are but dogs in his eyes.

As to our prospect, I expect nothing favorable for 15 to 20 years—i.e. we shall perchance grow—but it will be a while before 300 men shall be forced to lap water with their tongues. I have some notion I mentioned your brother's name to the Provost for entrance—and if so, clearly your Father did mention the subject to me. I will ask the P. [at] the first opportunity. I must tell you all about the Cambridge men, when I see you—do make a list of the things we have to talk about. I shall [be] with you for 10 days, if you will let me.

Ever yrs affectionately
John H. Newman

P.S. Old Palmer died about a week since

[*addressed*: The Revd. R. H. Froude, Torbay House, Paignton, Devon. *Postmarked* Au 9 1835. Oxford]

---

[1] *Sic.*

man's account of it cf. 'Palmer on Faith and Unity', *Essays Critical and Historical*, i. 143–85.

[a] John Keble had for some time been preparing an edition of Richard Hooker's *Treatise on the Laws of Ecclesiastical Polity*, cf. *Works*, 3 vols., Oxford, 1836.

[b] John Maguire (1801–65), professor at St. Edmund's, Ware, Wiseman's Vicar-General in London, until deprived in 1858 for siding with Archbishop Errington against him.

[c] Nicholas Wiseman, then head of the English College in Rome, had been visited there by Newman in 1833, and wrote to Newman in July 1835 that he intended to call on him in Oxford. The visit never took place.

[d] One of Newman's constant reproaches to the Roman Catholic body in the the United Kingdom was its alliance with the Liberals, among whom he counted the Irish liberator, Daniel O'Connell, and among whose ideological forebears he numbered David Hume.

Appendix IV

Chronology of the controversy in the columns of *L'Univers*

Author	Title	Newspaper	Date
J.-N. Jager	First Letter	*L'Univers*	30 August 1834
B. Harrison	First Reply	*L'Univers*	18 September 1834
J.-N. Jager	Second Letter	*L'Univers*	19 September 1834
B. Harrison	Second Reply	*L'Univers*	14 October 1834
J.-N. Jager	Third Letter	*L'Univers*	23 October 1834
J.-N. Jager	Third Letter (continued)	*L'Univers*	24 October 1834
J.-N. Jager	Fourth Letter	*L'Univers*	7 November 1834
J.-N. Jager	Fourth Letter (continued)	*L'Univers*	8 November 1834
J. H. Newman	Third Reply	*L'Univers*	25 December 1834
J.-N. Jager	Fifth Letter	*L'Univers*	25 December 1834
J. H. Newman	Third Reply (continued)	*L'Univers*	28 January 1835
J. H. Newman	Third Reply (continued)	*L'Univers*	29 January 1835
J.-N. Jager	Fifth Letter (continued)	*L'Univers*	30 January 1835
J.-N. Jager	Fifth Letter (continued)	*L'Univers*	5 February 1835
J.-N. Jager	Fifth Letter (continued)	*L'Univers*	6 February 1835
J.-N. Jager	Fifth Letter (continued)	*L'Univers*	20 February 1835
J.-N. Jager	Fifth Letter (continued)	*L'Univers*	21 February 1835
J.-N. Jager	Sixth Letter	*L'Univers*	26 February 1835
J.-N. Jager	Sixth Letter (continued)	*L'Univers*	6 March 1835
J.-N. Jager	Sixth Letter (continued)	*L'Univers*	12 March 1835
J.-N. Jager	Sixth Letter (continued)	*L'Univers*	27 March 1835

The Sixth Letter was still incomplete at this point. Jager then transferred the controversy from *L'Univers*, which was a daily paper, to the weekly *Moniteur religieux*, which enabled him to publish contributions in longer instalments. He inserted a note in *Le Moniteur religieux* (1 April 1835) to the effect that it was inconvenient to deal with such matters in a daily newspaper which was printed at night and where proof-reading had to be entrusted to men who were not familiar with the exactitude of theological language. The title of the periodical remained *Le Moniteur religieux* until it became *Le Moniteur de la religion* on 9 May 1835 (Stern, op. cit., p. 122, n. 86), running until 15 October 1836 (cf. E. Hatin, *Bibliographie de la Presse périodique*, 1866, p. 392).

Newman preserved a fascicule of *Le Moniteur* in which was printed the whole of Jager's *Seventh Letter*. He had it bound with a number of other tracts, but does not seem to have kept those issues in which appeared his own Fourth Reply, Part One, or later contributions by Jager. As a matter of interest, it should perhaps be pointed out that loose copies of *L'Univers* are kept with his correspondence; very usefully, since the file of that paper for the 1830s, preserved in the Bibliothèque Nationale, is incomplete.

Appendix V

Parallel passages showing Newman's use of the controversy in 1st and 3rd editions of *Lectures on the Prophetical Office of the Church*. References are given both to the first edition of the *Lectures* and to the third edition, printed as vol. i of *Via Media*

Newman's Second letter	*Prophetical Office, First Ed.*	*Prophetical Office, Third Ed. (Via Media, Vol. 1)*
p. 83 'That foundation . . . of the Gospel'	p. 259 'If we adopt . . . in the Creed.'	p. 217 'If we adopt . . . in the Creed.'
pp. 83–4 'Irenaeus says . . . she diligently guards'	pp. 261–2 'For instance; St. Irenaeus . . . she diligently guards.'	pp. 219–20 'For instance; St. Iranaeus . . . she diligently guards.'
p. 84 'Tertullian says . . . third day,' etc.	p. 263 'Tertullian, in like manner . . . the third day . . .'	pp. 220–1. 'Tertullian, in like manner . . . the third day . . .'
pp. 84–5 'When the Catechumen . . . world to come'	p. 264 'And so, again . . . world to come'	p. 221 'And so, again . . . world to come . . .'
p. 86 'The Semi-Arians . . . brethren'	p. 275 'So reluctant . . . at the word.'	pp. 230–1 'So reluctant . . . at the term.'
pp. 86–7 '. . . since those varieties . . . heaven and earth?'	p. 270 '. . . so in the formal symbol . . . by His Word?'	pp. 226–7 '. . . so as regards the formal . . . by His Word?'
p. 88 'Did Philip oblige . . . ultra-Protestantism.'	pp. 304–5 'Take the case . . . from the first?'	p. 255 'Take the case . . . from the first.'
pp. 88–9 'The Church recollected . . . attaches to them.'	pp. 305–6 'The Primitive Church . . . her Catholicity.'	pp. 256–7 'The Primitive Church . . . her Catholicity.'
pp. 89–90 'Every word . . . for Baptism presupposes.'	pp. 306–8 'Every word . . . for Baptism presupposes.'	pp. 256–8 'Every word . . . for Baptism presupposes.'
p. 90 'Next, she secures . . . of her children.'	p. 308 'She secures . . . of her children.'	p. 259 'She secures . . . of her children.'
pp. 91–2 'I refer firstly to the conduct . . . about the word.'	pp. 301–2 'It is Athanasius's conduct . . . about the word.'	pp. 252–3 'It is Athanasius's conduct . . . about the word.'

Newman's Second letter	Prophetical Office, First Ed.	Prophetical Office, Third ed. (*Via Media*, Vol. 1)
pp. 92–3 'To the same purpose . . . surmises.'	p. 302 'To the same purpose . . . surmises.'	pp. 253–4 'To the same purpose . . . surmises.'
pp. 94–6 'The Apostles' Creed . . . decrees of some others.'	pp. 296–300 'I say, then, that the Creed . . . truth in them.'	pp. 249–52 'I say then, that the Creed . . . truth in them.'
Newman's Third letter		
pp. 119–20 'And thus we are rid . . . little or great.'	p. 343 'Moreover this view . . . little or great.'	p. 287 'Moreover this view . . . little or great.'
p. 122 'The 6th Article . . . of the faith . . .'	p. 324 'Thus, in the sixth . . . of the faith.'	p. 271 'Thus in the sixth . . . of the faith.'
p. 122 'The Canons of 1571 . . . *canonical Scriptures*.'	pp. 322–3 'Again, in the Canon of 1571 . . . *Canonical Scriptures*.'	p. 270 'Again, in the Canon of 1571 . . . *Canonical Scriptures*.'
p. 122 'The sole question . . . are to teach.'	p. 324 'The sole question . . . is to teach.'	p. 271 'The sole question . . . *is to teach*.'
p. 122 'It has no reference . . . individuals.'	pp. 324–5 'It does not say . . . not even contemplated.'	p. 272 '. . . the question whether individuals . . . contemplated.'
p. 123 '. . . and in the 20th Article . . . of faith.'	p. 322 'For instance, in the 20th Article . . . of faith.'	pp. 269–70 'For instance, in the 20th Article . . . of faith.'
p. 123 'The very circumstance . . . written also.'	p. 346 'First, the New Testament . . . written also.'	p. 290 'First, the New Testament . . . written also.'
pp. 123–4 'God spoke . . . delivered it.'	p. 348 'In the Old Covenant . . . Ten Commandments.'	p. 292 'In the old Covenant . . . Ten Commandments.'
p. 124 'Consider too . . . Teacher and Prophet.'	p. 349 'All through the Gospels . . . Teacher and Prophet.'	p. 292 'All through the Gospels . . . Teacher and Prophet.'
p. 124 'And thus the Fathers speak . . . mystically delivered to thee.'	pp. 349–50 'And thus the Fathers speak . . mystically delivered to thee.'	p. 293 'And thus the Fathers speak . . mystically delivered to thee.'
pp. 125–6 'His conversation with Nicodemus . . . instance.'	p. 350 '. . . His discourse with Nicodemus . . . instance.'	p. 292 '. . . His discourse with Nicodemus . . . instance.'
p. 125 'I do not of course presume . . . live in charity.'	pp. 354–5 'To His own indeed . . . live in charity'	pp. 297–8 'To His own indeed . . . live in charity.'
pp. 126–8 'Bishop Jeremy Taylor . . . belief in them.'	pp. 356–8 'Is not all . . . must be accounted.'	pp. 299–300 'Is not all . must be accounted.'

Newman's Third letter	Prophetical Office, First Ed.	Prophetical Office, Third ed. (Via Media, Vol. 1)
p. 128 'Bellarmine indeed . . . salvation of believers.'	pp. 358–9 'It will be replied . . . salvation of believers.'	pp. 300–1 'It will be replied . . . salvation of believers.'
pp. 128–9 'Against this hypothesis . . . contained in the Epistles.'	pp. 360–1 'Now, this representation . . . doctrines of the Epistles.'	p. 302 'However, to this representation . . . doctrines of the Epistles.'
pp. 130–1 'Haec non cognoverunt . . . super tecta.'	pp. 364–5 'These things understood not . . . house-tops.'	pp. 305–6 'These things understood not . . . house-tops.'
p. 131 'Now it would be . . . similar way.'	p. 366 'Further; the last chapter . . . impatiently attempted.'	p. 307 'Further; the last chapter . . . impatiently attempted.'
pp. 133–4 'Now first I appeal . . . legitimate use.'	pp. 382–5 'Vincentius is commonly . . . explanation of Scripture.'	pp. 321–3 'Vincentius is commonly . . . explanation of Scripture.'
pp. 134–5 'Tertullian . . . take away.'	pp. 373–4 'Accordingly Tertullian . . . take away.'	p. 313 'Accordingly Tertullian . . . take away.'
pp. 135–36 'Origen . . . level with it?'	pp. 374–5 'Origen . . . was unwritten.'	pp. 313–15 'Origen . . . was unwritten.'
p. 136 'Cyril . . . on itself.'	p. 378 'Cyril . . . Tradition.'	p. 317 'Cyril . . . tradition.'
pp. 136–7 'Optatus . . . disciples' feet.'	pp. 377–8 'St. Optatus . . . disciples' feet'	pp. 316–17 'St. Optatus . . . disciples feet.'
p. 137 'Basil . . . superordinat.'	pp. 378–9 'St. Basil's . . . or addeth thereto.'	pp. 317–18 'St. Basil's . . . or addeth thereto.'
p. 137 'Augustine . . . believe it.'	p. 380 'St. Austin . . . believe it.'	pp. 318–19 'St. Austin . . . believe it.'
pp. 137–8 'Chrysostom . . . who are not.'	p. 379 'Let us now . . . who are not.'	p. 318 'Let us now . . . who are not.'
p. 138 'Anastatius . . . profit.'	p. 380 'Anastatius . . . profit.'	p. 319 'Anastatius . . . profit.'
pp. 138–9 'St. John Damascene . . . manifested to us.'	pp. 380–2 'With this view . . . manifested to us.'	pp. 319–20 'With this view . . . manifested to us.'
p. 139 'These extracts . . . Apollinarian.'	p. 382 'These extracts . . . on the mind.'	p. 320 'These extracts . . . on the mind.'
p. 139 'St. Athanasius . . . Testaments.'	p. 385 'Athanasius . . . Testaments.'	p. 323 'Athanasius . . . Testaments.'
p. 139 'St. Cyril . . . instruction.'	pp. 385–6 'The same contrast . . . instruction.'	
pp. 140–2 'In the following . . . opinion of the world.'	pp. 386–9 'In the following . . . opinion of the world.'	pp. 323–6 'Again; he recommends . . . opinion of the world.'
pp. 142–3 'Now then let us . . . holy and religious.'	p. 389 'I conclude with . . . holy and religious.'	p. 326 'I conclude with . . . holy and religious.'

Bibliography

The bibliography of Newman and the Oxford Movement is vast and constantly increasing. The purpose of the present list is therefore limited to showing the sources of the text and those works used either for verifying references or providing a background to the controversy. Within each section, the sequence is alphabetical, by title in the case of Newman's works, by author for the rest.

A. PRIMARY SOURCES

1. Manuscripts in the Archives of the Oratory, Birmingham (MS. draft of letter from Newman to Jager; Newman's first letter to Jager (Third Reply); Newman's third letter to Jager (Fourth Reply, Part Two: *Rule of Faith*); the correspondence between Newman and R. H. Froude; the correspondence with Harrison).

2. i. Text of controversy in letters published in *L'Univers* and *Le Moniteur religieux* (see Appendix IV).

   ii. Text of controversy in J.-N. Jager, *Le Protestantisme aux prises avec la doctrine catholique, ou Controverses avec plusieurs Ministres anglicans, Membres de l'Université d'Oxford, soutenues par M. l'abbé Jager*, t. i (all published), Paris, Debécourt, 1836, pp. 515.

B. SECONDARY SOURCES

1. *Newman's Works*

i. *Correspondence and diaries*

Autobiographical Writings, ed. H. Tristram, London, Sheed and Ward, 1956.

Correspondence of John Henry Newman with John Keble and Others, 1839–45. (ed. Fr. F. Bacchus) London, Longmans, 1917.

Letters and Correspondence of John Henry Newman during his Life in the English Church, with a brief Autobiography, ed. . . . by Anne Mozley, 2 vols., London, Longmans, 1898.

The Letters and Diaries of John Henry Newman, ed. C. S. Dessain. Vols. xi–xxvi, Nelson, later Clarendon Press, 1961 onwards.

ii. *Tracts for the Times*

Catena Patrum, No. 1 ('Testimony of writers in the later English Church, to the Doctrine of the Apostolical Succession') (No. 74).

On the Controversy with the Romanists (1836) (No. 71).

Tract XC. Remarks on certain passages in the 39 Articles. (Reprinted from the edition of 1841 with an historical commentary by A. W. Evans, London, Constable, 1933.)

The Via Media, i (No. 38) (1834).

The Via Media, ii (No. 41) (1834).

iii. *Other Writings*

Apologia pro vita sua, London, Longmans, 1882; also ed. with introd. by Wilfrid Ward, London, Oxford University Press, 1913; and by M. Svaglic, Oxford University Press, 1967.

The Arians of the Fourth Century (1833; London, Longmans, 1890, 7th ed.).

Discussions and Arguments on various subjects. New impn. London, Longmans, 1899. (Contains text of 'How to accomplish it' from the *British Magazine*, 1836; and 'Holy Scripture in its relation to the Catholic Creed', September 1838.)

An Essay on the Development of Christian Doctrine, London, Toovey, 1845; new ed. London, Pickering, 1878.

Fifteen Sermons preached before the University of Oxford (1833; 3rd ed., London, Longmans, 1872).

Historical Sketches (3 vols., London, Longmans, 1872; vol. i contains a short chapter on Vincent of Lérins).

Lectures on the Prophetical Office of the Church viewed relatively to Romanism and Popular Protestantism (1837; reprinted, with alterations and additions, as vol. i of *Via Media*, London, Longmans, 1877).

2. *Biographies of Newman*

Dessain, C. S., *John Henry Newman*, London, 1966.

Gondon, Jules, *Notice biographique du R. P. Newman*, Paris, 1853.

Middleton, R. D., *Newman and Bloxam. An Oxford Friendship*, Oxford, 1947.

Middleton, R. D., *Newman at Oxford. His Religious Development*, London, Oxford University Press, 1950.

Trevor, Meriol, *Newman. The Pillar of the Cloud*, London, 1962.

Ward, Maisie, *Young Mr. Newman*, London, Sheed and Ward, 1952.

Ward, Wilfrid, *The Life of John Henry Cardinal Newman*, 2 vols., London, 1912.

3. *Studies of Newman's Thought*

Boekraad, A. J., *The Personal Conquest of Truth according to J. H. Newman*, Louvain, Nauwelaerts, 1955.

Chadwick, Owen, *From Bossuet to Newman. The Idea of Doctrinal Development*, Cambridge, University Press, 1957.

Cognet, L., *Newman ou la recherche de la vérité*, Paris, Desclée, 1967.

Flanagan, P., *Newman, Faith and the Believer*, London, Sands, 1946.

Fries, H., and Becker, W., eds. *Newman Studien*, Nuremberg, 1948 onwards.

Guitton, Jean, *La Philosophie de Newman. Essai sur l'idée de développement*, Paris, Boivin, 1933.

Nédoncelle, M., preface to *Œuvres philosophiques de Newman*, Paris, Aubier, 1945 (5-204).

Tristram, H., and Bacchus, F., 'Newman', article in *Dictionnaire de théologie catholique*, Paris, Letouzey, 1931 (t. xi, cols. 326–98).

Walgrave, J. H., *Newman. Le Développement du dogme*, Paris, Casterman, 1957.

4. *Books and articles relating to the controversy with Jager*

Biemer, G., *Überlieferung und Offenbarung. Die Lehre von der Tradition nach John Henry Newman*, Freiburg, Herder, 1961.

Lease, Gary, *Witness to the Faith. Cardinal Newman on the Teaching Authority of the Church*, Shannon, Irish University Press, 1971.

Stern, J., *Bible et Tradition chez Newman. Aux origines de la théorie du développement*. Paris, Aubier, 1967, pp. 99–141.

Stern, J., 'La Controverse de Newman avec l'abbé Jager et la théorie du développement', *Newman Studien*, vi. 123–142.

Tristram, H., 'In the lists with the Abbé Jager' in *John Henry Newman: Centenary Essays*, London, Burns, Oates and Washbourne, 1945, pp. 201–22.

5. *General background to the Oxford Movement; Tractarian biographies*

Allies, T. W., *A Life's Decision*, 2nd ed., London, Burns and Oates, 1894.

Allies, T. W., *Journal in France in 1845 and 1848, with letters from Italy in 1847, of things and persons concerning the Church and Education*, London, Longman, 1849.

Brilioth, Yngve, *The Anglican Revival. Studies in the Oxford Movement*, London, Longmans, 1933.

Burgon, J. W., *Lives of Twelve Good Men*, 2 vols., London, Murray, 1888 (vol. i contains a chapter on Hugh James Rose.)

Chadwick, Owen, *The Mind of the Oxford Movement*, London, 1960.

Faber, F. W., *Sights and Thoughts in Foreign Churches and among Foreign Peoples*, London, Rivington, 1842.

Froude, R. H., *Remains*, 2 vols., London, Rivington, 1838.

Gondon, Jules, *Du Mouvement religieux en Angleterre ou Les Progrès du Catholicisme et le retour de l'Église anglicane à l'Unité*, Paris, Julien Lanier, 1850.

Guiney, Louise Imogen, *Hurrell Froude. Memoranda and comments*, London, Methuen, 1904.

Liddon, H. P., *Life of Edward Bouverie Pusey*, 4 vols., London, 1893–7.

Mozley, T., *Reminiscences chiefly of Oriel College and the Oxford Movement*, 2 vols., London, 1882.

Oakeley, Frederick, *Historical Notes on the Tractarian Movement* (A.D. 1833–1845), London, Longmans, 1865.

Ollard, S. L., *A Short History of the Oxford Movement*, London, Mowbray, 1915.

Overton, J. H., *The Anglican Revival*, London, Blackie, n.d. (1897).

Reichard, Adolphe, *Le Puseyisme*, Strasbourg, Berger-Levrault, 1859.

Ward, Wilfrid, *W. G. Ward and the Oxford Movement*, London, Macmillan, 1889.

6. *Ecumenism and early nineteenth century controversy between the churches*

Allen, L., ed. 'Two Letters from the Newman Archives', Durham University Journal, xlvii, March 1955, 57–68 (Dalgairns and Albany Christie writing to Newman from France and Belgium respectively).

Allen, L., 'Newman and Christopher Wordsworth', *Essays presented to C. M. Girdlestone*, Newcastle-upon-Tyne, 1960.

Allen, L., 'The Authorship of the Letter to the "Univers" ', *Notes and Queries*, March 1955, 124–6 (Dalgairns).

Brandreth, H. R. T., *The Oecumenical Ideals of the Oxford Movement*, London, SPCK, 1947.

Burnouf, Eugène, *Choix de Lettres*, ed. L. Burnouf, Paris, 1891. [A French Orientalist visiting Cureton in Oxford.]

Congar, M. J., *Divided Christendom: A Catholic Study of the Problem of Reunion*. [Trans. of *Chrétiens désunis*, by M. A. Bousfield, London, 1939.]

Gondon, Jules, *De la Réunion de l'Église d'Angleterre — Protestante — à l'Église Catholique*, Paris, Wattelier, 1967.

Hook, W. F., 'An attempt to demonstrate the Catholicism of the Church of England and the other branches of the Episcopal Church' (Sermon preached at the consecration of Bishop Luscombe and reprinted as No. 2 in *The Church and her Ordinances*, vol. i). Hook (1798–1875) was Dean of Leeds.

Lepappe de Trévern, J. F. M., *Discussion amicale sur l'établissement et la doctrine de l'Église anglicane et en général sur la Réformation*, 2 vols., London, 1817. (The author became Bishop of Aire and later of Strasbourg.)

Marsh, Herbert (1757–1839, Lady Margaret Professor of Divinity in the University of Cambridge), *A Comparative View of the Churches of England and Rome*, Cambridge, 1814.

Milner, John, *The End of Religious Controversy*, new ed. by Luke Rivington, Catholic Truth Society, London, 1898.

Milner, John, *Excellence de la religion catholique, ou Correspondance entre une société de protestans religieux et un théologien de l'église catholique romaine*, ouvrage traduit de l'anglais de M. Milner, 2 vols., Paris, A. Le Clère, 1823.

Tavard, George H., *The Quest for Catholicity. A Study in Anglicanism*, London, Burns & Oates, 1963.

Perceval, A. P., *The Churchman's Manual*, Oxford, 1833.

Wiseman, Nicholas, 'The Anglican Claim of Apostolic Succession', *The Dublin Review* (7, 1839, pp. 139–80).

Wix, Samuel, *Reflections concerning the expediency of a Council of the Church of England and the Church of Rome being holden, with a view to accommodate religious differences and to promote the unity of religion in the bond of peace* . . . London, 1818.

Wordsworth, Christopher, *Diary in France, mainly on topics concerning Education and the Church*, London, Rivington, 1846.

Wordsworth, Christopher, *Letters to M. Gondon*, 2 vols., London, Rivington, 1848 (Newman and *L'Univers*).

7. *Works of Anglican Divines used in the controversy with Jager*

Bull, George (1634–1710, Bp. of St. David's), *Defensio Fidei Nicaenae* (1685; trans. reprinted in 2 vols., Oxford, Parker, 'Library of Anglo-Catholic Theology').

Hall, Joseph (1574–1656, Bp. of Exeter and Norwich), *The Peace-Maker* (Cp. 1, Sect. 3 'Of the Fundamental Points of Religion'), in *Works*, vol. vii, Oxford, 1837.

Hammond, Henry (1605–1660, Archdeacon of Chichester), *Miscellaneous Theological Works*, Oxford, Parker, 1849, vol. ii ('Of Fundamentals in a Notion referring to Practice', pp. 69–189).

Laud, William (1573–1645), Abp. of Canterbury), *The Works of the Most Reverend Father in God William Laud* (7 vols., ed. W. Scott and J. Bliss, Oxford, 1847–1860).

Laud, William, *A Relation of the Conference between William Laud . . . and Mr. Fisher the Jesuit* . . . new ed. C. H. Simpkinson, London, 1901.

More, P. E., and Cross, F. L., *Anglicanism. The thought and practice of the Church of England, illustrated from the religious literature of the seventeenth century*, London, SPCK, 1935.

Stillingfleet, Edward (1635–1699, Bp. of Worcester), *A Rational Account of the Grounds of the Protestant Religion Being a Vindication of the Lord*

194 *John Henry Newman and the Abbé Jager*

Archbishop of Canterbury's Relation of a Conference, etc., in vol. iv of Works, 7 vols., London, 1709.

Taylor, Jeremy, *A Dissuasive from Popery to the People of Ireland*, London, 1664.

Taylor, Jeremy, *Works*, 10 vols., London, 1847–1854.

Waterland, Daniel (1683–1740), *A discourse of fundamentals, being the substance of two charges delivered to the Middlesex clergy at the Easter visitations of 1734 and 1735*, Cambridge, 1735. (Reprinted in vol. v of collected *Works*, ed. W. Van Mildert, Oxford University Press, in 6 vols., 1823, pp. 71–104.)

8. *Vincent of Lérins*, Commonitorium. *Translations and commentaries*

i. *Texts and translations of the Commonitory*

Vincent of Lerins, *The Commonitory*, in *Early Medieval Theology*, trans. and ed. G. E. McCracken and A. Cabaniss (vol. ix of The Library of Christian Classics, London, SCM Press, 1957).

Vincent of Lerins, *The Commonitory of Vincent of Lérins* (in vol. ii of *A select library of Nicene and post-Nicene fathers*, ed. H. Wace and P. Schaff, New York, 1890–9).

Vincentius Lirinensis (Vincent of Lerins), *For the Antiquity and Universality of the Catholic Faith against the profane novelties of all heretics* (Parallel Latin and English texts), London, Parker, 1886. (A reprint of the Latin and English texts published at Oxford in 1841. The English translation is a revision of one published in 1651; an Appendix contains extracts from Cranmer, Ridley, Jewel, Laud, Usher, Hammond, Bull, Jebb, Kaye, and Beveridge.)

Vincent of Lerins, *St. Vincent of Lerins on the tests of heresy* (*Records of the Church*, xxiv–xxv in *Tracts for the Times*).

ii.

Cooper-Marsdin, A. C., *The History of the Islands of the Lerins*, Cambridge University Press, 1913 (Chap. V).

Irons, W. J., *The theory of development examined with reference specially . . . to the rule of St. Vincent of Lerins*, 1846.

Jebb, John, *Pastoral Instructions on the Character and Principles of the Church of England . . .* London, Duncan, 1831. ('Peculiar Character of the Church of England as distinguished from other branches of the Reformation and from the modern Church of Rome', pp. 261–318.)

Madoz, José, S.J., 'El concepto de la tradicion en S. Vicente de Lerins', *Analecta Gregoriana*, 5, Rome, 1933.

Manning, H. E., and Marriott, C., eds., *Catena Patrum No. iii.* (*Tracts for the Times*, No. 78, 'Testimony of writers in the later English Church to the duty of maintaining *Quod semper, quod ubique, quod ab omnibus traditum est*'.)

Moxom, R. S., *Modernism and Orthodoxy. An attempt to re-assess the value of the Vincentian Canon in regard to modern tendencies of thought* . . ., London, 1924.

9. *The role of* L'Univers

Allen, L., ed., 'The Letters of Ambrose Phillipps de Lisle to Charles de Montalembert', *The Dublin Review*, Nos. 463–468, 1954–1955. (*L'Univers* as link between the Tractarians and France.)

Allen, L., 'Wiseman's Letter to Morini', *Victorian Studies*, Indiana, Bloomington, June 1960, 458–9. (Comment on the Tractarians and the French Catholic press.)

Bellanger, C., et al., *Histoire générale de la presse française*, publiée sous la direction de Claude Bellanger, Jacques Godechot, Pierre Guiral, et Fernand Terrou, 3 vols., Paris, 1969. (Vol. 2 covers the period 1815 to 1871.)

Hatin, Eugène, *Bibliographie historique et critique de la presse périodique française*, Paris, 1886.

Index